Sams Teach ▮▮▮▮▮▮▮ conventional wisdom a
modern twis ⟨ **T5-DIG-282** web sites, your step-by-step
career journey will become an adventure. The touch of a career counselor
is felt in this book as it navigates the high-tech World Wide Web. This is
the first book I've seen that comprehensively associates career planning
steps with the dynamic pages of the Internet. I highly recommend it to
anyone just beginning a career or considering a career change.

> Dr. Shayn Smith
> Assistant Director
> Career Services
> University of Colorado at Boulder

This book is comprehensive, helpful, and written in a reader-friendly style.
In a relatively painless way, it charts a course through the very important
(and often overlooked) process of self-assessment and then into the somewhat easier job search phase of job hunting. The authors acknowledge that
this is definitely not a "once and forever" effort…. All in all, the information provided is clear, accurate, helpful, and manageable. I will recommend this book to my son and daughter.

> Christopher Shinkman
> Author of *Career Development: Theory and Practice*
> Former Director of MBA Career Management
> Georgetown University

I both like and prize *Sams Teach Yourself e-Job Hunting Today* for several
reasons—the major one simply being that it accomplishes what the title
purports. Through easy-to-read-and-follow text, the authors concisely
cover all significant issues in creative and comprehensive career management, while focusing specifically on how the Web serves as the principle
resource in each step. This continual referencing of the top sites that deliv-
er expertise for each career management topic (including the top university
career development sites—which have always provided leadership in this
discipline) is exceptional.

> Thomas Bachhuber, Ed.D.
> Managing Director, University Resources
> Management Alliance Group, Inc.

e-Job Hunting

e-Job Hunting

Planning your career and searching for jobs online

Eric Schlesinger
Susan Musich

A Division of Macmillan USA
201 West 103rd Street, Indianapolis, Indiana 46290

Sams Teach Yourself e-Job Hunting Today

Copyright © 2000 by Sams Publishing

International Standard Book Number: 0-672-31817-2

Library of Congress Catalog Card Number: 99-067043

Printed in the United States of America

First Printing: April 2000

03   02   01   00   4   3   2   1

Trademarks

Warning and Disclaimer

Acquisitions Editor
Jeff Schultz

Development Editor
Alice Martina Smith

Managing Editor
Charlotte Clapp

Project Editor
Andy Beaster

Copy Editor
Gene Redding

Indexer
Eric Schroeder

Proofreader
Candice Hightower

Team Coordinator
Amy Patton

Interior Designer
Gary Adair

Cover Designer
Jay Corpus

Copywriter
Eric Borgert

Production
Brad Lenser

Dedications

from Eric

To my wife.

from Susan

To my father and my husband.

Table of Contents

Acknowledgments

Writing a book on e-job hunting is a lot like job hunting itself. It takes time, focus, and discipline. But more importantly, it takes support, feedback, and assistance to turn a good product into a great one. Here, we wish to express our deep gratitude to those who made it happen.

Yoshie Shibata, our colleague and friend, spent many late nights researching Web sites to recommend and include in this project. Her efforts added quality and substance to many of the chapters of this book. We also thank our colleagues and friends whose endless support and encouragement catapulted us into this subject in the first place. Helen Frick, our manager, for giving us the thumbs up and standing behind us throughout this project. Nedra Klee Hartzell, a career consultant and friend, for continually feeding us quality Web sites and cheering us on. Kathy Fishburne, knowledge guru, for rallying behind us and ensuring our knowledge of twenty-first century Internet technology. Christine Koenig, a gifted teacher and friend, who read each chapter, ensuring that non-techies could understand and comprehend the concepts and techniques and apply them with ease.

This book would not have been possible without the full support of our spouses: Shari Schlesinger and Eduardo Rodriguez. We thank them for tolerating late nights, busy weekends, and working vacations. We are also grateful to Eduardo's family, particularly Luis Rodriguez, who provided administrative and technical support while traveling in Costa Rica.

We are deeply indebted to the wonderful folks at Macmillan USA for standing behind us and believing in the value of this book. In particular, we thank Jeff Schultz, Acquisitions Editor, for his unwavering support, his flexibility with our chaotic schedules, and his gentle nudges to move this book into production. We also thank Alice Martina Smith, Development Editor, for her outstanding suggestions and changes that transformed this book's quality into truly top-notch stuff. We also thank the team of Charlotte Clapp, Managing Editor, for their tireless efforts in pulling this book together, including Andy Beaster, Amy Patton, Gene Redding, Eric Schroeder, and Candice Hightower.

Lastly, we are grateful to the thousands of job seekers we have met over the years who have inspired us and reminded us that it is still possible to make a difference in the world, one person at a time.

INTRODUCTION

Unfolding at lightening speed before our very eyes is a cyber-world filled with great opportunities to learn, to grow, and to thrive in our careers. Seek and ye shall find. And find it you will—more than you'll ever need and probably more than you'll ever want.

The Internet has reinvented the way we plan our careers and search for jobs. In many ways, it has simplified our approach. In other ways, it has added a level of complexity and sophistication that demands refined research skills and strict self-management.

By reading this book, you have declared yourself to be part of the Internet job search revolution. You are now actively taking part in one of the most exciting transformations in job search history. You are no longer just glancing at information on a 15-inch computer screen; you are looking into your future and defining your success.

Searching for a job in today's world may net you the best job you'll ever have. Getting a new job is a rare chance to get a fresh start by re-evaluating your interests and taking stock of your skills. It's an opportunity to develop career management skills that will catapult you into the world of work in the new millennium, which demands career resilience.

We know you're up to the challenge, or you wouldn't be reading this book. So grab a cup of java, warm up those fingers, turn the page, click online, and get ready to move forward.

Welcome to the e-job hunt—where preparation meets opportunity!

PART I
Career Decision Making

CHAPTER 1

Job Hunting in the e-World

Today we are in a position of great opportunity. No longer do we have to wait for the library to open or shove coins into a machine to copy reports from reference materials. We no longer *look* to the future of technology—we *live* it.

The promises of the Internet are being kept, and those promises are far reaching. Cyber-technology has dramatically changed the way we live, work, communicate, plan a career, and search for work. But as sure as we need oxygen to live, an objective to work, and a brain to communicate, we need a meaningful plan to thrive in a career and a viable goal to search for a job. It takes more than "getting wired" to land a job.

This book will help you in your pursuit of employment, and this chapter will help you start cyber-surfing your way to thoughtful and purposeful action.

Get Ready: Preparing Yourself Mentally

It isn't enough to find a list of Web addresses and start cyber-hopping the job- and career-related Web sites. Instead, take a few hours—more if necessary—to think through what habits you need to keep and what you need to leave behind, who will be responsible for your job search, and how you will manage your online career planning time. By thinking through these topics first, your job search will go more smoothly, be less anxiety provoking, and result in reaching your goals more quickly and with greater success.

What You'll Learn in This Chapter:

▶ How to prepare yourself mentally, physically, and environmentally.

▶ Where you can hook up to the Internet outside your home.

▶ The benefits of and problems with an online job search.

▶ How to evaluate job and career Web sites.

▶ What to look for in online career counselors, advisors, and coaches.

Job Search Habits

What job search habits do you need before you begin? We don't have a list to check off, just some simple guidance: Don't plan to sit in your sweatpants all day while cyber-linking from site to site. Job searching is not a spectator sport. You need to get out and meet people. The rules haven't changed—but the medium by which you access information and connect with people has improved.

More than 80% of jobs are obtained through some form of networking. Yes, some networking can now be done online, but this doesn't replace the human factor, meaning that you must meet face-to-face with others. Whether you are seeking employment at the entry level or the executive level, you need to meet and greet others. Chapter 10, "Networking: Online and Offline," covers this topic in greater detail.

If you're naturally outgoing, networking should come a bit easier to you. If you're not, you'll have to work at this skill, but you still have to do it.

You Are in Control

You, the job seeker, have control in the job search process. You will decide where you will work, for whom, and doing what. Of course you need to get a job offer, but you control where you apply and, ultimately, what offer you will accept.

Job Search Timeframe, Timeline, and Time Management Strategies

The job search can be a full-time job in itself. If you're employed, you don't have 35 to 40 hours a week to spare. Yes, you could probably do it, but you'd drive yourself crazy and end up starting the new job you land with very low mental energy.

We have a simple rule to follow: If you are working full-time, plan on spending 5 to 10 hours a week on your job search. If you need to find employment quickly, you may have to increase this time by adding one hour before work and including your lunch hour at work.

If you're unemployed, plan on spending 20 to 40 hours a week in your job search, depending on your other daily activities. The fewer activities taking your time, the more time you should commit to your job search. If you're unemployed when you begin your job search, we suggest that you keep a Monday-through-Friday routine, during business hours only.

We also think you should plan for six to eight months as a reasonable time for securing a new job. This is the average length of time for most job seekers, even in a strong economy. We're not saying that you won't find a job sooner—it's possible and has been done time and again. We do think, however, that if you plan for a 6-to-8 month job search, you're being more realistic and less likely to place unreasonable pressure on yourself. You'll also be less likely to accept the first job offer that is made if it is not the best option for you.

Many job search advisors suggest, on average, that you should allow one month of job search time for each $10,000 of salary you are seeking. Therefore, if you desire a $60,000 per year job, you could expect your job search, on average, to last for 6 months or longer.

If you can't afford to look for a job for this length of time, come up with an alternative source of income. There are numerous options to get you through the job-search period, such as working with a temp agency, working in a bookstore, or finding contract work. Brainstorm a list of what you can do that is safe, legal, and sure to cover the basic necessities to get you through this time period.

Finally, even if you have a great memory, it's a good idea to put into practice some good time-management principles. Write down your plans, your appointments, and notes for follow-up work. You will need a readily accessible calendar to mark down appointments. You can find a good online calendar at the Web Address Book site at *www.webaddressbook.com.* This site includes an address book, a calendar with email notification of appointments, a bookmark manager, a notepad to store messages, and a To-Do list for priority tasks.

All Work and No Play:
If you're already holding down a job as you begin a search for a new job, we suggest that you keep a Monday-through-Saturday schedule. You need at least one day off to play and rejuvenate.

A Few Chuckles Can Help!

You can ease the stress often brought on by a job search by adding some humor about work to your day. Check out Online's cartoons at www.workforce. com/section/01/ cartoons. Another great site is the Dilbert Zone at www.dilbertzone. com. After all, laughter is the best medicine.

Get Set: Preparing Yourself

When you're in the right mindset and ready to hit the information superhighway, we have a few tips to help you set up your work environment. First, you'll need to identify what additional job search strategies you'll have to develop during this time. You'll also have to establish a career planning/job search office.

Internet 101.

The acclaimed Yahoo! Web site has a page you can access to learn how to use the Internet. This page is straightforward and easy to digest. Go to *www3.zdnet.com/yil/filters/channels/netezuser.html* and click Surfing and Searching in the middle column; then click Search Rescue. Here you'll find great tips for narrowing your Internet searches and getting to the information you want—quickly!

Identify Your Job Search Strategies

There are numerous ways to plan your career and search for work. This book will help you navigate the greatest new highway of the millennium. However, we know that different folks may prefer different strokes—and that's okay, too. We still encourage you to tap the expansive resources on the Net.

If you're planning a career, you should consider consulting with a career counselor or accessing services through your university (if you're still a student) or your alma mater (if you're a graduate). You can find links to colleges and universities through the National Association of Colleges and Employers' Web site at *www.jobweb.org/catapult/homepage.htm*. You may also think about strategies such as networking, joining professional associations, participating in job search support groups, visiting community or nonprofit career centers, accessing library resources, paying for training courses on different aspects of the job search, and accessing information through the Internet.

Regardless of your resources, you need to know where they are, when they are available, what costs are associated with them, and what is available to you.

Of course, this book focuses on the Internet, which is available 24 hours a day and 7 days a week. But keep in mind that you need to balance this approach with some of the other tried-and-true methods we'll mention throughout this book.

Although you may not be ready to specify what other resources you will access, at least open your mind to the idea that there *are* other options available to you.

Job Search Office/Headquarters

You need a base for organizing files, notes, and other essentials in your job search. You should set up a place that you can always count on using during the hours you have set aside as your job search timeframe. This location may be where your home computer is, or it may be at a career center that rents offices for just this purpose (although this option can be costly).

We suggest a quiet corner of the house where you have a desk or writing surface, a telephone, preferably a home computer with email and Internet access, and a filing system. If you don't have these elements, you may need to separate your computer needs from the place you use to store your files and notes. The goal, however, is to be organized so that you're not spending time looking for what you need each day.

Get Wired! Where You Can Hook Up Outside Your Home

Millions of homes around the world are now wired for the Internet. But if you don't have one of those homes, there are plenty of techno-resources available that you can access.

Most local libraries are connected to the Internet and offer computer access at no charge. You can also find computers with Internet access at most community colleges and at many nonprofit organizations that offer career or research services.

One of the greatest resources available around the country is America's One-Stop Career Center System, which you can check out at *www.ttrc.doleta.gov/onestop*. This site includes links to more than 650 local One-Stop Centers nationwide. Most One-Stops have a physical location with computers that have access to the Internet. The One-Stop Career Center System is one of the best services that has developed out of the Department of Labor's

effort to cooperate with other organizations that offer career services to job seekers.

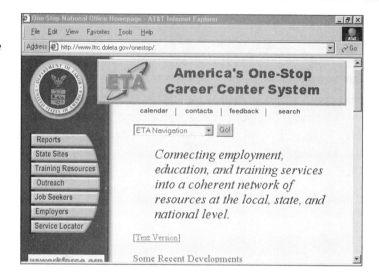

*If you don't have
Internet access at
home, chances are
you're not too far
from one of the
more than 650
One-Stop Career
Centers around
the country.*

Virtual Pros and Cons: The Good, the Bad, and the Ugly

There's no doubt about it. The Internet has revolutionized how we
plan our careers and look for work. It has simplified many of the
time-consuming tasks involved in the job search process. It has
made a once overwhelming task a manageable and exciting
opportunity. Given the new job market, this is not only good
news, it is outstanding news!

Yet there are very real concerns about what the Internet offers
regarding job search and career planning resources. Let's take a
look at the good, the bad, and the ugly. Spending a few minutes to
learn about each can keep you surfing smoothly while avoiding
the pitfalls many job seekers fall into.

The Virtual Good

The Internet can be helpful in many ways. It offers self-assessment exercises and helps you identify the skills you have to offer
(as described in Chapter 4, "Finding Yourself in the e-World").
You can now do most of your research on salary levels, career
industries, relocation issues, employer information, and much

more by linking to one of the many useful sites available at no cost to you! The World Wide Web connects you to career and job market information at the touch of a keystroke.

The most captivating information online for job seekers seems to lie in the expansive job databases (described in Chapter 11, "Finding the Perfect Job on the Net"). You can live in chilly Maine and identify job opportunities in sunny San Diego without ever leaving your home. You can be hooked up in Miami, Florida, and find out how much you need to earn to live at the same standard of living in Juneau, Alaska. It's amazing what you can find and learn online.

If you're new to the Internet (Net vets refer to you as a "newbie"), start your Internet action at Newbie-U (New User University) at *http://www.newbie-u.com*. This site has great tips on learning how to use the Web.

If you've used the Internet before, we suggest that you check out some of the great, up-to-date articles at *The Wall Street Journal*'s career site at *www.careers.wsj.com*. Click the Job-Hunting Advice link in the left column and then click Hunting on the Internet. You'll see a list of articles that cover some of the unique aspects of using the Internet in the job search, such as the article "The New Rules of Hunting on the Net." This article covers some of the problems Internet job seekers experience when using email and posting their resumes. Another great article is "Time Management Is Key when Job-Hunting Online," which covers the time traps that catch many job seekers who use the Internet as their only job search medium.

If you're new to the Web and need to learn more of the basics so that you're ready to tackle the job search, try visiting Newbie-U, the New User University, where you can quickly learn the ins and outs of the Web, email, and other Internet activities.

▼ **Try It Yourself**

1. Go to *http://www.newbie-u.com*.

2. Under the Courses heading, click The Web.

3. Read through the curriculum and click the Go to Class button at the bottom of the page.

4. Read through the six topics under the Before We Begin heading. This information is brief and will familiarize you with jargon and instructions used throughout the online course.

5. When you're ready, scroll down to the section called "OK, Let's Go!" The entire course is listed there. It's short and clear and will get you surfing in no time at all. If you don't want to go through the entire course, read through at least the first four sections on URLs, bookmarks, search engines, and searching sites.

Congratulations! You're ready to surf!

The Wall Street Journal's career site offers excellent articles on timely topics about the Internet job search.

The greatest strengths of the Internet are that you can access information easily and efficiently and the cost is nominal (approximately $20 to $25 per month for unlimited access through a home Internet service provider). In some cases, you can access the Internet for free through local libraries, community colleges, or nonprofit organizations.

Because you can start on one page in search of information and link immediately to a different site if that page has a hot link, you can take a non-linear approach to research. This means that you can cover a lot of ground in one sitting by linking to information that may broaden or narrow your focus. The downside is that this approach also means that you can lose a lot of time if you don't stay focused on what it is you're looking for.

The Virtual Bad

With all these benefits, what could possibly be a problem? The Internet offers a false sense of hope that it is a one-stop job search medium. Don't be fooled by this untruth. The bottom line is that many people hold on to the hope that they can conduct their job searches from start to finish online. Although you can work through many of the stages online, if you're not in a high-tech field, you still need to get out and meet the masses—that is, your potential employers. Even in high-tech fields, you will ultimately have to meet your potential employer for a face-to-face interview. Remember: Job searching is a "contact" sport!

You also need to strike the right balance of preparation, research, networking, and action. The Internet offers opportunities in each of these areas, but it offers the most value with the research aspect of your job search. There are literally millions of jobs online, but there are millions more that aren't. Think about it this way: How many people do you know who have looked for work in the last year, and how many of them found that job online? Chances are, you don't know anybody. If you do, it's probably only one or two out of many, many more.

For some reason, many people think that if the information is available online, then it's got to be good. This belief is dead wrong! Because the Internet is in its relative infancy, anybody can post just about anything he wants online. Just as you can't believe everything you hear, you can't believe everything that's posted.

We've seen innumerable Web sites that offer somebody's personal tips on how to write a resume or get a job. Although the strategies may have worked for that individual, that doesn't make the advice applicable to anyone else's job search. Like any type of advice from friends and family, always be selective about what you use and disregard the rest.

The Virtual Ugly

On the good side, there are incredible opportunities to network and meet others through online chats, listservs, and email messages. On the ugly side, there are many people out there who are looking to *flame* listserv or newsgroup participants. A *flamer* is one who makes inappropriate, sarcastic, or ugly remarks about you or the message you posted to a group. Unfortunately, because the Internet allows for instant reactions, there are many who type before they think or who believe their opinions are more important than your feelings and reputation.

You can avoid some flaming by making sure that you join appropriate listservs and chats (more on this in Chapter 11) and reading through the rules of the group before participating. In fact, we suggest that you wait for one or two weeks after you join a discussion group and simply "lurk" to get a feel for the conversation's tone and appropriate topics.

If you get flamed anyway and you've done nothing to provoke the flamer, keep in mind that others on the list probably already know about this individual and also ignore that person's comments.

You should plan to come across a lot of wrong and downright bad advice about the job search process. Don't be fooled by many of the cyber-masked, self-purported experts. You need to know what's good and what's not. If you don't, you're going to have trouble.

How do you know what to read and what to use? We'll tell you the sites that have good information and offer some tips on sites to steer away from. As a matter of fact, in the next section of this chapter, we'll provide some guidance on how you can evaluate a job search Web site to determine if it's worth your time.

E-Valuating Job and Career Web Sites

After you read this book, you should feel quite comfortable with the virtual job search process. Chances are, however, that new Web sites we haven't mentioned here will pop up, and you'll want to use them. How do you know if the Web site is worth your time? There are three steps you can take to get a good sense of whether or not a site has reliable information.

1. Who is operating the site and why?

    You need to know the credentials of the person or company
    offering the information on the Web site. Anybody can hang
    a sign identifying himself as a career expert. You want to
    know how long the person has been in the business, does he
    have formal education in a related field (such as counseling,
    human resources, or management), and is he a member of a
    relevant professional association. Most reputable career
    experts are members of at least one professional association
    related to the field. The association provides guidance on
    ethics and keeps the professional up to date on current trends
    in the field.

2. Is the information free? Why or why not?

    You can find just about any job search–related information at
    no cost on the Web. Usually this information is provided as a
    service to help meet the needs of a particular community.

    Educational institutions such as universities usually offer
    career information Web pages. In general, this information is
    developed by career counselors and is pretty reliable. Other
    sources of free online information are government sites, such
    as the Department of Labor or your state government.
    Associations and nonprofits usually offer free career informa-
    tion to help their members or to help others entering a career
    field related to their mission.

    Of course, the most popular job search sites are free to job
    seekers but charge employers a fee to list jobs. These sites
    frequently offer job search guidance to help the job hunter
    apply for jobs. Many of the larger sites, such as Monster.com
    at *www.monster.com* and *The Wall Street Journal*'s career site
    at *www.careers.wsj.com*, have done an outstanding job of
    providing accurate and solid career information. We're start-
    ing to see more and more special-interest sites offering simi-
    lar services for women, minorities, and other populations.

3. Is the site updated regularly?

At the bottom of the home page, you can often find the date or month the site was updated. This is particularly important for job listings because you don't want to waste your time applying for jobs that have been filled.

Also, you don't want to read outdated industry information. For example, if you are looking for a job in accounting or financial services, you don't want a site that still refers to the key firms as the Big Six (two of these firms merged and now this group is referred to as the Big Five). A simple mistake like that in a cover letter could cost you your credibility with a future employer.

Online Career Counseling, Advice, and Coaching

Individual online career advice from career counselors, advisers, or coaches is a growing trend. We're seeing an increasing number of shingles being hung on the Web to offer assistance with career planning and the job-search process. Our piece of advice: Identify what you're getting, know your source, and determine the cost.

Online counseling is a hotly debated topic among career professionals. Some insist that counseling is a face-to-face interaction; others say that offering counseling online has expanded the reach to individuals who would never see a counselor in person.

Regardless of the current debate, the bottom line is that you need to know what it is you're asking for. If you want advice, you need to be clear about the type of advice you're looking for. If it's related to a sensitive topic, such as why you've been fired from your last three jobs, you may want someone who can do more than send back a few lines about how to improve your resume. Not only that, you may not want that negative personal information traveling across the wires.

If you decide to have a virtual counseling session, know that there may be limitations to what can be achieved in these sessions. Ask a counselor for a listing of his credentials. Ask for a local professional contact in the event of an emergency. Ask how he will ensure confidential interaction. Finally, always ask for references and check them out. If the online counselor can't do any of this to your liking, move on.

Although anybody can *say* he is a career counselor, real career counselors have advanced training (usually at the master's level) in counseling, social work, or psychology. If the individual has anything less, don't be fooled by the title. An ethical individual will practice within the areas for which he is qualified based on his experience, training, and competence.

If a Web site offers counseling services, be sure to look for a list of credentials, such as licenses, certification, education, and training. In addition, the counseling staff should have information explaining its competence in the use of technology for online counseling. Two Web sites offer in-depth information about online counseling. We suggest that you spend some time researching this topic before you take the plunge. Check out Counseling Net at *www.counselingnet.com*, which offers online counseling services and links to related information on this topic. It also addresses how counselors should interact with you through email or in a chat room. You can also find great information about the ethical issues regarding online counseling at *http://www. counseling.org/resources/codeofethics.htm*.

If a Web site offers counseling services, ask if this means the site can address the varied situations that may affect your job search, such as family, social, or personal issues. Also ask if the site or its counselors will help you in the assessment process to relate your interests, values, and skills to the world of work.

More and more, career professionals are calling themselves "career coaches." Often this label indicates that there will be less emphasis on the counseling process and more of an emphasis on setting goals and reaching them. Of course, this is also part of the counseling process, but counseling focuses more on discovering who you are while coaching focuses more on where you want to be.

Putting It All Together

Congratulations! You've taken the first and most important step in the online job search process: You set a solid foundation and framework. You learned that this is to ensure job search success.

You now know that you need to prepare yourself mentally for the job search. You need to put your thoughts and plans in order. To do this, your work environment for the time you spend searching for a job must be practical, convenient, and organized. If you don't have a computer or an in-home connection to the Internet, there are lots of places nearby where you can hook up for free.

The Internet has a lot of power, both good and bad. Know the difference. Make sure that you are getting the best information you can. Whether your information is coming from a Web site or a Web counselor, you must ensure the credibility, reliability, and dependability of the source.

Next stop: Learning how to use this book!

CHAPTER 2

Using This Book E-ffectively and E-fficiently

We take it that you didn't buy this book because of the surprise ending. Keeping this in mind, we decided that it might be helpful to offer you some guidance on the variety of approaches you can take with the contents of this book. This chapter will go through each of the sections of this book and give you tips on how to use this book to your best advantage. Good luck with the job search!

If you're not sure where to begin with your career planning or job hunting, you'll be glad to know that this book was written in a logical sequence to help you. Career planning is an ongoing process, but if you've never thought about it before, then start with Chapter 3, "e-Career Mapping and Job Search Planning," and move forward one chapter at a time. If you have worked on planning your career but think it's time for an overhaul, jumpstart, or tune-up, we suggest that you, too, should start with Chapter 3 and move forward one chapter at a time.

A Quick Scan of the Contents

We divided the book into five parts:

- Part I, "Career Decision Making," is an introduction to the job-search process.

- Part II, "Establishing Personal Goals," focuses on making career decisions using a self-assessment process, given the changes in employment approaches in the last few years.

- Part III, "Developing Job Search Tools," helps you develop your job search tools, such as the resume.

What You'll Learn in This Chapter:

▶ How to find and use foreign embassies and consulates on the Web.

▶ How National tourist offices differ from embassy and consulate sites and why they are useful.

▶ How to navigate and find what you need: A case study of the British Tourist Authority's Web site.

▶ How to find useful information at state and local convention and visitors bureaus.

- Part IV, "e-Job Search Strategies," helps you develop your job search strategies.

- Part V, "Strategies for Success," covers strategies for career success once you have found your job.

We've also compiled all the Web sites referenced in this book. You can find this Web Directory in the appendix section at the end of the book.

In each chapter, you'll find helpful tips and opportunities to get online and try it yourself with our step-by-step exercises. These Try It Yourself exercises will show you how to navigate your way through a Web site that can be of particular use to you in the job search.

Here's what you'll find in each of the chapters.

Chapter 3, "e-Career Mapping and Job Search Planning"

Chapter 3 gives you an overview of the world of work. It will help you to map out a career path as you plan for your career in the twenty-first century. It covers what kind of work is out there and how you can make career decisions to find your fit. This chapter also offers some good suggestions for organizing your job search and setting career goals.

Chapter 4, "Finding Yourself in the e-World"

Chapter 4 helps you learn more about yourself by using online tools and resources to identify your values, skills, abilities, interests, and needs. This chapter will help you to brainstorm careers and identify job preferences. Most importantly, it will guide you in identifying any job search barriers that may be keeping you from finding meaningful employment.

Chapter 5, "What in the World of Work Is Out There?"

This chapter helps you explore career options through different types of research. We offer great tips on how to use the Internet to facilitate this process but also balance online research with some more traditional methods.

Chapter 6, "Finding the Right Industry, Employer, and Organization"

In this chapter, you learn how to find valuable information about industries, employers, and organizations. We will show you how to find information about the private sector, the government, and nonprofit organizations.

Chapter 7, "Writing Resumes: The Printed Word"

In this chapter, we discuss how to use your resume as a marketing tool. By understanding this concept, you can better position yourself in the job market. We will go through the components of the resume and cover important areas such as the language to use and how to design your resume for maximum attention.

Chapter 8, "Sending Resumes: The Electronic Word"

You've heard about electronic resumes, but most people don't know what they are, how to write them, or how to use them. This chapter covers online resumes, emailed resumes, and scannable resumes. We also refer you to some great sites to get started in using this electronic self-marketing medium!

Chapter 9, "Writing Letters for the Information Age"

Whether you're being introduced to your friend's contact or submitting a resume with email or snail mail, you will still need to write a cover letter. This chapter takes you through the basics of good letter writing and offers samples on how to write letters to request information meetings, to submit a job application or resume, and to thank an individual for a meeting or an interview. Written communication is key!

Chapter 10, "Networking Online and Offline"

No matter what type of job you apply for, you'll need to network. This seven-letter word sends chills down the spine of even the most seasoned professional. We'll show you how to do it effectively, how to do it well, how to do it electronically, and how to keep your network working!

Chapter 11, "Finding the Perfect Job on the Net"

Most likely, you'll jump to this chapter before you read the pages that precede it. If you do, you'll find some great sites, but you'll be aimlessly wandering around in those great sites for a long, long time. However, if you take the time to go through the preceding chapters, the investment will be well worth your while, and the job sites will be better resources for you. This chapter is rich with information, tips, and advice, but do yourself a favor and make sure that you're not cheating yourself out of a thoughtful job search process. If you don't have a career and job search goal yet, go directly to Chapter 3. Do not pass 4. Do not collect any more Web addresses (for the time being).

Chapter 12, "Interview Techniques Online"

There are many different interview styles. This chapter explains the more commonly used ones and shows you how to prepare for each stage of the interview. In the end, the Internet is just a link. You will have to "sell yourself" directly to an employer.

Chapter 13, "Job Offers: E-valuating and Net-gotiating"

Interestingly, one of the most difficult decisions in the job search process can be whether or not to accept a job offer. This chapter gives you guidance on how to make a decision, as well as how to negotiate your salary and benefits.

Chapter 14, "Starting Work: e-Ideas for Success"

The first impression lasts forever. This chapter offers tips on how to make a great first impression, take charge of your career, and balance the work/life scale.

Chapter 15, "Change and Transitions"

It's common today for people to change careers. Chances are that you will change careers several times in your life. You may be doing that right now, which is why you are reading this book. This chapter offers some guidance on how to manage this transition. Relocation is another major life transition, and this chapter gives you guidance on how to plan for relocating within the United States or overseas.

Chapter 16, "Continuing Education and Training"

Lifelong learning is quickly becoming the buzz. If you're thinking of continuing your education and maintaining your edge in the job market, we have some hot tips for you in this chapter.

Show Me the Links!

For your convenience, we've compiled all the Web page addresses listed in this book and created a Web Directory, which is contained in the appendix section. This quick reference will help you use this book as a continued reference throughout your job search. As you find Web sites we haven't included, write their addresses in this section of the Web Directory so that you have your own personalized directory. Also, be sure to send in the form in the back of the book and let us know what sites you found that are not in this book that you think we should include in the next edition.

Show Me the Updated Links!

If you're struggling to find a Web site that we've listed in this book because of a broken link, you can find the updated Web address or link directly to the site through Susan Musich's Web site, Career Kiosk, at www.careerkiosk.org.

Can't Connect?

If any of the links in this book don't take you to the site we specify, you still can find the site in a snap. Just delete all information following the first single slash (/) in the address we give. This shortened URL will take you to a higher level of the site. Then follow the instructions on the site to reach the page you want.

For example, if the site manager made some address changes, you may get an error message when you go to Western Illinois University's career site to find information on interview styles at *http://wiuadm1.wiu.edu/mioip/interview/l_type.asp*. Edit the address to *http://wiuadm1.wiu.edu* (because immediately following *edu* you see the first single slash), and you will end up on a major entry page that directs you to the page on interview styles.

File Not Found

If you type a Web address and a message pops up saying *File Not Found*, *404 Access Denied*, or *404 Not Found*, the Web page no longer exists or has changed its address. On the Web, this happens occasionally. You can find the page by searching on Yahoo! at *www.yahoo.com* or MetaCrawler at *www.metacrawler.com*. Type the name of the site in either of these search engines; the search should uncover the site's current address. Be sure to write the correct address in this book for future reference.

We also suggest that you use the contact information on the "Tell Us What You Think" page at the back of this book to note any changes of Web site addresses you have discovered. The day this book is printed, we guarantee that some of the sites we list between the covers will be outdated. It's impossible for a printed book to offer perfect links to career and job sites in a virtual world that changes by the millisecond. But as we repeat throughout this book, virtual career planning is not a spectator sport. We can give you the guidance to use the virtual tools, but you can do a few things to make sure you don't ignore outstanding career information just because you don't have the current address.

Putting It All Together

We think you'll find this book to be a valuable resource for your job search—both offline and online. Our quick tips are

- If you're just getting started with your career planning and are not sure what exactly it is you want to do, start with Chapter 3 and work through each chapter in order.

- If you know your career direction but need some specific help in getting there, go to the chapters whose titles represent the help you need. But don't hesitate to glance into other chapters. We can always improve our tactics.

- If you know what you want and what you need, and you just need some great leads on Web links to help you move forward, scan the chapters and then go to the Web Directory in the back of the book.

Next stop: Making decisions about your career!

CHAPTER 3

e-Career Mapping and Job Search Planning

Somebody once said, "If you don't know where you're going, how will you know when you get there?" Simply put, you won't. Yet most people hurl themselves into the job search without a plan, a map, a guide, or a goal. *Finding a job* isn't your goal. You know that you can find a job, but you're looking for one that means more to you than cutting grass or handing out restaurant coupons at a busy intersection. You want a career that meets your professional interests and financial needs, accommodates your personal lifestyle, and allows you to thrive. To find this job, you must plan and prepare for your career journey…and so you don't get lost, you need a map.

What You'll Learn in This Chapter:

▶ How to map out your career path and prepare for a career in the twenty-first century.

▶ How to make good career decisions.

▶ How to set effective career goals.

Mapping Your Career

If you are planning for the trip of a lifetime, you will probably put in a lot of effort, time, and thought to ensure that your itinerary meets your interests. Similarly, a job search requires thoughtful assessment, research, and planning. For the tens of thousands of hours you will work during your life, planning your career carefully is worth the time.

You may be wondering how you can plot the longevity of a career in a world that is changing so fast. It is virtually impossible to stay on top of all the latest jobs, career trends, and employment contracts. Although there are things you can do to speed up the job search, you must first have a career plan. If you don't have a map, how will you know when you get there? This chapter is about designing that map without necessarily knowing where you might need to stop or refuel along the way.

Do You Know Where You're Going?

If you don't know where you're going, how will you know when you get there?

Preparing for Twenty-First Century Careers

Here are some suggestions for what you should do to prepare yourself for the job search and for satisfying employment in the twenty-first century:

- **Master the art of managing transitions.** Companies will continue to reinvent themselves, you will continue to develop your skills, and the workforce will continue to change at high speed in a high-tech world. The better you can manage change, the better prepared you'll be for work in the twenty-first century. Go to the William Bridges and Associates Web site at *http://www.wmbridges.com.* On the home page, click the Articles link and check out one or two of the archived articles on transitions, such as "How You Can Handle Change Better." William Bridges is a leader in the field of career management and life transitions.

The site for William Bridges and Associates at www.wmbridges. com is a great site to find excellent articles on managing change and transitions.

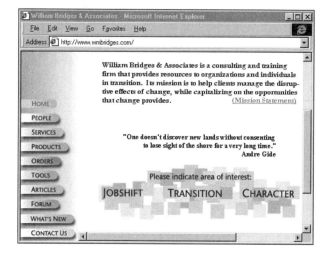

- **Become your own career manager and prepare to change jobs regularly.** We've passed the age of job security. You can expect to change not only jobs but careers as well. Twenty-first century workers will not wait for the employer to take care of them. Instead, savvy workers will take charge of their own careers and futures by continually upgrading and diversifying their skills, ensuring security through solid financial planning, and providing value to the employer by working beyond the parameters of the job description.

- **Nurture your network.** In the twenty-first century, it's not only who you know, but who knows you. Your professional network will be critical for some degree of employment security and career success. Taking charge of your career means developing longer-lasting relationships with those you can connect with regarding professional interests and those you can turn to for professional support. In turn, these contacts can count on you to do the same.

- **Strengthen your communication skills.** If you are comfortable hiding behind a computer or quietly filing your work, it's time to think again. The twenty-first century demands a workforce that can continually communicate its assets, its needs, and its value to a company. In addition, you will be forced to take on multiple roles that involve working on teams and sharing the load of numerous tasks, including writing, speaking, reporting, and organizing.

- **Develop a career portfolio that includes techno-skills.** If you haven't yet considered expanding your portfolio of skills, now is the time to do it. You will need skills that allow you to be flexible in the work environment and fit into a variety of projects. To survive and thrive in changing times, you will need to wear multiple hats. You need to continually add to your repertoire of skills the latest and greatest of technology skills relevant to your field.

To determine the direction you're headed, you first need to do a bit of research to figure out what you want, what you need, the time it will take, and the best route to get there. Effort put into prep work has a direct impact on the road to be traveled. With the Internet, the research is faster, easier, and often more current.

To help you determine your career path, you must more fully understand yourself, your opportunities, and the specifics related to your career interests.

Going, Going, Gone:

Before you walk down the career road less traveled, you need to learn more about who you are, what you need, and how you're going to get there.

Constant Change:

Most workers in the twenty-first century will change careers five to seven times during their lifetimes. On top of that, workers will probably change jobs three to five times within each career!

So how do you get from here to there? The next three chapters will take you through this process and lead you to the point where you'll have to make decisions and set goals. If you've already gone through most of this research, you may want to jump to the "Making Decisions" and "Setting Goals" sections later in this chapter. However, if you have some doubts, a bit of time to build a foundation may be just what you need to get a sturdy start.

Where Will You Be in Five Years?

Most people can't answer this question. However, many people do have a sense about their career interests and aspirations. Although you may not know where you'll be down the road, you might have an idea about where you would *like* to be. If you have some idea, you can plan for success. If you have no idea, you're riding on chance.

This does not mean you must commit to one career. It does mean, however, that you need a plan of action—one that allows for changes, updates, and additions. This is not a prescription for life, but a road map that provides direction. Roads, as we all know, need repair once in a while, but without them, it's tough to get anywhere.

Career Planning in the Twenty-First Century

Tremendous changes in society have resulted in major changes in the skills required to succeed in business today. Because these changes are happening at lightening speed, many experts agree that twenty-first century job hunters need a well-developed portfolio of skills that can easily adapt to an employer's needs.

You may change careers five to seven times during your lifetime. On top of that, you may change jobs numerous times within each career. To prepare for this constant change, you need to know a lot about yourself and how your personal characteristics affect your career and job choices.

Planning your career is a continuous process. Your plan must be clear, but you will have to revisit and update it regularly. In general, however, there are some basic steps to help you develop your plan.

Five Steps to Planning Your Career

1. **Explore how your interests, values, skills, and abilities fit in the world of work. Determine what skills and education you need to be competitive—and how you will get them.** This requires self-assessment and research. Chapter 4, "Finding Yourself in the e-World," will show you how to do this. Self-exploration is an ongoing process. Chapter 4 will help you with your initial evaluation about what you have to offer, but the research you will do in Chapters 5, "What in the World of Work Is Out There?," and 6, "Finding the Right Industry, Employer, and Organization," may further clarify what it will take to stay competitive in your career field.

2. **Decide on what you need and want in a career or job and identify the obstacles that may interfere with achieving your goals—and plan the steps you can take to overcome them.** Chapters 4 and 5 will help you articulate your professional needs. Chapter 4 will also help you identify barriers to employment and give you suggestions for moving past them.

3. **Create a clear, immediate job/career goal and a long-term career goal.** We provide some guidance for setting career goals later in this chapter, but you need to know more about who you are and what you want before you can do this. As you uncover more information about yourself, your goal may be altered or change completely. *Long-term* can be defined as five years or longer. The bottom line is that you need to know what you want to do now and have an idea about what you want to do in the future so that you can take appropriate steps to move in that direction. This chapter helps you define your long-term career goal.

4. **Research careers, work trends, employers, and organizations.** If you're new to the world of work, you first need to find out what's out there. If you've been part of the world of work, you need to know what has changed. Chapters 5 and 6 will help you learn more about who and what is out there.

5. **Connect to sources of support, such as a mentor or professional group, and develop a solid network.** This is critical both during the job search and after the job search. You need others to offer you positive and professional feedback and support. You need others to cheer you on and encourage you to stick with it when the going gets tough—as well as when the going goes nowhere for awhile. To succeed in today's job market, you need to develop and maintain a professional network. Chapter 10, "Networking Online and Offline," will help you learn how to do this for your job search; Chapter 14, "Starting Work: e-Ideas for Success," will briefly discuss the value of nurturing your network after you're employed.

Are you ready to use the Internet to do some quick career planning? Here are some Web sites you may want to explore to get
started with your planning.

1. To take a look at the overall career planning process, try
   going to Bowling Green State University's Career
   Planning/Competency Model at *www.bgsu.edu/offices/
   careers/process/process.html*. This model is an outstanding
   guide for taking you through career planning and exploration.
   Start your career planning here by clicking the Self-
   Assessment link. Of course, Chapter 4 in this book will cover
   career planning in greater detail.

2. If you are changing careers or want to learn more about what
   career options may be related to your degree, go to the
   University of Delaware's Major Resource Kits. The Career
   Services Center has compiled kits for more than 70 academic
   majors. The kits include job titles related to the major, profiles of a day on the job, links to other sources of information
   about the field, how to enhance your marketability in the
   field, and considerations for further education and experience. Now it's your turn. Go to *www.udel.edu/CSC/mrk.html*
   and click your major. Bookmark this page so that you can
   return to it again as needed.

   If you don't find your major listed at the University of
   Delaware site, try the University of North Carolina at
   Wilmington's site at *www.uncwil.edu/stuaff/career/
   majors.htm*. On the site's Career Services page, called "What
   Can I Do with a Major In…?" you'll find more than 35
   majors. The listing of job titles is excellent, but you won't
   find specific guidance about how to make yourself more marketable.

   Liberal Arts majors will find a great list of majors and titles
   at the College of Mount St. Joseph's Kaleidoscope of Careers
   page at *www.msj.edu/academics/career/kocfields.htm*.

If you can't .find your major at any of these sites, try Michigan's Occupational Information System (MOIS) at *www.mois.org/clusters.html*. MOIS has an excellent list of career fields and relevant job titles.

If you still can't find your major, check out the University of Milwaukee's site at *http://www.uwm.edu/Dept/CDC/ internet-research.htm*. Go to the second section on this page to find links to numerous Web sites that give options for career fields and majors.

3. If you think you want to continue in your current career field and want to take a look at its outlook, go to Job Star's site at *www.jobsmart.org/tools/career/spec-car.htm*. Click the name of your career field and review what the outlook is for the twenty-first century. Here you will also find information about how to plan for a career in your chosen field.

4. Visit Web sites that will help you develop a career plan. Go to Mapping Your Future's Career Plan at *http://www. mapping-your-future.org/planning/careerpl.htm*. Click the Career Goals link to review the importance of career goals and then click the link to review a sample career plan. Now see if you can write a career plan of your own. If you can't, go through the next three chapters of this book one page at a time; return to this Web site after you have completed your research..

What's Out There?

Extraordinary variety exists in the world of work: career fields, industries, job titles, employers, organizations, work environments, salaries, locations, and more. Such variety means you need to make some choices. But before you can make any choices, you need to know what you want or prefer.

Many career opportunities exist and are changing every day. Businesses and industries are redefining themselves daily as the world of work becomes more global. And new businesses are popping up left and right.

There are many questions to answer before narrowing down your options. Take employers, for example: Do you know what type of employer you want to work for? Do you prefer an organization with a mission statement that is aligned with your values? Do you prefer an organization that offers services, one that produces goods for trade, or one that operates internationally? Do you prefer working for a non-profit organization, a Fortune 500 company, a small or mid-size company, or the government? There is much to learn about each before you decide which employer you may want to target. If you're not yet clear about which employers interest you, Chapter 6 will help you explore your options.

You may have some idea about the career you want or the organization for which you want to work. Images may come to mind when you picture yourself employed. But you need to look thoroughly and thoughtfully at your options to know if you are limiting yourself to a job that just pays the bills or seeking a job that pays *and* holds potential for career growth.

Your first step is to match your skills and interests to the world of work and identify the skills you have to gain and maintain to be competitive in the job market. There is much to do—both inner research (who you are) and outer research (where you fit).

Getting Organized

If you're not organized, not only will this increase your stress level, but you may miss out on some golden opportunities during your job search. Whether or not you are a college graduate, go to College Grad's site at *www.collegegrad.com/book/6-1.shtml*. Read through the guidance on how to set up your job search control center.

Here are some additional tips to help you get and stay organized during your job search:

- An expandable—but transportable—file that holds copies of job leads, your resume, references, letters, and employer information can help you stay organized. To find such office supplies, you can either go to a local store or purchase them through one of the many online office supply stores. To find

an online supply store, go to Metacrawler's search site at
www.metacrawler.com and click the Shopping link. Click
Office Products, and then click Office Supplies. On the
resulting page, you'll find a selection of dozens of links to
office supply sites, including some of the large chains such as
Office Depot and Staples.

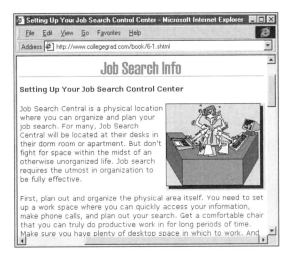

*You can learn how
to set up a job
search control cen-
ter for yourself at
the College Grad
site at www.
collegegrad.com/
book/6-1.shtml.*

- You will need a calendar to jot down appointments, "to do"
  lists, and follow-up appointments. Be sure to mark ahead on
  the calendar when you plan to follow up with an individual,
  call about an interview, or telephone to reschedule an
  appointment.

- Keep a detailed profile on each person in your network. Be
  sure to include his mailing address, email address, fax,
  phone, company, title, dates you met or spoke on the phone
  or sent a thank-you card, and short notes to remind yourself
  about each person's career and interests. You can find different types of profile sheets designed for this purpose. Go back
  to your list of online office supply stores to find one that suits
  you.

Making Decisions

Making decisions can sometimes be the toughest part of the job search. Sometimes we don't have enough options; other times we have too many options; and still other times we have competing options. Because decisions always involve some level of risk, your threshold for taking risks may determine the level of challenge.

We all employ different styles of decision making. Some styles make decision making more difficult than others; other styles leave us with decisions that may not be in our best interest. Some processes have a logical flow, while others involve only instinct. In any case, we all make decisions on a daily basis—many decisions are easy to make, but others require more thought as the stakes increase. When push comes to shove and you need to buckle down, decide, commit, and focus, how do you know that your decision-making strategy will work for you?

The Internet can help you weigh your options carefully. Some sites provide steps for effective decision making, such as the Career Development Manual by the University of Waterloo at *www.adm.uwaterloo.ca/infocecs/CRC/manual-home.html* and North Carolina State University's Career Key at *www2.ncsu. edu/unity/lockers/users/l/lkj/decision.html*. Other sites offer rules, guidelines, strategies, and checklists, such as California State University's site at *www.csulb.edu/~tstevens/c15-carp.htm*. Either way, your best bet is to use a site that does not make the decision for you based on a formula but instead offers insight into what you need to consider when making a decision. The sites mentioned here will help you do just that!

Five Steps to Making a Decision

1. Brainstorm all options and consider alternatives.

2. Write down the personal and professional risks or consequences of each option. For example, you may consider it a risk to look for work in certain jobs that may involve more travel than you want. Or it may be a risk to start a new career because it might be starting at the bottom of the field.

3. Narrow down the list by ranking them from highest (most important) to lowest (least important) according to what is most important to you. For example, salary may be more important to you than location, or opportunity for professional development activities may be more important to you than salary.

4. Choose the items ranked highest and develop a strategy for addressing the risks and consequences. For example, if salary is most important to you, but it means that you may travel more than you want to, perhaps you can look for companies that have positions for local travel. If career development opportunity ranks high on your list, but it means a lower salary, think about what you can do to address this issue, such as listing how much you need to get by and how much you can earn as you develop more skills.

5. Determine which decisions are the most viable based on this exercise.

If you're ready to make career decisions, first check out a good online model of decision making, such as the University of Waterloo's career planning site at *www.adm.uwaterloo.ca/ infocecs/CRC/manual-home.html*. Not only does this site include great career planning guidance, its approach to career decision making is one of the best we've found online—and it's easy to use. If you're not a college student, you may need to make some changes to accommodate your current situation.

▼ **Try It Yourself**

1. Go to the University of Waterloo's career planning site and click each of the four steps in the Decision-Making area in succession. Here you'll find help in making personal decisions about your career, establishing career objectives, and exploring lifelong-learning decisions and volunteer considerations.

2. Scroll to the bottom of the page and click Let's Begin.

3. Click Career Objectives and then click Personal Objectives.

4. If you're considering community service, click Community Service and answer the questions asked.

5. Lastly, we think you should click Lifelong Learning and go through the model questions. Notice that the questions are geared toward college students; if you're not a student, substitute a timeline that is more appropriate to you. For example, for Year 1, you might cross off some of the irrelevant information about course work and change the timeframe to the first quarter of the year.

The site at www.adm. uwaterloo. ca/infocecs/CRC/ manual-home. html will help you work through the entire career-planning process. We found that the four-step decision-making process outlined here is outstanding!

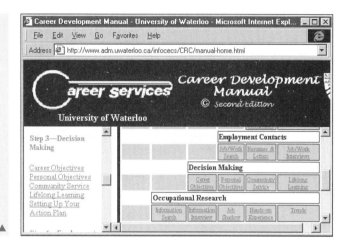

Choices in the Job Search Stadium

Making decisions in the job search is tough. Many job hunters wrestle with decision making because they don't want to pigeonhole themselves into one type of career or one type of job.

But making career decisions is a lot like purchasing tickets to a sporting event at a stadium—and the job is the field where it all comes to life.

Imagine you've never been to this stadium before, so you want to check it out to see what seats are best. When you arrive, you find that there are numerous gates (career paths) to enter the stadium. You must decide which one you will walk through. Some will be more crowded than others, and some will get you to your seat (employer) faster, but you can only go through one—for now. You can choose a different gate (job/career) at the next game (job search).

Next, you have a choice of 44+ rows, but you can pick only one—for now. You decide to go to Row 13. Why Row 13, when Rows 10, 11, 12, and others look just as good? You decide on 13 because you need to make a decision—for now. You can choose another row another time.

Next, you have 20+ seat choices (job options), but you must choose only one (to focus your resume)—for now. You decide on Seat 7. You can always choose a different seat or ask someone to switch with you during the game.

Congratulations! You're ready for the game to begin. Sometimes your team will win; sometimes it won't. But that doesn't discourage you from returning to the stadium to join in the action of another game.

So, what's the point here? Look over what just happened. It seemed like there were limitations when you had to make a decision, but each time you made one, more options became available. Also, this analogy makes the point that there will be many good options, but those options will also be there in the future. You don't need to make a lifetime commitment just because you make a decision to go in one direction—for now.

Setting Goals

What do you want to do? Where do you want to work? If you are holding out for the perfect answer, you probably won't find it. Career goals can be both simple and complex. You may know that you want to work in the field of your college major, but you're not sure where, because you don't think you have researched all your options.

Your goal is to find a job, but not just any job. Therefore, a broadly stated goal simply does not work. Goals must be specific if they are to help you stay focused and directed. However, you are not always going to find a job that matches all of your interests, so the goal must be flexible enough to allow for creative alternatives in some areas.

Most resumes begin with a job objective. In some ways, this can be considered a part of the person's career goal but, in and of itself, it is *not* a goal, because it is too broad. The job objective, however, illustrates the formation of a goal. It identifies the job seeker's career aspirations and often includes a brief description of the type or style of an ideal or preferred organization.

Most objectives are stated briefly, such as "to work as a manager in a progressive international company." This objective states the kind of work the job seeker wants, and it appears to be a reachable goal. However, to create a goal based on this objective, you must consider and include specific information. This information includes, but is not limited to, what must be done to find the job; the strategies you will use; the timeframe you will work within; and the measurable results that will indicate when the goal has been met.

At this point, you may not be ready to develop detailed career goals. In fact, your only goal right now might be to assess your interests, values, and abilities so that you can brainstorm career options. When you are ready, return to this section and visit the suggested Web sites, to help develop career goals that will lead you toward a meaningful career.

Goal-setting is tough because it means making choices. However, this doesn't mean you must conduct exhaustive research to create good career goals. It's perfectly okay to say "I thought this through and this is the best decision I can make at this time with the information I have."

Five Tips for Setting Effective Career Goals

1. Make the goal specific. You can find some great guidance on how to do this at About.com's site at *http://7-12educators.about.com/library/ weekly/aa121997.htm?iam=mt.*

2. Use strong, specific verbs. Verbs can help you be clear about what you want to achieve. If you say you want to "expand" your network, you know you'll have to take specific action to build connections beyond what you already have. However, if you state that you want to "nurture" your network, you'll have to work on what you already have.

3. Quantify the goal's outcome. Do you want to apply for two jobs, seven jobs, or only one job each week? Do you want to try to conduct two informational meetings per day or only two per week?

4. Be realistic about what you plan to achieve. If you are already working, you need to allow more time for your job-hunting efforts. You can't work every lunch and every break. You must give yourself breathing time as well.

5. Set a timeframe within which you'll reach your goal. Set your goal to change careers within three months (obviously, your own personal deadline may differ from this recommendation).

The Internet offers many sites that help you develop career goals and objectives. However, it's important to remember that your career goal is not written simply for your resume or the job search. Instead, it represents your career plan. Although you may change—and should update—your career goal, try to write a career goal for the next five years of your life.

To write an effective career goal, there are many things to consider that may affect your goal. To write an initial goal, review your skills and interests, identify preferred career fields and occupations, and develop criteria with which to prioritize your plans. To further develop your career goal, you will need to research your career interests carefully and thoroughly. These approaches are covered in the following chapters.

It's a lot of work, but taking these steps to write clear, measurable goals and objectives will help you make the best career decisions. Your career satisfaction is worth it!

Putting It All Together

You know now that careers and the skills needed for careers in the twenty-first century are changing at a rapid pace.

To be effective with your career planning in the twenty-first century, you have to make good decisions about where you're going and how to get there.

Now that you have an overview of the career planning process, you need to develop your personal career map. Your career map will guide you on your journey to finding meaningful work.

Next stop: Finding out who you are.

PART II

Establishing Personal Goals

CHAPTER 4

Finding Yourself in the e-World

If you don't know who you are, then it'll be a long and weary road trying to convince an employer that you know you've got what it takes to do the job well. Self-assessment is a fundamental and critical step that is often overlooked by job hunters. You want to find work that you can do well and enjoy thoroughly. To accomplish this, you must be clear about what you can do, what you like, what you have to offer, what you know, what you need, who you are, and what personal and professional barriers are stopping you from getting there. Job seekers who skip the inner research in favor of speeding up the job search usually end up employed, but also end up on the job search trail again, sooner rather than later. Our experience is that those who take the time to do the ground work described in this chapter often spend less time in the actual job search and usually find more meaningful employment.

Questions to Answer Before Searching for a Job

Here's a list of seven key questions you should ask yourself—and answer—before you start searching for a job. The rest of this chapter approaches each question and helps you sort through the sometimes-conflicting information so that you can come up with answers that are meaningful.

- What do I like to do?
- What do I have to offer?
- What do I know that can help me in a particular job?

What You'll Learn in This Chapter:

▶ How to identify your interests, skills, and abilities.

▶ How to connect what you enjoy doing with career options.

▶ How to identify specific knowledge and accomplishments you want to apply to your career.

▶ What values you have that will affect your career decisions.

▶ How to identify your job search barriers.

- What must I have to meet my professional needs and stay satisfied in a job or career?

- What values do I have that make me who I am?

- What is it about my personality that may influence my career and job decisions?

- What is stopping me from identifying a meaningful career or finding the job I want?

A Word of Caution About Online Assessment Tools

Many sites on the Internet can help you answer these key questions. Generally, many Web sites developed at the career centers of universities and community colleges have various assessment tools, checklists, or inventories that focus on interests, skills, abilities, achievements, values, or personality.

Many of the tools we found on the Internet were mostly abbreviated versions of assessments used by career counselors. Keep in mind that these assessment tools usually require a trained career counselor to help you interpret the results. We suggest that, if you are going to use online assessment tools, you should remember that the results are not prescriptive about who you are and what you should do.

Proceed with caution. It's important to note that no test can determine what you could do or what you should do. Instead, these online tools provide information that represents just a few pieces of the complex puzzle you are.

What Do You Enjoy Doing?

Although not all interests can be translated into meaningful careers, all meaningful careers are based on some kind of interest. Those interests that don't match or fit your career can probably be fulfilled through other activities. By weaving your interests throughout both your career and your non-career activities, you are creating a lifestyle that provides purpose and meaning.

Think about the activities you enjoy. Can you picture yourself working in a specific job or career field? By factoring interests into the job search equation, not only are you going to be happy with what you do, but you'll probably be successful, too.

You may have a degree in a specific field, but it may not drive your interests. You may have a degree in a field that you love, but you don't know where to go. Or you may not have a degree at all, but want meaningful employment. It all can be oh-so confusing!

Naturally, if you are highly interested in something, your motivation soars. One way to begin thinking about your career plan is to brainstorm what it is that interests you and what it is that you really enjoy doing. If you follow the three steps outlined in the following sections, you're probably going to end up with some exciting career options to explore in the following chapters.

Step 1: List 10 Favorite Activities

Think about 10 activities that you truly enjoy. At this point, do not concern yourself with whether or not you have the finances, education, or training to engage in the activities regularly. You can list hobbies, sports, or anything you want—just keep it legal. Think about all areas of your life. Interests can be diverse and unrelated, such as reading a book, building model airplanes, and organizing youth programs. If you can't think of 10 things, try thinking about your favorite courses in college or activities you would enjoy doing if you had extra time or if you won the lottery, or what you will do when you retire. Try to list at least 10 things.

As Easy as 1-2-3!

To identify your interests and relate them to a career, simply list your interests, rank them, and brainstorm jobs that involve them.

Career Brainstorming, Part I: Activities I Like

1. _____

2. _____

3. _____

4. _____

5. _____

6. _____

7. _____

8. _____

9. _____

10. _____

Step 2: Rank Interests from Highest to Lowest

Now rank the list of interests you just created in order from 1 (most interesting to me) to 10 (of interest to me, but not as much as the others listed). If you are having trouble doing this, think about which items on the list you talk about on a regular basis.

Step 3: Brainstorm Related Jobs

Pick your top five interests and list them on the first line of each space in the *Career Brainstorming, Part II*. Next, think of three jobs, careers, or skills that have any interaction with the items you listed. If, for example, *soccer* is one of your top five interests, you might write down *coach, player, referee, stadium manager, waterboy, ticket seller, or team administrative staff*. If you think of more than three related jobs, pick the three that are of greatest interest to you.

Career Brainstorming, Part II: Activities I Like and Related Jobs

1. _____
   a. _____
   b. _____
   c. _____
2. _____
   a. _____
   b. _____
   c. _____
3. _____
   a. _____
   b. _____
   c. _____
4. _____
   a. _____
   b. _____
   c. _____
5. _____
   a. _____
   b. _____
   c. _____

Can't Think of Jobs Related to Your Favorite Activities? Try This Shortcut

Go back to the list of your five favorite activities and try to add an action verb in front of each activity. The verb should describe your involvement and specific interest in that activity. For example, if you wrote *guitar lessons*, you might add *teaching, studying, writing,* or *practicing.*

In reviewing this list, think about how you could turn any of these interests into a career. If you get stuck, think about an organization or an association that is involved with activities surrounding your interests. Jot these ideas next to the activity.

Also, look at the list to see if you find any verbs that repeat themselves. Look for verbs that reflect other verbs, such as *teaching* and *training, designing* and *writing,* or *playing* and *coaching.*

Congratulations! You now have a general list of jobs and careers to explore. There is more to do before you actually explore these jobs, so stick with us as we walk through the next steps of developing what you need for your journey.

You can find some great Web sites to help you identify your career interests and relate them to possible careers.

▼ **Try It Yourself**

1. You can gather great ideas on careers related to your interests by checking out the Career Interests Game at *http://web. missouri.edu/~cppcwww/holland.shtml.* It's quick and easy to do: Simply go to the site and select one of the six groups of people with whom you prefer to interact. Then find your second and third preferences and investigate career interests based on these three choices.

2. If you're stuck and can't think of any careers related to your interests, go through the Career Interests Checklist at *http://icpac.indiana.edu/infoseries/is-50pl.html.* This is a simple inventory of your interests. After you check off the items of interest to you, submit your answers, and the program returns a list of possible careers to explore.

The Career Interests Checklist at http://icpac. indiana.edu/ infoseries/ is-50pl.html is a quick and easy way of developing a list of possible careers based on your interests.

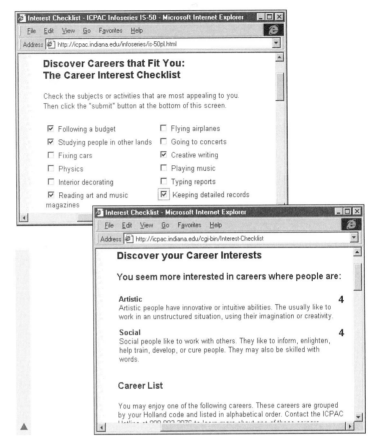

After submitting your interests, the Career Interests Checklist provides a list of potential career fields to explore with links to additional information about those careers.

What Do You Have to Offer?

Each of us has unique skills and abilities that reflect our competency at work and affect our success in a career. Skills are the building blocks of your career. With these same blocks, you can build different job structures to support different career models simply by arranging your skills in a different order.

Your Skills

You have many abilities that have helped you get to this point in your life, and you may have invested time and money in developing professional skills. Your skills are your strengths, and your strengths are what makes you a valuable asset to an employer. There are three kinds of skills you will need to identify: work-specific skills, self-management skills, and transferable skills.

Work-Specific Skills

Work-specific skills are probably the easiest to list. They are those that have been learned or honed through professional education, training, or work experience. Often these skills apply to a specific career or job and require you to have a certain level of knowledge or expertise in order to be considered competent. In several professions, such as medicine and law, some form of credential or license is required.

Work-specific skills involve the how to knowledge within a particular job or industry, such as civil engineering, accounting, software development, woodworking, human resource administration, graphic design, and fiction writing. You can find a great list of work-specific skills at Cal Berkeley's Career Site at *http://career.berkeley.edu/Prep/PrepSkills.stm*. We suggest that you print out this page and use this information to inventory your skills.

Your Work-Specific Skills

Work-specific skills are those you learn through professional education, training, or experience.

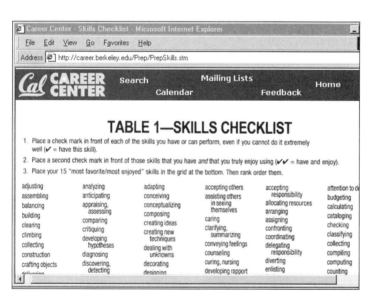

The Cal Berkeley Career Site has an outstanding checklist of skills.

Self-Management Skills

Self-management skills are personal characteristics or traits that you use to navigate different situations. These skills are not always specific to one particular job, but rather to how you manage yourself on that job. These traits may come naturally to you, such as reliability or the ability to stay organized. On the other hand, they may be skills that you have developed, such as being on time to meetings.

There are few thorough online checklists for self-management skills. We think that the Washington University's Self-Management Skills Worksheet at *http://career-3.wustl.edu/cps/self/manage.htm* will help you identify the adaptive skills that best characterize you. This list is excellent, but limited. We suggest that you complement this list with the list found at Creative Job Search's Online Guide at *http://www.amby.com/worksite/cjs/cjsbook2/skill6d.htm*.

Transferable Skills

Transferable skills are functional skills that can be applied to many different work situations. These skills usually refer to your interaction with people, data, or things. It is this group of skills that you will focus on if you are changing careers, returning to the workforce, looking for your first job, or seeking more challenging opportunities.

Your transferable skills may include the ability to analyze and synthesize information, conduct research, build structures, organize projects, write, communicate effectively, pay attention to detail, meet deadlines, work well with teams, supervise, and facilitate workshops. We recommend the Skills Zone's list of transferable skills at *www.pch.gc.ca/Cyberstation/html/szone2_e.htm*. We've found this list to be one of the most comprehensive and relevant lists online!

Your Abilities

Abilities are sometimes more difficult than skills to identify, because you may not be aware of the value of some abilities that are natural to you. For example, you may have spent time learning techniques that are often used in marketing and sales in order to be more persuasive in speaking to groups of people, and that *skill* may be well honed. The *ability* you have, however, may be in doing so with minimal time to prepare, or it could be the ease with which you connect with a specific audience, such as teenagers. The *skill* is persuasive speaking, but the *ability* is truly a gift or talent that may be difficult to develop if it is not natural. Another example of a skill is playing the guitar. However, some individuals can play music by ear. This ability is a gift not shared by all musicians.

You probably have more skills and abilities than you realize. The online skill checklists and inventories we mentioned earlier in this chapter will help you identify skills, categorize them, and record them for future reference. By going through this process, you are also identifying information that you will include in your resume or share during an interview. (You'll find more about presenting your skills in resumes and interviews in Chapter 7, "Writing Resumes: The Printed Word," and Chapter 12, "Interview Techniques Online." However, listing your skills and abilities is only the first step in evaluating them.

As you surf through the different Web sites that offer skill checklists, inventories, or assessment tools, you will notice that many sites cover one, two, or all three of the skill categories just discussed. In identifying your skills, try to think of projects or activities in which you have been successful. Think about what it took for you to accomplish what you did. Consider what you had to do to ensure the success of a project or activity.

After identifying your skills, review the list to see if your skills tend to fall into clusters. A cluster of skills may indicate areas of strength. We often prefer to lead with our strengths because success breeds success.

The next step is to cluster your skills under a broad heading or theme—similar to the way the skills are clustered in the Web sites you visited earlier in this chapter.

For work-related skills, a major heading may be *education skills*. Under this general heading, there is a list of related skills, such as *tutoring*, *teaching*, *demonstrating*, and *training*.

For self-management skills, you might list *people skills* as the major skill heading, with sub-categories of *good listener*, *friendly*, and *mitigates conflict*.

For transferable skills, you may choose a heading such as *management*, with a list that includes *managing projects*, *coaching others*, *leading teams*, *managing budgets*, and *coordinating activities*. Examples of clustered transferable skills can be found at the University of Minnesota Deluth's career site at *www.d.umn.edu/ student/loon/car/self/career_transfer_survey.html*.

Sometimes your strengths are skills that you don't want to use in your next job. It's a good idea to go back through your lists and cross out skills that you know you definitely don't want to use in the future. We suggest that you be conservative in crossing out skills, so as not to limit brainstorming in future exercises. A conservative approach would be to look just at the skills on the work-related list and cross out those that are specific to an industry or job to which you don't plan to return.

Often the more diverse experiences you have in life, the more skills you can add to your repertoire. Maintaining a comprehensive list of your skills in the three key skill areas (work-specific, self-management, and transferable) will help you with other processes and tasks throughout your job search. Print out those lists and hold onto them for future reference!

What Job-Specific Knowledge Do You Have?

Skills Versus Knowledge: You need both skills and knowledge for career success, but knowing the difference can give you a leg-up in marketing yourself to employers.

If you have been working in your career field for many years, you have probably expanded your knowledge regarding the career field itself. Knowledge is usually gained through learning, training, and experience. Identifying what key career areas of knowledge you have can help you in understanding more about who you are in the world of work and what you have to offer to an employer. You need to be able to highlight the key knowledge areas you have that make you valuable to an employer. For example, a firefighter must have good knowledge about the addresses and streets in a particular area.

What's the difference between *skill* and *knowledge*? Being able to memorize information is a skill, but having this information in your head is knowledge. Therefore, you need to consider what particular bodies of knowledge you have that might help you in a job or career. It's no surprise that what one person knows can vary significantly from what another person knows. You can have knowledge of the similarities and differences of minority populations; someone else may have knowledge of the coldest cities in North America; and someone else may have knowledge of the different airplanes used during World War II.

You might not be ready to identify which specific bodies of knowledge are going to be relevant to your career. However, we suggest that you start a list of your areas of significant knowledge, regardless of whether or not you think they are relevant. This list may spark ideas for career opportunities and will help you see strengths that may not have been clear to you before.

What You Need to Survive and Thrive

The key to balancing work and life is to ensure that you have considered both when making a career decision.

What kind of work environment will help you feel comfortable and at ease? Do you prefer to work in a fast-paced environment or a more relaxed office? Some people are attracted to a bustling office with heavy work traffic, while others prefer a quiet workspace peppered with manageable projects. These, among other environmental preferences, are important to consider. Think about it: Do you prefer to work outdoors or indoors? Would you rather live in the city and work in the country or live close to where you work? Do you want to live near relatives, or can you maintain relationships over distance?

To learn more about your work preferences, try the Birkman Career Style Summary at *www.review.com/birkman/birkman.cfm*. This assessment tool is one of the best we've seen online. It asks you a series of questions and then presents the results from your answers. It offers some insight into what work environment may work best for you. This information will help you to target organizations that offer an environment that's compatible with your work preferences.

Protect Your Environment!
When making career decisions, you need to consider your lifestyle, personal needs, and leisure activities.

There are also many personal needs to consider, such as salary, benefits, location, company size, growth opportunities, and transportation. If you are looking for work in New York City, for example, your personal needs may be significantly different than if you are searching in Flagstaff, Arizona. Take a look at the working conditions at the Career Search site at *http://cbweb9p.collegeboard.org/career/html/searchQues.html.* If you have the time, it's worth going through this career questionnaire from start to finish. This tool not only asks you about your preferred work environment, it asks you about your work style, temperament, and interests. After submitting your information, the program returns a list of careers that match the combination of your answers.

List 10 lifestyle factors that you consider most important when planning for your career or job. Think about location, climate, spouse employment opportunities, and children's educational opportunities. Also consider organization size, travel, proximity to other locations such as home and leisure activities, time commitment to work activities, flexibility with work hours or telecommuting, autonomy versus teamwork, and any others that you have identified. If you want to take a look at a list of lifestyle factors to consider, check out Bowling Green State University's site at *www.bgsu.edu/offices/careers/process/exercise.html.* This list covers some of the basic financial and living considerations.

Bowling Green State University's site has an inventory that allows you to reflect on how important different lifestyle factors are to you.

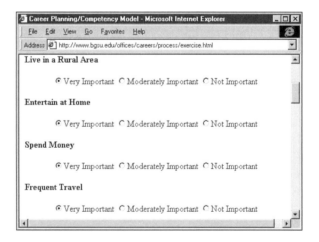

Lifestyle Considerations I Value

1. _____

_____

2. _____

_____

3. _____

4. _____

5. _____

6. _____

7. _____

8. _____

9. _____

10. _____

Next, list at least 10 areas of personal need (more, if necessary) that you must consider with a job. Such needs include salary, benefits, health care options, relocation expenses, housing options, and disability assistance, such as an ergonomic chair or keyboard. Include other needs that are important to you.

Personal Needs in a Job

1. _____

2. _____

3. _____

4. _____

5. _____

6. _____

7. _____

continues

continued

8. _____
_____
9. _____
_____
10._____
_____

Lastly, list 10 leisure activities that you consider important. Think about hobbies, sports activities, children's activities, involvement with close friends, arts and entertainment, weekend travel, religious activities, volunteer opportunities, and any others you can think of.

Leisure Activities I Value

1. _____
_____
2. _____
_____
3. _____
_____
4. _____
_____
5. _____
_____
6. _____
_____
7. _____
_____
8. _____
_____
9. _____
_____
10._____
_____

Once you have gone through all three exercises, go back through each and rank all the items in order of preference (number them from 1 to 30). Keep this combined list available for future reference.

Who Are You?

Our values influence the way we live, work, and make decisions. By identifying your values, you can establish important criteria with which to evaluate careers and eventual job offers. Values guide both our actions and our reactions. A job that is in sync with your values will most likely be more personally satisfying and rewarding.

So how do you identify values that may influence work decisions? First, it's important to understand that values evolve from life experiences, are highly personal, and have varying degrees of conviction attached. It's important to understand your current values and whether or not they are important to your career decisions. Keep in mind that values need to be realistic. Few people would choose a career with significant filing work. Yet, most jobs involve these clerical activities—even if you're the CEO of a Fortune 500 company. You'll need to stay in touch with these values, however, because they may alter with new or changing life events.

You can find some great Web sites to help you identify your career interests and relate them to possible careers. Follow these steps to locate some helpful online resources:

1. One of the best Web sites for identifying work values is Career Perfect's Work Preference Inventory at *www. careerpower.com/CareerPerfect/cpWorkPrefInv.htm*. At this site, you check activities that resonate well with your personal work values. The inventory then summarizes your work values and presents them to you in an easy-to-use format.

The Value of Values:

Being aware of the values that are of greatest priority to you can help you make meaningful life and career decisions.

▼ **Try It Yourself**

The Work Preference Inventory is a quick and easy way to identify how you prefer to interact in different work situations.

Based on your decisions, the inventory shares the characteristics of your work style.

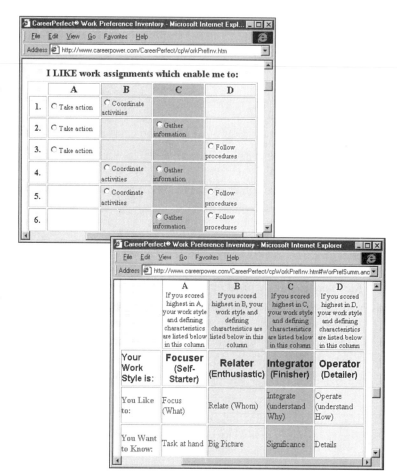

2. We suggest that you complement Career Perfect's inventory with the information on values at the University of Minnesota, Morris's career Web site at *http://www.mrs.umn. edu/services/career/Career_Planning.* You will want to print out the information and inventories because they are designed to be done with pencil and paper. There are three sections that will give you a comprehensive overview of how your values may influence your work decisions. The first section is a questionnaire; the second section is a values assessment; and the third section prioritizes your values. We suggest that you go through all three sections.

Identifying Your Values

Circle those areas that you value or which are important to you. If there are other values not listed here, add them to this list.

- Challenging assignments
- Chance to see actual results of your work
- Decision-making options
- Distance to work
- Employment security
- Geographical location important
- Good advancement options
- Good promotion opportunities
- High tech/low tech
- High-risk assignments
- Independence of action, without a lot of direction
- Independent or team work style preference
- Income level
- Maintain large career network
- Manage others
- Opportunity to relocate/not relocate
- Options for vacation/time off
- Type of boss
- Prestige
- Relaxed atmosphere
- Small, developing company
- Small/mid-size/large organization
- Stimulating work
- Structured environment
- Time for family allowed
- Travel opportunities
- Well-known employer
- Unpredictability in work or daily activities
- Variety in work
- Work in a leadership role
- Work in an office/outdoors
- Work overtime/work regular hours
- Work with things/people/data/ideas

The next step is to rate each value as *very important*, *somewhat important*, or *not important* when choosing a career or job. Hold onto this list for future reference.

What Have You Done and What Do You Know?

Your accomplishments to date give you a leg up in the job search and, even before that, in thinking about your career choice. Whether you are 22 or 52 years old, you have achieved a lot, and it's worth taking the time to review what you've done, whether you consider your accomplishments to be relevant or not. What accomplishments did you like and why? What achievements did you *not* like and why?

We haven't found many online accomplishment inventories, but we know there exist some excellent tools that involve a modest fee that are both valid and reliable. You can take the Self-Directed Search at *http://www.self-directed-search.com* for less than ten dollars. This tool helps you look at how your skills and interests may relate to different careers. If you don't want to fork out the money to pay for this inventory, it might be worth your time to print out the skill assessment worksheets at The University of Waterloo's site at *http://www.adm.uwaterloo.ca/infocecs/CRC/manual/skills.html*. This site has a good worksheet to help you identify your achievements. Remember that your accomplishments set you apart from the crowd and can provide a foundation upon which to build other skills and abilities.

Try It Yourself ▼ It's important to have a good understanding of your accomplishments and achievements. You can develop a list of your own by going to the University of Waterloo's site at *http://www.adm.uwaterloo.ca/infocecs/CRC/manual/skills.html* and doing the following:

1. Read through the introduction to clearly understand the definitions for the skills and achievement terms used throughout the exercise.

2. Print out the Web page you just read.

3. Work through the first section to identify 18 specialized, communication/interpersonal, and general skills. Be sure to identify whether or not you like to use the skill and whether or not you are proficient with the skill.

4. Pick the five skills you most want to use and give examples of your past use of them as indicated.

5. Go through the next section and list your significant life experiences. You will probably need extra pages of blank paper to work through this section.

6. List the achievements you are most proud of.

7. Go through the additional exercises on Knowledge and Learning Style and Values, if you want.

8. Hold onto this information—you will reference it in Chapter 5, "What in the World of Work Is Out There?"

Identify Your Barriers

Many of us get stuck from time to time. You may have read through everything in this chapter—or possibly even the entire book—and said, "But I've already done all of this, and I still don't know what to do or where to go with it." Rest assured, this cliffhanger is common but conquerable.

Taking a step back often helps bring perspective. In reviewing your values, interests, skills, accomplishments, do you see any patterns emerging? If not, do you see significant differences from one item to the next? Sometimes the barrier has nothing to do with the patterns. If you've recently emigrated, you may find that different laws are not permitting you to work in your career field. If you're having a tough time identifying your barriers, check out Geocities at *http://www.geocities.com/Athens/Academy/5450/3main.html* for an excellent presentation of employment and job search barriers. This site covers various barriers, from personal and financial to language and technological. The site nicely organizes barriers by category to help you better understand and consider potential barriers in your job search.

The key to successfully moving past your barriers is to be honest about what they are and to develop strategies for dealing with them effectively. Once you can identify your personal, professional, or legal barriers, you are closer than you think to overcoming them. However, you need to be realistic about what you can do to overcome them. Is there something you can do or try that you haven't done yet? Is it that you need to continue your

Breaking Down Barriers:

Knowing what may be stopping you from moving forward in your job search is the first step in moving past career-blocking barriers.

education or find professional training to round out your skills and abilities?

You can find the best-organized inventories on job search and employment barriers at Geocities.

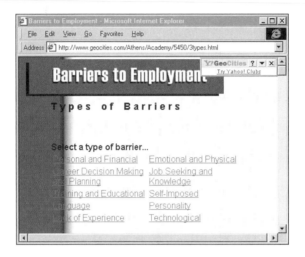

Or is it simply that your self-assessments aren't accurately representing what they should? If this is the case, it may be helpful to ask a friend to review what you've completed and offer input. Others often can help us identify skills that we don't realize we have or accomplishments that we don't see as being significant.

Finally, if you are struggling with how to move past your barriers, we encourage you to seek out a career counselor. Chapter 2, "Using This Book E-ffectively and E-fficiently," offers guidance on how to do this.

Putting It All Together

Congratulations! You did the groundwork by taking a closer look at your skills, interests, abilities, and values. This information will help you better target your job search, define what you are looking for, and ultimately help you with informational meetings and job interviews.

Now that you have looked at what you enjoy doing, what you're good at, what you know, what you want and prefer, what you've accomplished, and what's keeping you from moving forward, you're ready to connect all this golden information to relevant careers and jobs.

Next stop: Researching careers and the world of work.

CHAPTER 5

What in the World of Work Is Out There?

Exploring career options on the Internet can be both exciting and overwhelming. With the multitude of career sites on the Internet, you can easily get sidetracked on topics that may be of interest but not relevant at this point. Simply put, if you're not focused, you can easily get lost in cyberspace. You'll find career information—but you'll find more than you can use and some things that you just don't need. This chapter offers proven strategies on how to effectively and efficiently explore the world of work in the world of cyberspace. With persistence and a sense of adventure, you can begin to figure out where you fit in the real world.

What You'll Learn in This Chapter:
- ▶ How to explore the world of work online.
- ▶ How to determine what you need to research.
- ▶ How to pick careers to research.
- ▶ How to research a career both online and offline.
- ▶ How to decide on your best career option.

Did You Know...

- There are more than 60,000 different job titles listed in the U.S. Dept. of Labor's *Dictionary of Occupational Titles.*

- Most people will change careers five to seven times during their lifetimes.**

- Seventy-two percent of adults would seek more information on career options if they could start over.**

- Eighty-eight percent of people who found career information rated it as useful.**

- Fifty-three percent of those surveyed see a need for more education or training to increase earning power.**

- Global competition will result in a need for new high-skilled jobs and reduce demand for low-skilled workers.*

- Twenty occupations with the highest earnings all require at least a bachelor's degree, and occupations that require a college degree are growing twice as fast as others.*

- Half of all homes have a personal computer (1999).*

continues

continued

- Nearly 1 out of 10 workers fits into an alternative work arrangement, and nearly 4 out of 5 employers have some form of non-traditional staffing.*
- Full-time independent contractors earn more than the average traditional worker.*
- Small businesses employ nearly half of the U.S. workers in the private sector.*
- Young people hold an average of 9 jobs before age 32.*
- In five years, almost half of all workers will be employed in industries that produce or are intensive users of information technology.*
- The average American has been in his current job only four years.*

*Department of Labor/Bureau of Labor Statistics.

**Results of a Gallup survey representing 171.2 million U.S. adults. Full report: Learning to Work: The NCDA Gallup Survey, 1995, by Kenneth B. Hoyd and Juliette N. Lester, published by the National Career Development Association: Alexandria, VA.

A Changing World of Work

The world of work is changing faster than you can download a Web page. The information you find today might not reflect the reality of tomorrow. We are in the midst of a major information revolution—one that is creating, restructuring, and redefining jobs and careers altogether.

These changes can create problems for job seekers, who must stay current on career trends in their fields in order to be competitive in a changing job market. Although staying on top of these changes isn't always easy, there is no need to feel overwhelmed. You're in luck! You have three great resources at hand: the Internet, this book, and your tenacity. By using the Internet as a tool in your job search, you will find this process much faster and easier than it used to be. By using this book, you have the scoop on some of the best Web sites to find good career information.

Learning more about current careers, jobs, and the world of work is helpful only if you know *what* you're looking for and *where* to find it. Once you gather information relevant to your career interests, you will inevitably make thoughtful career decisions with confidence.

What Are You Looking For?

What do you need to research to learn about relevant careers? In general, you should be able to identify information in four areas:

- Skills you have and want to use.

- Your preferred career field(s).

- Your preferred occupational environment or industry.

- Your most important personal/lifestyle considerations (for example location, part- or full-time, Fortune 500 or non-profit, and so on).

The assessments, inventories, and checklists of your interests, values, personal considerations, abilities, and skills that you completed in Chapter 4, "Finding Yourself in the e-World," help point you in a direction to learn about who you are and what makes work satisfying for you. Now it's time to use the conclusions and assumptions you can draw from your self-assessments to research career opportunities. Integrating your results and findings so that they reflect who you are and researching viable career options that support those personal conclusions can give you a broad-brush picture of how you fit into the world of work. Here's how to get started.

Four Areas to Consider in Career Research:
- Your skills
- Career interests
- Your occupational preferences
- Your lifestyle

Getting Started

You now have a sense of the elements needed to establish attainable goals. In addition, you have already identified what personal qualities and factors are important to you in a career. Now it's time to start exploring what's out there—and there's a lot!

So where do you begin? It depends on whether you are exploring career options or searching for information concerning your chosen field.

If you are exploring career options, you will need to prepare for your research by first brainstorming career options based on interests, career tests and assessments, needs, preferred work environment, and any other factors important to you.

On the other hand, if you are researching a specific career field, you will need to define the career field in both broad and specific terms. For example, you should list the general types of employers (for example, large or small companies), industries, and other areas of interest that you wish to incorporate in your career.

For both situations, you will need to develop a list of questions and then access all possible resources to find the answers. Follow the step-by-step instructions on how to do this.

Your Career Research Road Map

It's a good idea to begin drafting a research plan—your career research road map—to help keep you from clicking astray or cyber-wandering onto pages that don't address the research questions at hand. Your goal here is to stay focused, on track and, in the words of grade school teachers, "on task."

Here's a list of steps you can follow to develop your personal career research road map. Each step is detailed in the sections that follow.

1. Create a list of careers.

2. Develop a list of research questions.

3. Identify online sources.

4. Identify non-electronic sources.

5. Identify individuals for informational meetings.

Step 1: Create a List of Careers to Research

By now you should have some idea of your general interests, skills, values, and needs. If you are unsure, go back to Chapter 4 and try some of the online assessments, checklists, and inventories.

I'm Still Not Sure Who I Am!

If the online assessments didn't help you clarify your interests, skills, values, and needs, check in with a career counselor to help you interpret the meaning of the results or to administer other assessments. Believe it or not, it's not that difficult—and, in some cases, not too expensive—to find help. Look for career counselors at some of these places:

• If you are currently a student, your university/college career center is the best place to find a trained career counselor. These services are free.

- Most universities offer career services to alumni—some are free and some have a fee. Check it out!

- Community colleges serve the community in general. Check with your local college to see what career services it offers.

- Check the blue pages of your phone directory for local government career services. Most, if not all, states have implemented some form of "one stop career service." To find the one near you, you can also check online at *www.onestop.almis.org*. These services vary by provider, but generally they are outstanding and often at no or low cost.

- Look in your phone directory under "Careers," "Jobs," or "Vocations." You're bound to find a list of career counseling providers. Keep in mind that these services come with a price. Shop around and ask for references.

- Many career counselors/advisers are now hanging a virtual sign on the Internet. The jury is still out on the effectiveness and ethics of this service. Read more about this in the Introduction of this book.

Remember to consider non-traditional employment. *Alternative careers* are those that do not fit the pattern of the traditional 40-hour, 9:00 a.m. to 5:00 p.m., Monday-to-Friday job at an office.

Alternative careers can be an exciting, adventurous, necessary, or welcome change to routine or stagnant careers. Many individuals are seeking short- and long-term careers in different settings— even in different countries. Stay-at-home moms and dads are re-creating their roles by developing part-time or full-time home-based employment, such as the following:

Times Are A'Changing: More and more workers are turning to non-traditional employment. These options are helping workers to better manage family time and personal interests.

- **Home-based business owner**   Millions of Americans are opting to start their own businesses from home. Such businesses range from tax preparation and consulting services to buying and selling items on Internet auction sites.

- **Travel writer**   Roaming from Alaska to Africa, writers are finding lots of markets interested in printing stories about their journeys.

- **Entrepreneur**   Such business people start antique stores, software development companies, consulting firms, and just about any other business that can market and sell a product or service.

- **Telecommuter**   More and more businesses are allowing employees to work at home during part or all of the work week. Employees often stay connected to the office using email, phone, and fax setups.

- **Consultant/contractor**   Professional services range from interior decorating to business consulting.

Most career assessments offer lists of possible careers based on your personal results. Your personal score or result is often related to interests, abilities, values, or personality. This score is compared to careers that share similarities with the combination of items represented by your unique score or result. Do any of the careers or jobs listed pique your interest? If so, mark them down in the spaces provided in Chapter 4 as careers to explore.

Also, go back through the list of careers you brainstormed in Chapter 3, "e-Career Mapping and Job Search Planning." Look at your list of interests and the jobs associated with them. Based on your general knowledge of these jobs and careers, could any of them fit with what you learned about yourself through the assessments?

Create a list of up to 10 career options that you want to research and write them in the space provided. If you can think of more than 10, go ahead and include them as well. Now is not the time to omit or make final decisions on what you really want to do, but rather the time to think big and broad.

Careers I Want to Research

1. _____

_____

2. _____

_____

3. _____

_____

4. _____

_____

5. _____

_____

6. _____

_____

7. _____

8. _____

_____

9. _____

_____

10. _____

_____

If you are looking for lists of careers to help you brainstorm, don't forget to check out some of the sites where you input information on interests, values, and skills. For example, if you complete the Career Interests Checklist at *http://icpac.indiana.edu/infoseries/is-50pl.html* or Career Search at *http://cbweb9p.collegeboard.org/career/html/searchQues.html* and submit your information, the program returns a list of careers that reflect your interests.

If you are a college graduate, are currently in college, or have a preferred career field, you should check out the University of Delaware's Major Resource Kits at *www.udel.edu/CSC/mrk.html.* This site covers 70 majors and provides job titles related to each major. Not only can it spark ideas for jobs and careers to explore, it gives you a start by providing job profiles and links to information about different careers.

▼ **Try It Yourself**

1. Go to the site at *www.udel.edu/CSC/mrk.html* and scroll down until you find the career field or major of interest. Click it.

2. Scroll to the second section: the lists of related job titles. Do any of these grab your attention?

3. If you're interested in this career field, either bookmark or print out the page so that you can use the resources it provides in your career research.

The University of Delaware's Major Resource Kits at www.udel.edu/ CSC/mrk.html offers a great list of 70 career fields and numerous related career titles to help you pinpoint careers to research.

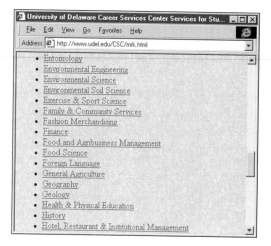

If you don't find your career field represented at this site, check out the following sites until you find your major or career field of interest:

- University of North Carolina at Wilmington at *www.uncwil.edu/stuaff/career/majors.htm*

- College of Mount St. Joseph's Kaleidoscope of Careers at *www.msj.edu/academics/career/kocfields.htm*

- Michigan's Occupational Information System at *www.mois.org/clusters.html*

- University of Milwaukee at *http://www.uwm.edu/Dept/CDC/internet-research.htm*

The most important thing to remember when looking at career information is to ensure that it is up to date. Check the dates on Web pages, books, handouts, and other sources. If the information is more than two years old, then it's too old to reflect the major technological changes that have affected many careers. If you are exploring the technology industry, then the information needs to be less than six months old.

Step 2: Develop a List of Research Questions

A list of questions will help you target specific, relevant information, which will not only accelerate the decision-making process but also make it easier. By developing a thorough list ahead of time, you will save yourself the painful process of revisiting Web site after Web site to fill in the gaps. Following is a suggested list of questions. Feel free to make additions or deletions that reflect your needs.

Twenty Questions to Research Careers

As you research careers and occupations, try to find answers to the following questions:

Technical and Professional

1. What are the duties and responsibilities of this career field?

2. What general or special skills, credentials, or licenses are needed? What experience is required to enter this career at the entry, middle, and senior levels?

3. Am I competitive in this field? At what level? Entry-, middle-, senior-, or executive?

4. Do I have the required skills and abilities? What am I missing? Do I need more training or education? What skills will require continual updating? Do I need to start in a different position in the same field to gain experience?

5. What other types of jobs are related to this career field?

Work Environment

1. What kind of work environment is typical for this work?

2. What types of employers generally hire people for this work?

3. What is a typical day like for someone in this career field?

4. Where are the jobs in this field located?

Personal Interests and Values

1. Is this a career I can see myself doing every day for the next 5 to 10 years?

2. How much of my skills, interests, values, and other considerations will be affected if I choose this career or job?

3. How does this career fit with my short- and long-range career goals?

4. What is an entry-level salary? mid-level? senior-level? executive?

5. What time commitment is required with this job? Can I work full-time, part-time, as a consultant or contractor, or as a temporary employee?

6. Is job satisfaction high in this field?

continues

continued

7. Does this career provide opportunities to fulfill personal interests, such as travel or working outdoors?

8. What are the promotional opportunities?

Employability and Sustainability

1. What is the unemployment rate in this field?

2. Where can I find further information about trends and changes for this career?

3. What is the projection for growth in this field during the next decade?

Step 3: Identify Online Sources

Once you have a list of questions, you need a list of resources from which you will gather information. Chances are that you will be able to do most of your research online. However, online information for some professions may be limited. In general, however, you should consider including the following in your list of online sources:

Online Research Resources:

- Career information sites
- University career sites
- Business sites
- Mailing lists

- General career information sites, including Web services such as Monster.com and subscriber-only online career centers such as the one run by America Online. However, the best online source for career information is the Occupational Outlook Handbook, which is provided by the Department of Labor at *http://stats.bls.gov/ocohome.htm*.

  We also suggest that you complement this information with the information found on America's Career InfoNet at *http://www.acinet.org*. The information contained in this site provides greater detail about the job market for specific career fields and offers a profile of the occupation by state.

- Career sites of universities that are well known in this field (if they are relevant). You can link to different university career sites through Catapult at *http://www.jobweb.org/ catapult/homepage.htm*. This page links you to career centers in the United States, Canada, Australia, and Great Britain.

- Web sites of related professional associations. Two sites provide excellent links to professional associations. First try My

Job Search at *www.myjobsearch.com/network/associations. html.* Here you can link to almost 2,000 associations. If you strike out at this first site, try Yahoo!'s Guide to Professional Associations at *http://dir.yahoo.com/business_and_economy/organizations/professional.*

- Relevant business sites. You can find an excellent database of businesses by industry at Yahoo!'s site at *http://dir.yahoo. com/business_and_economy/companies/.*

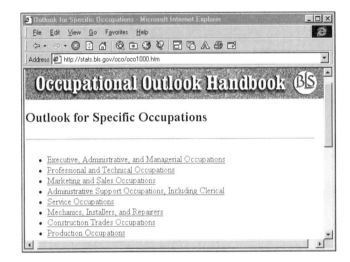

Yahoo! has an outstanding database of links to business sites at http://dir.yahoo.com/Business_and_Economy/Companies/. Click your occupation or area of interest to find an extensive listing of business Web directories and sites.

- Relevant mailing lists. Toward the end of this chapter, we cover mailing lists in greater detail. For now, you can get the latest scoop and trends on different career fields by joining mailing lists that are relevant to your career field. The Liszt at *www.liszt.com* is the best database for identifying appropriate lists and learning how to use them.

The Occupational Outlook Handbook (OOH) is one of the best resources you can find to get a realistic picture about a particular career.

▼ **Try It Yourself**

1. Go to the OOH site at *http://stats.bls.gov/ocohome.htm.*

2. Click the Perform a Keyword Search link.

3. Type a career field and click Search Now.

4. Select the abstracts that interest you most.

5. Review the information on that career field. The information available includes the nature of the work, working conditions, employment, training, other qualifications, advancement possibilities, job outlook, earnings, related occupations, and sources of additional information.

The Occupational Outlook Handbook at http://stats.bls.gov/ocohome.htm offers detailed information on more than 250 occupations.

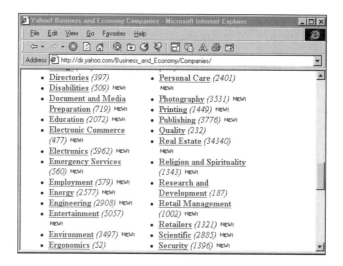

Step 4: Identify Offline Resources

A wealth of career information is also available in print. Although many printed materials are now available online, here are several printed resources you should add to your research list:

Offline Research Resources:

• Association materials

• Career books

• Business articles

• U.S. Department of Labor

• Career brochures and trade journals available through professional associations.

• Books specific to the career field.

• Newspapers and their business sections.

• Government agencies.

• Department of Labor career directories.

Step 5: Identify Individuals for Informational Meetings

A significant amount of valuable information comes from the "insiders." By speaking with people who currently work in the field of your interest or who maintain connections in the field you're interested in, you can gain insight into the day-to-day activities, opportunities, benefits, and frustrations of the field.

Remember, however, that what individuals tell you is biased information. Therefore, you should try to meet with several individuals who work in different organizations to gain a balanced perspective. Try to speak to at least two or three individuals about each career you are researching.

You can find individuals by using some of the resources listed in Chapter 10, "Networking Online and Offline." You may want to explore the Telephone Directories on the Web site at *http://www.teldir.com/eng*, which links you to more than 350 different online phone directories in 150 countries. The contents of these directories vary, but generally include the phone number and sometimes the email address of the person listed.

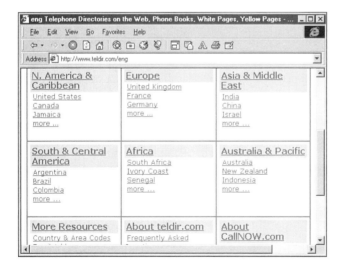

You can find email addresses, telephone numbers, street addresses, and more in any of 350 directories covering more than 150 countries.

What Is an Informational Meeting?

Informational meetings serve the purpose of gathering additional information from an expert in the field. This will help you make well-informed career decisions, and these contacts also help jump-start your network.

With Whom Do You Meet?

You can meet with anyone who is involved in an occupational field or organization of interest. As you get a clearer idea of the kind of job you want, you should interview both the employees working in that field and their supervisors or managers. Supervisors can offer information about expectations on the job as well as advice about related work within their organizations.

An individual working in the career field can offer you a realistic picture of what it is like to work in that field on a day-to-day and year-to-year basis. In addition, he may be able to provide insight into the types of organizations that hire people in the field. He may be able to recommend a professional association to join, and he may be willing to offer additional contacts for future informational meetings or networking.

Don't forget about high school teachers and college professors. If they are involved in a related academic field, they may be able to provide valuable information.

You can read through an actual information meeting at Career Chase's site at *http://www.careerchase.net/INTERVIEWS.htm*. This site houses responses to questions asked of professionals working in 20 different career fields. The professionals who offer information about their career fields are identified by gender, age, educational level, and position. This is a great place to gather some initial information as well as to gather ideas for questions to ask your own contacts.

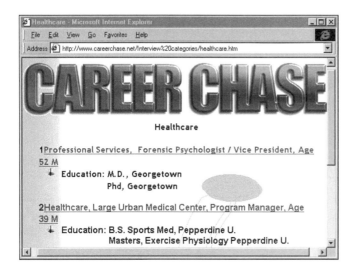

Career Chase at http://www.career chase.net/ INTERVIEWS.htm has dozens of answers to questions asked of professionals about their career fields.

Setting Up the Meeting

You have already listed several possible information sources on the career research road map. However, if you have only one or two sources, consider asking for referrals from your family, friends, former employers, former colleagues, college alumni, and contacts from social or religious groups. Remember that the easiest and best way to set up an informational meeting is to have a personal referral from someone you know who knows the person you want to interview.

If you can't get a personal referral and don't know anybody to contact, try calling a person you would like to speak with and ask him for a brief appointment. Be sure to emphasize that you only want to speak with him for informational purposes, not to ask for a job.

When you connect with the person, be honest and communicate your request clearly and concisely. For example, say "I'm interested in the work you do and would like to talk with you about it." You might say "Janet Smith gave me your name and said you are an expert in the field of retail sales. I am researching this field to see if it may be a career interest and would like to meet with you to learn more about what you do and why you enjoy what you do."

Information Only!

When contacting somebody for an informational meeting, be sure to make it clear that you are seeking career information only and not a job.

Four Talking Points for Informational Meetings

When talking to somebody for the first time, you should try to get across four points in your opening line:

1. Your name and why you chose this person to interview.

2. An indication of what kind of information you are seeking.

3. Something complimentary about the person's skill or experience.

4. A request for 15–20 minutes of time at his convenience.

Conducting the Meeting

Beyond the Information:

Although you're only asking for information in these meetings, the contacts you develop will help you build your network.

You are responsible for conducting the informational meeting, so you must prepare. You must be clear about what information you are seeking and what questions you want to ask. You want to leave the meeting with a real-world picture of this contact's job and to have additional information about the career field. However, you also want to develop contacts for future meetings and for network development.

Twenty Questions to Ask in an Informational Meeting

1. In general, what credentials (degrees, licenses, academic majors, and so forth) are required in your line of work?

2. How did you get into this field and why did you choose it?

3. What do you find most and least rewarding about this field?

4. What types of employers generally hire people for this line of work?

5. What is a typical career path?

6. What is the future outlook of this field?

7. Do companies in this field like to promote from within? What is the turnover rate?

8. What would you do differently if you could begin your career search again?

9. What other jobs did you have before this one?

10. What is a typical day or week like?

11. What skills and abilities are needed to be successful in this field?

12. What other career areas are related to this job?

13. What are entry-level (mid-, senior-) salaries? What is the financial potential?

14. What are the opportunities for travel in this field?

15. What is the best way to conduct a job search in this field?

16. How do you keep on top of the trends and changes in your field?

17. Do you recommend any relevant associations or organizations with which I should be affiliated?

18. May I keep in touch with you to let you know how my job search is going?

19. Do you know anybody else who would be willing to speak with me about this career?

20. Would you be willing to offer feedback on my resume?

Ten Tips to Maximize Your Twenty-Minute Meeting

Before the meeting, you should prepare yourself. Following are some tips for organizing yourself:

1. **Clarify what you want to get out of it**   You don't need to collect the same information meeting after meeting. Determine what you're looking for, such as information about the company, trends in the industry, or what type of career path is typical in this line of work.

2. **Collect your thoughts on paper**   Write out everything you want to know from an individual about the career field or organization. The more meetings you have, the more information you will acquire.

3. **Prepare a list of interview questions and prioritize them**   Use the list in the preceding section as a starting point, but feel free to add, change, or delete any items that aren't relevant to your information needs. Then list the questions in order of importance to you. Chances are, you won't be able to ask more than a few questions at each meeting, so make sure that you ask first the questions most important to you.

4. **Prepare to direct the conversation by being precise in your questions**   Rather than asking "What do you do?" try being more specific, such as "What is a typical work day like during your busy season?"

During the meeting, you have to remain focused on your purpose. Here are some tips to help you stay on track while you're in the meeting:

1. **Learn what the person does in his job**   Ask questions about the person's duties and responsibilities as well as what kinds of unique projects pop up from time to time.

More than Showing Up:

To make the best of an information meeting, you need to prepare questions ahead of time.

2. **Learn how the person feels about the work and what he likes and dislikes**   Try to get a sense of why this person likes or dislikes aspects of the job. Is it because of a personality conflict? Or is it because the job is routine and the person prefers variety?

3. **Be clear in your information requests**   If you are looking for information about the negative aspects of the career field, clearly state that this is what you want to know. Don't try to beat around the bush trying to get at this information.

4. **Take notes**   Bring a pad of paper and a pen   These tools will also keep you from fidgeting with your hands.

5. **Request a business card or contact information for follow-up**   If your contact doesn't have a card, ask for the correct spelling of his name and title. Also be sure to ask for a mailing address.

6. **Ask for the names of one or two others who can speak with you about their careers**   Be sure to ask permission to use your contact's name as the one who referred you to him. Remember to get his contact information; follow up with these new contacts within a few days.

Review Your Meeting

More than Saying Goodbye:

After you finish the meeting, it's important to review how it went and what changes you need to make in future meetings.

After your meeting, take some time by yourself to think about how your contact responded to your questions. Think about what you might ask next time. Also consider how well you established a rapport with the contact. Was the person relaxed and interested in speaking with you? Were you comfortable talking with him?

Reflect on how you acted, reacted, and felt throughout the conversation. Were you enthusiastic, friendly, courteous, attentive, calm, bored, defensive, or nervous? Did your contact sense these feelings or reactions? Perhaps the other person felt the same. It's normal to experience many of these emotions, but what is important is how they affect your conversation, if at all.

Was your contact willing to share solid information and names of others who may be of help? If not, think about what you might do next time to obtain better results.

Think about the type and level of language your contact used. If you did not understand something, did you ask for clarification? How did this person respond to you? It's helpful to pick up on the company or career jargon. Although you may not want to write down this information in front of your contact, it's a good idea to jot it down as soon as you leave. The terminology used can tell you more about the career field. What did you learn from the terminology used in your meeting?

Also think about what burning questions you have that were not answered. What can you do to get answers to those questions?

Lastly, what did you learn from this meeting? What did this contact gain or learn from spending time with you? What were your strengths and weaknesses in conducting the meeting? Remember that, not only are you gathering career information, you are building a network.

Remember to record your information about this meeting in a notebook you can use for future reference.

Following Up

After your informational meeting, it is important to follow up with a thank-you letter. Mention specific information that proved especially helpful to you or one suggestion that you're planning to follow through.

One Day in the Life of...

One of the best ways to learn about a career is not online. To observe or experience a career or job first-hand catapults you into the "insiders" world of career information. Aside from informational meetings, think about spending a day, week, or longer "shadowing" at least two individuals at different places of employment who are already doing what interests you.

Ask your family, friends, neighbors, colleagues, and peers for recommendations of whom to contact to make such requests. Next, contact the person and explain that you are interested in learning more about his career and would like to share a day with him at his place of employment. The following is an example of what a job seeker may find through this type of research.

One Day in the Life of Michelle

John has been working as a local sports journalist since graduating from college. He's now interested in changing his career to physical therapy. He knows from his informational meetings that he needs to go back to school, so before he invests a lot of time and money in this pursuit, he decided to experience a day in the life of a physical therapist.

John asked a career counselor at his alma mater to recommend somebody working in that field so he could spend a day at her place of employment to see what her work is really like. John followed Michelle, a physical therapist with three years of experience, for one day at the rehabilitation center.

In one day, John saw Michelle work with 15 clients who had varying needs. He watched as Michelle hopped from patient to patient, placing hot and cold presses, using different machines to stimulate muscles, therapeutically massaging weakened areas, and teaching exercises to help them build strength.

Michelle stayed extremely busy, with little time for breaks or lunch. When one patient left, another arrived. When she had a spare moment, she was busy filling in charts or filling out forms. The work kept her running and the day flew by. This resonated well with John, who enjoys the hustle and bustle of being a sports journalist.

What caught John's eye the most were the athletes who visited the clinic. There seemed to be many injuries from local sports activities. John's interest in sports initially led him to sports journalism. Now he realizes he doesn't have to give up his personal interest in sports to make a career change that also allows him to work in a helping field.

John ended the day with the knowledge that his interest in physical therapy would be mostly directed toward athletes, so he decided to specialize in that area. He realized that the work pace matched his personal work style and that the interaction with patients met his desire to help others.

Following the Road Map

Now that you have your career research road map, you're ready to start your investigation. Plan to spend anywhere from a few days to a few weeks thoroughly researching the careers on your list.

Begin by making one copy of the research questions for each career you are investigating. Be sure to leave plenty of whitespace between each question to write notes and jot down ideas, thoughts, comments, and concerns. Also include Web addresses for sites you may wish to return to for future research. (Tip: You can write the site's name with a brief annotation and then bookmark the site for an easy return.) Use the resources you outlined in your road map and follow the steps in the following sections.

Step 1: Check Out Those Web Sites

Start your research by going through the various Web sites you have identified. As you go through these sites, you'll undoubtedly come across links to other sites of interest. Visit those sites if they are relevant to your research needs. If not, then bookmark them and return to them when you are not working on your career plan.

As you go through the Web sites, try to answer all questions from the list you developed. If you end up with different answers to the same question, be sure to provide enough details to jog your memory as to the Web site you viewed and the context of the information. You want accurate information, so it's important to understand why you may be getting conflicting information.

To determine if the information is accurate, cross-check it with other sites. Also, look for the source of the information. Is it a company's site? What is its reason for sharing this information? Does it have a specific interest in grabbing your attention with the information offered?

Be sure to look at any information offered by a professional association. You can find professional associations through the Web sites listed earlier in this chapter. There are thousands of associations, representing workers in career fields that range from dairy farmers and dancers to engineers and educators. Most associations offer some type of career information or service to assist members or to educate those who are interested in entering the field. Some associations have more comprehensive information than others, but it's worth the effort to see what is online. If you don't find anything online, then e-mail, call, or write to the association and request its career-related literature.

What's a "Bookmark"?

A bookmark is a way of saving a Web site to revisit it in the future without having to retype its address. A bookmark is also referred to as a "favorite site" in a "Favorites folder."

Who's the Source?

If you're using information from a Web site that is not recommended in this book, be sure to identify the individual or organization providing the information to make sure that the information is provided in good faith and is not based on unreliable sources.

Step 2: Visit Career Centers

In general, most university and college Web sites offer up-to-date and reliable information about many careers. The content is developed for the students (and alums) of their institutions, but most Web sites are available to the public. Take advantage of this access, but double check to ensure the information is current or recently updated. Use the sites mentioned earlier to locate online university career centers.

Step 3: Gather Information from Professionals

Once you have gathered sufficient information from Web sites, you need to balance your research findings with information gathered by meeting with people currently working in the field. There are several ways in which to do this. Some may be faster and easier, but not necessarily better, than others.

Listservs or Mailing Lists

These are email services that allow groups of people to communicate using email. Any *subscribed* member (there is usually no cost to subscribe) may send a message that all subscribers will automatically receive by e-mail. Lists are maintained by an individual or organization. There are thousands of different lists, covering just about any topic or career field you can think of. You can find mailing lists at The Liszt at *www.liszt.com*. This site's database contains information on more than 90,000 mailing lists. If you want a quick look at mailing lists by topic, check out Topic.com at *www.topica.com*. This site does an outstanding job of categorizing mailing lists.

We recommend that you join one or two lists related to your career field, but observe only at this point. We strongly caution against asking questions until you observe the list's *netiquette*. List participants often remember the people who do not use the list appropriately. For more information on netiquette, visit the Netiquette Home Page at *http://www.albion.com/netiquette*. This site offers the rules of the road for communicating in the cyberworld.

Your purpose at this point should be to observe the discussion to gain perspective on the current topics and trends in the field.

Associating with Associations:

Professional associations can be some of the best resources for finding career information. Be sure to check out what is available through an association that represents your career field of interest.

Seven Ways to Ask Professionals for Information:

1. listservs
2. chat rooms
3. email
4. letter (regular mail)
5. fax
6. phone call
7. face-to-face meeting

Later in this book, we'll discuss how to get involved in a listserv or mailing list for networking purposes.

However, you may choose to join a list that is specifically for job seekers. Although it is acceptable to discuss your job search, we still recommend observing for a few days and reading the rules carefully before participating.

Chat Rooms

Online chat rooms are areas in which you can participate in a live discussion. Some sites that support chat rooms offer rooms by topic. Subscribers to America Online have access to numerous chat rooms on varied topics, including the job search. Other chat rooms can be found by going to Yahoo at *www.yahoo.com* and typing **Chatrooms**.

Email

Email has quickly become the communication choice for many organizations, individuals, and employers. However, most people consider their email to be quite personal. We discourage you from emailing somebody for career information, unless human resources is his job.

It is easy to find the email address for just about anybody. There are entire Web sites devoted to helping you find people. You can also find email addresses for many employees and employers by going to their Web site. Keep in mind that many employees don't have a choice about whether or not their name and contact information is placed on a company Web page; they may not be keen about others contacting them through this medium. Also remember that most people do not like to receive unsolicited email.

Unless you have been referred to an individual by somebody he knows, it's best to avoid using email to find career information. You can find email addresses through the Web sites listed earlier in this chapter.

Approach Letter (Snail Mail) or Fax

Writing letters or sending faxes can work well for you if you know how to use them appropriately. A letter, for example, can be written to request a face-to-face meeting or to request a telephone conversation. However, we discourage you from sending a letter with a lot of questions. Most people don't have the time to send a reply or may not feel comfortable responding to somebody they don't know.

We suggest that you don't send faxes to request career information or informational meetings. It lacks confidentiality for the individual on the receiving end.

You can learn how to write a good approach letter in Chapter 9, "Writing Letters for the Information Age."

Phone Calls

Phone calls are appropriate for requesting an informational meeting or literature from a company or association. If you decide you want to talk to a person on the phone to ask questions about his career field, we suggest that you leave a message asking permission to set up a phone appointment.

Face-to-Face Meetings

There is something to be said for looking someone in the eye and making a connection. This is probably the best and most valuable form of communication. Not only are you able to ask your questions, but you are developing a network as well. A face-to-face visit results in a human response that you can't get from a telephone, letters, or email.

Making Decisions at the Crossroads

Once you have researched enough about each career, you are probably ready to narrow down your list of career options. Chances are, your research helped de-select several career options and left you with only a few that really stood out from the rest as meeting your personal and professional needs. If you're having trouble narrowing down the list to three or fewer, go back to the information on how to make a decision in Chapter 3 to help you weed out some options.

Keep in mind that as you narrow down the list, you don't need to close the door on other options—particularly if they may hold some interest for you in the future. Maybe they don't fit your short-range or immediate career plan, but they may fit your mid-range or long-range plans. Hold onto the information that you think will be helpful in the future. Remember, you will probably change jobs/careers within the next one to four years.

Just When You Think the Research Is Over, There's More!

Now that you have a clearer picture of the type of career that interests you, you're ready to move on to other areas of research. You may already have some information from the career exploration you conducted or from the self-assessment process.

However, if you have not yet explored your personal considerations, now is the time to do it. Take your top one to three career interests and think about what you need and what you want. Do the necessary research to see how your career interests match your personal needs.

Salary and Benefits

The bottom line is that you need to earn a living. Consider what your bottom line is. What do you need to survive? What do you need to thrive? Consider what benefits you need, such as health insurance, maternity/adoption leave, professional training, and life insurance. If you are already covered by health insurance, maybe you don't need that. If you are relocating, what expenses would you need covered? Learning about what salary and benefits you want and need will help you as you research career and job options.

Part-Time or Full-Time Employment

Do you want to work 20, 40, or more hours a week? Keep in mind that some full-time jobs mean more than 40 hours and some part-time jobs mean more than 20 hours. Determine what it is that you want and need to work. Also think about whether you prefer traditional hours or evening and weekend hours. Nurses, for example, often work only three days per week but work 12-hour shifts, often at night. This information can affect your decision on some careers and jobs.

Don't Forget to Consider:

- Salary and benefits
- Part-time, full-time employment
- Family needs
- Continuing education
- Environmental needs
- Travel
- Predictors for success and satisfaction

Family Needs

If you are a single or married parent, there are many considerations, such as childcare, school hours, sick days, maternity leave. Many factors can also affect the time you spend with your family, such as travel, deadlines, work pressure, and self-imposed pressure. Think about how much time you want to spend with your family and how your career decisions may affect this. You should consider all aspects of your home life and family needs, because these weigh on your career decisions.

Continuing Education

If you plan to continue your education, are you interested in an employer who will be flexible with your work schedule or who may subsidize your education? If this is important to you, you may want to investigate these opportunities as they relate to your career choices.

Environmental Needs

Do you prefer to work in an urban or rural environment? Do you prefer an artistic or a conventional environment? Do you want a creative environment or one that has specific guidelines and rules? Would you prefer to work for a large or small organization? Do you want to work in an office or outdoors? There are numerous environmental considerations. What are yours? Your environmental considerations should be taken into consideration as you make career decisions.

Travel

If you want to travel, how often? Do you prefer to travel domestically or internationally? Would you prefer to travel to a specific region? Whether or not you want to travel should be an area you consider as you research career options.

Predictors for Success and Satisfaction

What do you need to thrive? Is it the opportunity for promotion? Greater responsibility? Stability? Change? Less responsibility? Write it all down and see if it matches what is offered through the careers and employers you are exploring. You should consider these factors as you explore your options and make career decisions.

Personal Considerations Checklist

- Salary and benefits _____

  _____

  _____

- Part-time, full-time employment _____

  _____

  _____

- Family needs _____

  _____

  _____

- Continuing education _____

  _____

  _____

- Environmental needs _____

  _____

  _____

- Travel _____

  _____

  _____

- Predictors for success and satisfaction _____

  _____

  _____

Putting It All Together

Congratulations! You have now explored your career interests by using both high tech and traditional methods.

You integrated your assessment results from Chapter 4 with the career information you uncovered online, through college or community career centers, and through informational meetings.

You now know how to conduct informational meetings and probably feel much more comfortable talking with others about who you are, who they are, and how you both fit in your careers. Yes, you have started the networking process and are ready to move forward!.

Next stop: Researching employers, industries, and organizations.

CHAPTER 6

Finding the Right Industry, Employer, and Organization

Now that you have narrowed your career interests to one or more career fields, it's time to start looking at industry information and trends, as well as organizations and employers.

Researching Industry Information

Integrating industry information with your research on specific employers gives you a clearer picture of company options. You want to learn about the products and services of the industry, how the industry divides labor into function areas, industry jargon, and career path opportunities within an industry.

To find more detailed information about a particular industry, try the WetFeet.com site at *http://www.wetfeet.com*. WetFeet.com is an outstanding resource. Simply click the Research Industries link in the left column and you're there. WetFeet.com is one of the best compilations of research information online. It covers industry trends, an overview of what's good and not so good about the industry, key companies in the industry, job tips, key positions within the industry, and links to materials you can purchase if you want even more detailed information. However, what is offered on the site appears to be sufficient; you probably won't have to purchase additional materials.

What You'll Learn in This Chapter:
- ▶ How to research industry information.
- ▶ How to research employers and companies online.
- ▶ How to find private sector employers quickly online.
- ▶ Where to find information about federal, state, and local government employers.
- ▶ Where to find online information about non-profit organizations.
- ▶ Where to find information on geographic locations.
- ▶ Where you can research salaries and benefits.

WetFeet.com at www.wetfeet.com serves as a one-stop resource for finding great industry information online.

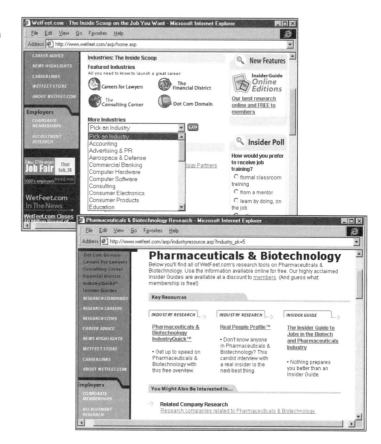

After you select an industry to research, you will be offered a menu of choices, just like the one on this page.

One of the handiest features on WetFeet.com is the section on What's Great and What's to Hate in the industry.

Let's take a look at WetFeet.com's Web site for excellent profiles on different industries.

▼ **Try It Yourself**

1. Go to *http://www.wetfeet.com/asp/industryresource_home.asp* and click the Research Industries link in the left column. You should now see the industry research page.

2. Take a look at the featured industries at the top of the middle column and begin by looking at those pages, if they represent your industry of interest.

3. If the industry you're interested in is not at the top of the column, scroll down the middle column and review the list of industries. Click the name of the industry that best matches your interests or career field.

4. You will be offered a list of information options, including an overview of the industry, a profile of somebody working in the industry, and a link to an Insider Guide, which highlights a company in the industry.

5. Scroll down further to find links to additional relevant information, such as links to companies working in the industry and other related research.

Researching Companies and Employers

There are different online and offline ways to research companies. Online, you can look at company listings by size, by industry sector or a breakdown of each industry, and other factors. Offline, you can find company information at university or community career fairs, libraries, and career centers, as well as directly from the company. Overall, this approach will lead you to major companies, but this is not necessarily the savviest direction to take.

By looking only at major for-profit employers, you are missing out on other options that may better meet your needs and interests. You must consider the different types of employment sectors in order to determine the direction in which you should go.

Changes in a Decade

In the 1990s, many professions required skills now considered obsolete. Although the overall duties may be the same for many professions, the skills required have changed dramatically in just the last decade. For example, if you were an accountant, that job used to require you to write checks by hand, operate a calculator, and track finances in ledgers. Now, accountants crunch numbers much faster with computers, and employers want them to have skills in spreadsheets, databases, and accounting software.

You need to know about the changes and trends in your career field. The changes are happening daily, and you are responsible for staying on top of them. The best way to track industry trends and employers is to join a professional association.

You can locate associations through a search on My Job Search at *www.myjobsearch.com/network/associations.html*. My Job Search has links to nearly 2,000 associations. We suggest that you visit and bookmark the Web sites of the organizations that address your interests. Often they have good career information, trends in the field, and links to related sites.

Types of Employers and Organizations

There are three major employment sectors that you will need to research to determine which is the right fit for you: private sector, public sector, and nonprofit sector. Each sector has various arenas—each with its own set of advantages and disadvantages. It's worth taking the time to explore each of these sectors. All sectors provide employment opportunities for most jobs and careers; however, the role or function of such positions will vary from sector to sector. Each of these three sectors is detailed later in this chapter.

Applying Traditional Employer Research Methods

In the old days, a paper cut was a greater threat to job hunters than computer eyestrain. Savvy job hunters spent days in libraries, career centers, and organizations' reception areas reading anything they could dig up on employers. They searched for information in pricey business directories, local newspapers, business magazines, professional trade journals, company profiles, and employer literature. Eventually, they were introduced to exclusive and expensive technology that manifested itself in information databases and CD-ROMs. They requested annual reports and detailed literature directly from the company or pumped recruiters for the latest information at career fairs. They conducted numerous informational meetings with insiders, and they called their professional associations for assistance.

As for the resources used today, not much has changed—except for the technology that allows you to access much of this information from the comfort of your home, 24 hours a day, 7 days a week. Now, savvy job hunters tap these same resources through myriad Web sites devoted to providing just the information you need.

Keep in mind, however, that not all employer information is online. For example, many employers may have Web sites, but they won't necessarily post information on their missions, departments, staff, and job listings. If you don't find it online, you need to balance your Web research with some of the more traditional research methods.

What You Need to Know About Employers

The Internet is your electronic librarian, but without a degree in Library Science. You can find all kinds of employer information, but you need to know what you're looking for, because the Internet search engines are not as "educated" as a librarian who would give you the right sources.

So, what is it you want to know? Arming yourself with key information about a company will help you determine whether it's the type of company for which you want to work. Some of the questions will depend on your personal preferences but, in general, you should be able to find data about the company you're interested in so that you can respond to the following questions:

- What industry is this company part of? What is its product or service? Does the product or service interest you?

- What is the overall working environment of the organization? Is it appealing to you? Is the location acceptable to you?

- How are the company's functions organized? What is the workflow? Does it reflect your personal work and organizational style? What is the typical work environment like?

- What is the management style and philosophy? Do they match yours?

- What jargon is used in the company's literature?

- What are the career path opportunities within the company and industry? Do they reflect your longer-term career goals?

- How stable is the company and what are its long-term prospects and risks?

- How has technology and business trends affected this industry and organization? Are you on a par with their technology? Do you have the required skills?

- Where are the positions that interest you located?

- What are your prospects for employment and how could you enter the company?

- What is the salary range for positions that interest you and what are the benefits and perks?

Keep in mind that you want to identify and research companies that support your personal interests, values, and goals. The Internet is exploding with valuable information for different groups of people and people interested in working in nontraditional positions. Also, remember to ask those in your network to offer any inside information on specific employers.

The Private Sector

The *private sector* spans the business of profit-making. Businesses trying to sell a product, a service, or an idea are competing with other companies that are vying for the same market.

Globalization is changing how businesses run and how business is done. It is making a significant impact on the way the private sector operates and the way people work. Because a shifting paradigm always means new rules of the road, researching organizations is essential to an effective and efficient job search.

In general, the private sector can be divided into five groups, based on size: Fortune 500 companies, large companies, mid-size companies, small companies, and the self-employed. Your objective is to figure out which suits you best. Although the self-employed are considered to be a group in the private sector, the topic of self-employment is much too broad to cover in this chapter. However, it's important to understand that this segment of the working population belongs to the private sector; many people who are independently employed sometimes contract out their work.

The Private Sector:

The private sector is made up of for-profit businesses and the self-employed.

Most job hunters expect the majority of jobs to exist within the large corporations. Not true. Small businesses—those with fewer than 100 employees—make up more than 80% of the workforce. Be sure to explore your options before making assumptions and decisions. Go back through the list of questions to answer when researching employers. Using the Web sites appropriate to your industry, you should be able to respond to most of these questions.

Sizing Up Private Sector Employers

The private sector includes the following five groups of employers:

- Fortune 500 Companies: top ranked companies, usually more than 5000 employees
- Large Companies: non-Fortune 500, more than 1000 employees
- Medium-Size Companies: 100 to 1000 employees
- Small Companies: 1 to 100 employees
- Self-Employed: 1 employee or more (and does not fit in one of the other four categories)

Finding Company Web Sites

It's easy to find an employer's Web site. There are two shortcuts to getting there:

- Go to a basic search engine, such as Yahoo! or AltaVista, and type the name of the company in quotes, such as *"Proctor & Gamble"*.
- In the address line of your Web browser, simply type the name of the company between *www.* and *.com*, such as *www.proctor&gamble.com*.

Tips for a Local Employer Cyber-Quest:

If you are researching a particular company, find out the location of its headquarters. Search the online newspapers and magazines from that area to uncover the latest news relevant to the community.

General employer information and profiles can be found on the Internet. Many companies have developed sophisticated Web sites to present their company information. In researching larger companies, you often can find details on new ventures, as well as company products and services. However, many smaller companies have yet to establish a Web presence. You will have to rely on traditional research methods in order to be inclusive.

To uncover details that an employer may not include on a Web site, you can check the periodicals. The Web has sites dedicated to linking you to news-related information. Many of these sites offer a search feature, which makes it easier to identify an archived article that references a specific company or industry. The site with the best compilation of business news sources is @Brint.com. Go to *http://www.brint.com/newswire.htm* and scroll down the page until you find a news source that reflects your industry or company of interest.

The BizTech Network's @Brint.com site is an excellent site to link to business resources on the Net.

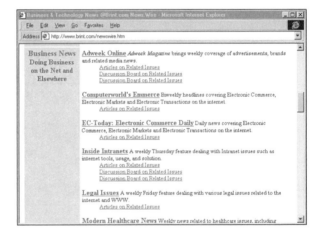

Try It Yourself ▼

Try finding company information in archived news articles. Here are some steps to guide you in this process:

1. Go to *Business Week*'s Web site at *http://www. businessweek.com/search.htm*. This page allows you to search issues going back five years. If you are a current subscriber to *Business Week*, there is no charge to access these articles.

However, if you are not a current subscriber, you can still perform searches and find out what information is available. The search will return the first 40 words of the story, which is probably enough for you to determine whether it's worth purchasing the article or not.

2. If you don't yet have a company name you want to research, scroll down to the bottom of the page and type **Coca Cola** as a sample search term in the box next to the word Go.

3. Click Go and then review the articles that turned up. You'll find a detailed selection.

4. Repeat steps 2 and 3 using other company names that are of interest to you.

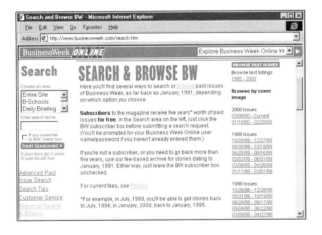

Business Week's Web site at http://www. businessweek.com/ search.htm allows you to search articles from the past five years of their weekly magazine.

Even if you can't find company details, you still have online tools to get you where you need to go, such as electronic telephone directories to find a company's location and phone number.

Best Places to Find Company and Organization Information

Hundreds of businesses add new Web sites to the Internet each day. Such sites will continue to join the cyber-world at lightening speed. Because there is no lack of companies to research, the online challenge is to determine what information you want so that you can target specific employers.

We found some sites that we think are your best online bets.

General Business Information Sites

The Web now provides outstanding business information through one-stop shopping sites, referred to as "business meta-sites." You can find a variety of links to information on companies, industry, employment, trends, and more at My Job Search's company research page at *http://myjobsearch.com/cgi-bin/mus.cgi/ employers/research.html* and the site's Directories page at *http://myjobsearch.com/cgi-bin/mus.cgi/employers/directories.html*.

The My Job Search site at http:// myjobsearch.com has an outstanding collection of links to online directories and research pages that provide company information.

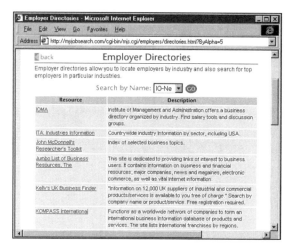

Try It Yourself ▼

Are you ready to look for company information by using one of the online directories? Let's try this together:

1. Go to My Job Search at *http://myjobsearch.com/ cgi-bin/mus.cgi/employers/research.html*.

2. Suppose that you are interested in the airline industry. Because you don't see a directory listing only for airlines, scroll through the pages and select Hoovers Online. This online directory has access to thousands of company records. Click that link to go to the Hoover's Online page.

3. Click the Companies and Industries link. This link takes you to a page on industry updates.

4. Now find the link to the airlines industry and click it. You should see a listing of airline companies with links to information about each one.

5. Click the link to the airline that interests you most and read all about it.

Offline, you can find general information through your local Chamber of Commerce, library resources, and the Small Business Administration.

Sites about Company Profiles and Directories

Profiles and directories can be found on the Internet and in local libraries. They offer excellent information on company size, location, ownership (public, private, or foreign), and type of business. The information varies from directory to directory, so make sure that you cross check the companies that are of greatest interest to you.

Company Information Sites

You can find information about many employers on their Web sites. Most large and medium-size employers have or are developing sites. Many small employers are getting on board, but not all are there yet. You need to supplement the online information and Web sites you find with some traditional methods, such as company directories, annual reports, and news.

International Business Information Sites

If you're interested in working in international commerce, tourism and recreation, development, or some other arena, you need to find the key international players. On the Web, you can find international business directories. The best compilation of international business resources is Michigan State University's Center for International Business Education and Research (MSU CIBER) at *http://ciber.bus.msu.edu/busres/company.htm*. Here you will find links to company and business information worldwide.

Offline, you can find this information in the business directories in your library, through a professional association, or through the Department of Commerce.

> **Researching Employers Through Informational Meetings**
>
> General company information will be instrumental when making decisions, targeting employers, and interviewing for jobs. But you must balance your research with information obtained through informational meetings.
>
> Informational meetings help you acquire insiders' knowledge about a company or industry, which you would never catch sight of online.
>
> Review Chapter 3, "e-Career Mapping and Job Search Planning," for details on how to plan and conduct informational meetings.

Employers and Different Populations

When it comes to hiring individuals from certain populations with special interests, some employers are considered friendlier than others. If you are a member of one or more of these groups, such as women and minorities, you should identify and check out employers who are known to support your group(s).

Discrimination Still Exists:

In the year 2000, mostly women hold secretarial jobs and mostly white men hold senior management positions. Your goal is to find an employer that supports your values and what you have to offer.

Don't assume that employers will be open to your issues just because your rights to equal employment are protected by law. Discrimination exists in all employment sectors. You need to research organizational policy and management's track record within the division where you would most likely work. Some of this can be found on the Web, including online articles and newspapers. However, you need the inside scoop. This only comes from insiders' knowledge. Use your contacts from informational meetings and your networking strategies will pay off.

Most career Web sites offer sections for minorities, women, career changers, and other unique groups. You can find an outstanding list of links to different sites at the Riley Guide (*http://www.dbm.com/jobguide/diverse.html*). The Riley Guide provides links to career resources for women, minorities, military, the disabled, and other affinity groups and audiences.

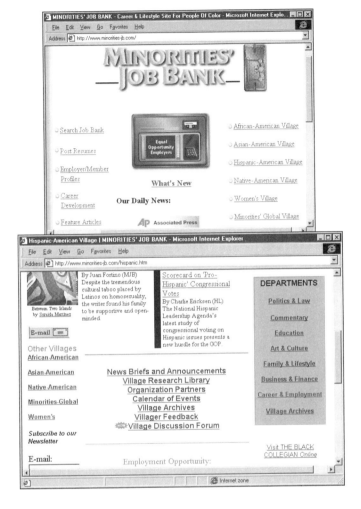

The Minorities' Job Bank at http://www. minorities-jb.com is a great resource for minorities and women to use to connect to career information rele-vant to them.

After clicking a specific village, scroll down and click the Careers & Employment link in the left column. You'll see current news arti-cles related to that group of people.

If you're looking for information on employers and careers that support the interests of special populations, follow these steps:

▼ Try It Yourself

1. Go to the Riley Guide at *http://www.dbm.com/ jobguide/diverse.html*.

2. Scroll through the long list of links to Web sites that address career issues of different populations. For example, scroll down and click the Minorities' Job Bank link.

3. Note that the Minorities' Job Bank is more than just a collection of jobs for minorities. It also includes articles of interest to different populations. Check them out. For example, click Hispanic-American Village.

4. Scroll down and look in the left column. Click Careers & Employment. This link takes you to a list of articles regarding employment issues of Hispanic-Americans. Each of the villages in the Minorities' Job Bank has a Careers & Employment section. It is an excellent way to stay on top of trends and companies addressing issues of different populations.

Public Sector

The public sector's bottom line is not the dollar. Instead, the public sector is organized to provide services for and assistance to the taxpayers who fund the government.

The public sector includes the federal government, state governments, and local governments. The federal government has more than two million employees, making it the largest U.S. employer and one of the largest employers in the world. The United States Postal Service is the largest department, with nearly one million employees.

In the mid-1990s, the federal government made an effort to downsize and decentralize operations. Although the downsizing is slowing, the federal government continues to hire more than 300,000 people each year to fill positions that have been vacated.

Jobs with the Feds!

The federal government hires nearly 300,000 people a year, making it the largest employer in the country.

Contrary to public opinion, less than 10 percent of all federal jobs are located in the Washington, D.C., area. There are more than 400 different occupations within the federal government that include nearly every career field. These jobs pay a wide range of salaries and offer a variety of benefits.

The federal employment system is often complicated, convoluted, and confusing. Most job hunters don't know how their experience fits in with federal job requirements. There are also many questions concerning the process for writing a resume for the federal government and completing job applications.

Federal Government

Fourteen cabinet departments and over 100 independent agencies comprise the federal government system. These departments and agencies have offices in all corners of the world. The size of the agencies varies considerably. The larger the agency, the more diverse the opportunities. These large agencies hire to fill a broad spectrum of occupations, both professional and unskilled labor positions.

If you want to travel, government jobs offer abundant opportunities to relocate within the 50 states and throughout the world. Twelve federal agencies and departments offer employment abroad for over 60,000 U.S. citizens. The Department of Defense Dependent Schools system employs hundreds of teachers for military dependent schools overseas.

There are numerous employment paths available: full-time, part-time, and job-sharing positions, cooperative education hiring programs, internships, student employment, job opportunities for veterans and the handicapped, and summer work programs.

The best way to find out about government employers in your preferred location is to look in the blue pages of your telephone directory.

These pages will enable you to identify local government offices. This listing is much easier to use than a similar electronic directory, so use it first if you are particular about location.

Once you have an idea of where you want to work, your next step should be to gather as much information as you can about the agencies you have identified. Check out their Web sites for publications, press releases, programs and services, and archived speeches. You can link to just about any government Web site through the World Wide Web Virtual Library's page on U.S. Government Information Resources at *http://www.nttc.edu/ gov_res.html.* If you have a specific query, such as *government careers in California,* it's easier to use Govbot at *http://ciir2.cs.umass.edu/Govbot,* which is an effective and easy-to-use searchable database of U.S. government Web sites.

State and Local Governments

Thousands of state and local government opportunities exist nationwide. Most government branches reflect the organization of federal programs. For example, all states have a division of health as well as housing. Some states have tourism bureaus and overseas trade representatives. All governments have administrative and managerial opportunities.

As a rule, the federal and state governments tend to be more concerned with the big picture, or national interests, while county and municipal governments work on local aspects of the same topics. For example, a state social service organization might be concerned with evaluations and budget making, while the county counterpart would deal with more hands-on duties.

You can find the Web sites of state and local governments through the Piper Resources Guide of State and Local Governments on the Net at *http://www.piperinfo.com/state/states.html*. Again, if you have a specific query, try using Govbot at *http://ciir2.cs. umass.edu/Govbot*. Also, be sure to talk with people who already work within the system to learn more about its organization and opportunities.

Nonprofit Sector

Volunteers soliciting charitable donations, selling candy, or constructing homes is often the picture conjured when you refer to "nonprofit" work. In general, nonprofit work is stigmatized as no-pay or low-pay and not professionally challenging. We beg to differ. In fact, many nonprofits offer competitive salaries and meaningful, professional employment. We think you should check them out.

From small and simple to big and bureaucratic, there are more than one million vastly diverse nonprofit organizations whose bottom line is not monetary but mission and purpose. Millions of Americans are employed in these organizations, which generally focus on education, health, social services, religious services, business, philanthropy, culture and the arts, the environment, or research.

Here are some examples of the kinds of services and programs offered by the nonprofit sector:

- **Culture and the Arts**   historical, performing arts, visual arts, music, cultural affairs

- **Education**   community education, private schools, educational institutions

- **Environment**   advocacy, environmental awareness

- **Health**   hospitals, cancer, heart, other illnesses, clinics, nursing homes

- **Philanthropy**   foundations

- **Professional & Business**   associations, societies, trade, employment

- **Religious Services**   churches, synagogues, other religious institutions

- **Science and Research**   scientific and research, think tanks

- **Social Services**   poor/disadvantaged, international, food/clothing/shelter, youth, women, minorities, cooperatives, economic and community development

Most nonprofits offer services and programs at the community level, but some have national or global operations. They vary significantly with regard to their sizes, missions, locations, communities served, organizational cultures, salaries, promotional opportunities, and work opportunities.

Because budgets tend to be smaller in nonprofit organizations than in large corporations, the majority of nonprofits depend heavily on the voluntary work of affiliated individuals or community members. However, full-time employment opportunities still exist in thousands of organizations.

Ranging from entry-level to executive-level, nonprofit jobs often attract individuals who believe in the mission of the organization. The skills most successful nonprofit job hunters need to demonstrate to a potential employer include commitment to its mission, strong writing and communication skills, and the flexibility to deal with changes and ambiguity.

Here's a short list of some of the jobs you can find in nonprofit organizations:

- accountants

- administrative staff

- computer specialists

- conference and meeting coordinators

- fundraisers

- lobbyists

- managers

- membership coordinators

- policy analysts

- presidents/executives

- program specialists

- public relations/marketing

- writers/editors

Online Information About Nonprofits

You have many career options with nonprofit organizations. Fortunately, your research is manageable, since most nonprofits are on the ball and have some form of Web presence. Nonprofit information is generally organized on the Web in four ways: by local or national organization, by online directories, by arena, and by category on other career sites.

The easiest route is to visit one of the online directory Web sites that offer an overview of nonprofit employment, employer profiles, links to organizations, job banks, and trends in the field. Our favorite site is Idealist at *www.idealist.org*. Idealist has information on more than 20,000 nonprofit organizations in over 140 countries.

If you're looking for information on nonprofit employers, first try these steps:

▼ **Try It Yourself**

1. Go to Idealist at *www.idealist.org*.

2. Click the Find an Organization link. This link will take you to a search page.

3. You can search by the organization's name, if you know it. If you don't, the easiest way to find organizations in your field of interest is to search by combining the area of focus and the location. Select a focus and location and click the Search button.

4. You will see a list with links to profiles of organizations that match your search criteria. Each profile also provides a link to the organization's Web page, if one exists.

Idealist at www.idealist.org is one of the best Web sites for finding and researching nonprofit employers.

You can narrow your search focus by filling in more than one field in the search form.

Other Areas Related to Employer Research

Researching employers involves more than simply finding information on the organization. You need to know where the organization is located and what salaries and benefits it offers. Fortunately, you can do a lot of this research online—we'll show you how.

Location, Location, Location

Geography is key when you're researching potential employers. In order to determine where to look for work, you first need to know where you want to live. Maybe you are flexible and willing to move anywhere. Perhaps you'd prefer to move overseas. Maybe you'd prefer a change of climate. Of course, you may want to stay where you are.

You need to determine the location factors that are important to you. Many people love living in New York City, but others won't go near it. Each of us has different stress buttons that when pushed can send us through the roof. Make a list of what you can't live without. Then add what you must have to live a satisfying life. Money.com at *http://pathfinder.com/money/depts/real_estate/bestplaces* offers an annual listing of the best places to live in the United States. This article includes information on both big cities and small towns and covers a range of factors, including employment, crime, and education. You can also use its screening tool to find a place that matches your own interests. If you don't find a city here that you want, try USA City Link at *http://usacitylink.com*. This site has a comprehensive listing of cities nationwide, with links to other relevant Web sites.

Try It Yourself ▼   You can find out what cities meet your needs by following these steps:

1. Go to Money.com's Best Places to Live page at *http://pathfinder.com/money/depts/real_estate/bestplaces*.

2. Look at the left column and click the Find Your Best Place with Our Exclusive Screening Tool link.

3. If you want to do a quick search, you can look for cities based on any of the following nine factors: weather, economy, housing, health, education, crime, transportation, leisure, and arts and culture. Click the factors that are most important to you and submit your request. The factors you selected will be broken down into subsections. Fill in the blanks and submit your request for a list of cities that match your interests.

4. If you want a more detailed search, click the All 63 Factors link and submit your request. This action divides the nine factors into greater detail. For example, the economy factor is broken down into the cost of living index, sales and income taxes, job growth in the past year, projected job growth, and unemployment rate. After you submit your responses, the site returns a list of cities that match your criteria.

Money.com is an excellent source for information on living in more than 300 cities in the United States.

Location: Ten Things to Consider

- cost of living
- low unemployment
- real estate
- climate/weather
- schools/educational opportunities

continues

continued

> • arts, cultural events, sports, activities
> • crime and safety
> • medical access
> • commute/transportation
> • family and friends

Salaries and Benefits

When researching employers, you can't ignore your financial needs. Although everybody has different financial concerns and constraints, we all have basic needs to be met. Your goal is to find an employer that can offer you a compensation package that meets your financial needs. The following sections offer information on what to think about as you research salaries and benefits.

Salary: Ten Things to Consider

> • life insurance
> • health insurance
> • retirement plan
> • savings plan
> • appropriate salary for cost of living
> • relocation expenses
> • earnings of others with equivalent experience and education
> • emergency fund
> • stocks and investment opportunities
> • sick leave/pay

Benefits: Ten Things to Consider

> • professional development and training opportunities
> • contributions to retirement accounts
> • travel
> • profit-sharing
> • professional and club memberships
> • sick leave, vacation, and holidays
> • child care benefits
> • relocation assistance
> • performance bonuses and holiday perks
> • flex-time, telecommuting, alternative work options

Salaries in the Private and Nonprofit Sectors

Most people spend more time planning a vacation than researching salaries. The problem is that if you don't spend your time doing the research, you may have to forego the vacation. You need money to survive, and you need more money to thrive.

Not only does research help you determine what jobs and careers you can or cannot afford, it also helps you rule out areas that may be out of your cost-of-living range. You can do most of your salary research at Job Star at *http://jobstar.org/tools/salary/index.htm*. This site has links to more than 300 different salary guides, calculators, and surveys. It's the most comprehensive collection we've found online.

Researching salaries also helps prepare you for confident salary negotiations. After interviewing, the ability to negotiate salary is the least-honed skill of job hunters today. But those who have done their research and developed the negotiation skills almost always come out ahead.

The Internet has simplified the general research and even some of the detailed research. First, you need to make a list of what you need to earn to cover your basic expenses. Next, you need to anticipate future expenses, such as children, continuing education, or an ailing relative. Putting all of this together gives you a sense of what you need (and what you are worth).

Salaries in the Public Sector

Many job seekers flock to the government because of stable wages and the generous benefits packages that are offered.

Most federal white collar positions are under the aegis of the Office of Personnel Management (OPM) and are known as General Schedule (GS) positions. All GS positions are classified according to a numerical career series, and each job within the series is assigned a grade to reflect level of duties and responsibilities. Grades range from GS-1 to GS-15. The higher numbers reflect higher level positions and salaries. You can find out what the current salary scales are by going to Federal Government Pay Scales at *www.opm.gov/oca/payrates/index.htm*.

Salaries are determined by the amount of education and relevant experience you bring to a position. In general, a GS-5 salary range requires a bachelor's degree or three years of general experience. This experience is expected to provide a good, basic knowledge of the principles of organization, management, and administration.

A GS-7 position requires a year of experience relevant to the position, a bachelor's degree with superior academic achievement, or one year of related graduate study.

A GS-9 placement requires an additional two years of related experience, a related master's degree, or two years of graduate study.

By researching all the GS levels, you will gain enough knowledge to determine the level for which you qualify. Keep in mind that the hiring process is market driven and usually requires more than the minimum qualifications for certain salary levels.

Although benefits vary from agency to agency, the government benefits tend to be more limited than those offered by the private sector. Still, the benefits are good and are similar to the basic benefits offered in the private sector. One perk is that government employees, in general, have a dozen days off throughout the year in observance of federal holidays.

State and local government pay ranges will vary according to many factors, such as position and geographic location. The government typically rewards length of service and provides stable pay. Pay is based on some combination of performance and seniority. Annual cost-of-living increases are relatively common in the public sector. Increasingly, employers in the public sector are also including variable pay, pay for performance, bonuses, and skill-based pay in their compensation programs. Ask your prospective employer what reward systems are available.

Putting It All Together

You've done it! You have enough information to make some job search decisions. Now is the time to define your career objective and target your job search. Review and refine your career goals. You're on your way to a satisfying career!

You now know more about your career industry and possible employers in the private, government, and nonprofit sectors. By determining your preferred location, salary, and benefits, you have developed a solid job search foundation and should now have a focused career goal.

By pulling together the information you've gathered in this and the preceding three chapters, your analysis and "hunches" should point you in a direction in which you feel confident and enthusiastic.

Now it's time to start developing some job search tools so you can market your skills and experience. Good luck!

Next stop: Writing a powerful resume.

PART III

Developing Job Search Tools

CHAPTER 7

Writing Resumes: The Printed Word

Ask 100 career counselors how to write a resume, and you'll get at least 100 different answers. There is no one right way to write a resume! Our advice is based on more than 40 years of combined experience working with resumes and job seekers. More importantly, our experience includes significant contact with employers across the country and around the world. This, perhaps, is where we've culled most of our resume writing guidelines. We've taught these techniques to thousands of job seekers, and we've seen great success.

Still, writing a resume is tough and takes time. This chapter will demystify the resume-development process and show you how to use the Internet to help you write your resume. This doesn't mean it'll take less time to write your resume, but it will help you develop a more powerful marketing tool for your job search.

This chapter will guide you in creating an attention-grabbing resume. However, new technology has opened the door for job hunters to post resumes online, submit resumes for scanning, and email resumes to employers. But you first need to know how to write a powerful resume. Nail down the basics in this chapter before jumping to the next, which will guide you in developing the latest and greatest electronic resumes.

Your Resume Is a Tool That Markets You to Employers

The resumes of today are not the same as those of yesterday. A resume that grabs attention, makes a statement, and has the best chance of convincing an employer to invite you to an interview is

What You'll Learn in This Chapter:

▸ How to use your resume as a marketing tool.

▸ What employers look for in a resume.

▸ The difference between chronological and functional resumes.

▸ How to write a powerful resume.

▸ How to make your resume look great.

the one that meets the needs of today's employers. You need to understand what the employer is looking for and respond to that need by connecting your experience to his requirements.

If you are currently looking for a job, chances are you have written or tried to write a resume already. In fact, you may have created one to share during your informational meetings or networking opportunities.

Maybe you wrote a resume before you even knew what you wanted to do. After all, what's so complicated about writing one or two pages about your accomplishments? For starters, if you have already written a resume, you probably wonder if it's complete, if it's effective, or if it's what the employer wants to see. Maybe you had trouble boiling down four or five years of experience into one or two pages. Perhaps you're changing careers and think that your resume doesn't reflect relevant experience for jobs that interest you now.

Your resume is a word picture of you, describing your background and relating it to your goals and the needs of the employer. The bottom line is that your resume is a unique document that presents your life and work experiences as they relate to your professional goals as well as the employer's needs. Whew! That's a lot to accomplish on one or two pieces of paper. We know you can do it, and we believe you can do it well. Just follow the steps in this chapter, and you're on your way to developing a powerful job search and self-marketing tool.

Contemporary Resumes for the New Millennium

What differentiates a contemporary resume from a vintage one? The answer is simple but critical for you to know and keep in mind when writing your resume.

A resume used to serve as a personnel document that contained a description of your work history, documentation of your abilities, and a listing of job descriptions. Not any more. Now, your resume serves as a marketing tool instead of a personnel document. It describes what you have to offer by listing work accomplishments and documenting core and transferable skills that you enjoy using. To do this effectively, it focuses on the future (the vintage resume focused on the past).

If you can grasp these concepts and apply them, you'll be in good shape!

Will a good resume get you a job? The easy answer is *no*! A resume is *not* going to land you a job. Do you know anybody who was offered a job based on his resume alone? Probably not. Not many people are offered jobs based solely on the contents of a resume. Instead, your resume needs to grab the interest of an employer so that you will be invited to interview for a job.

When Do You Use a Generic Resume Versus a Targeted Resume?

Since you'll need to target your resume to the needs of employers, you're probably wondering what to do if you don't know what an employer needs. You also will need a resume for informational meetings or network contacts who want copies for their own reference or to pass around.

For these situations, you'll need to develop a powerful generic resume that you can carry with you to meetings and networking functions. It will also serve as your framework for developing tailored resumes for specific jobs you'll eventually apply for.

To develop your generic resume, follow the same steps that we outline in the rest of this chapter. The only difference is that you'll need a lot of feedback from your contacts to ensure that you are representing yourself well for the industry's general needs and that you're using appropriate buzz words for the industry and employer.

If you have interests in more than one industry, you need to develop a generic resume for each. Then, as you develop contacts in those fields, ask for their feedback on your resume. Your contacts will help you tweak different areas to power it up!

Know Your Job Objective Before Writing Your Resume

Before you even think about writing your resume, you need to know what kind of career interests you. By now, you should have assessed your skills, interests, abilities, values, and personal needs. If you haven't, go back to Chapter 4, "Finding Yourself in the e-World," before beginning this process.

Job Objectives and the Laundromat:

You must have a clear job objective about what you want to do or you'll spin in circles like a sock with static stuck in a dryer at the neighborhood laundromat. You'll eventually end up in somebody's laundry basket, but probably not the one you really want to be in!

You must know what your job objective is *before* you write your resume! You're probably wondering, Don't I write the objective *on* my resume? Perhaps. But, whether you do or not, your job objective is what drives your job search and the contents of your resume. The information included in your resume must support what you want to do.

Imagine you spent the last five years in three different jobs as a telemarketer. You're sick of being on the telephone, so you want to change careers. Although you don't know what you want to do, you decide to write a resume to get your job search started.

You include all of your phone experience and make it sound like you're quite the expert in phone sales. You pass along your resume to friends of your parents, and they pass it to an employer who has several positions open: a front office manager, a receptionist, and a marketer.

You are thrilled when the employer invites you to interview for her company. When you get there, the employer mentions how impressed she is with your telephone skills. You talk fervently about your phone expertise, thinking this will show her how good of an employee you are. Instead, she says that she has a dire need for someone with solid phone skills and offers you the receptionist job. You sheepishly, but politely, mention your interest in the marketing position, but she's quick to point out that it doesn't seem like you have the experience for that—even though you do!

What happened here? You pigeonholed yourself into being a telephone communications expert! Not exactly the career change you were looking for.

Imagine now that you are interested in becoming a marketer. You certainly have relevant experience, but you didn't pitch it that way in your first resume because you didn't have a clear job objective. You focused on your job *duties* instead of on the accomplishments, skills, and functions related to marketing-type positions. We'll talk more about how to focus on these later in the chapter.

Resume Rules for the Road
- Know your job objective.
- Know what skills employers want.
- Get feedback on your resume from those in your network.
- Make every word count.
- Make sure that the final product reflects the best you have to offer.

You'll find a lot of great information online to help you produce the best possible resume to market yourself effectively. Most colleges and universities offer information about how to write a resume. Most of the larger online job banks also offer resume writing information. Proceed with caution. Find out who is writing this information and what credentials and experience they have that makes them authorities.

Generally, you can count on the resume sites that are referred to on the Job Hunter's Bible at *http://www.jobhuntersbible.com*. The author of the site is Richard Bolles, author of *What Color Is Your Parachute?* He keeps the site's information updated and is a credible source.

Richard Bolles' site, the Job Hunter's Bible at www.jobhuntersbible.com, *is an excellent reference point for identifying the best and most helpful resume writing information online.*

Try It Yourself ▼

Are you ready to find some great sites that offer tips on how to write a powerful resume? If so, the Job Hunter's Bible site offers excellent references. Check them out for yourself:

1. Go to the Job Hunter's Bible site at *www.jobhuntersbible.com.*

2. Scroll down the page until you see the Resume link in the left column. Click it.

3. Read through the Fairy Godmother Report to get the scoop on what you can and can't expect from some of the sites listed here.

4. Go the Build section and click the Best Online Articles link. This link takes you to a review of this site.

5. Click the site and scroll down. You'll find some of the best material online about how to write your resume.

6. Read the reviews on the different articles and select the one that interests you the most and is appropriate for your needs.

▲   Congratulations! You did it!

What Employers Look for in a Resume

Translating Résumé

The word *résumé* is a French word that means *brief*. The French write it with the accents over the letter *e*. Most Americans, however, drop the accents (´) but pronounce it virtually the same as the French do.

This is not the time to be verbose. Don't include everything you've ever done since you started kindergarten! Remember this: The French word *résumé* means brief. Employers don't want to read your life's history. If they're interested enough, they'll invite you in for more in-depth conversation or an interview and ask you more questions about your experience and education. Ultimately, the resume's purpose is to get you an interview, not a book contract.

This means that you need to focus on what will grab the employer's attention—and then get rid of the rest! What grabs the employer's attention? Whatever solves his problems!

Unlike days gone by, employers no longer want to know whether you'll be happy with the company long-term. It's not that they don't want you to be happy, but they are looking for someone who can jump on board with minimal training and minimal time to get up to speed.

Most employers won't *expect* you to commit to their companies beyond a few years. Other employers won't *offer* you employment beyond a few years. Hence, they need to know you are ready to go, so that they are getting maximum productivity from you in the short time you are working with them.

The changes in the world of work greatly affect the style of your resume. Ignoring these changes is toxic—and the Internet is filled with resume toxicity. There are plenty of old-style resumes that just don't fit with the new way of work. We caution you to be judicious about using other people's resumes as examples. And before trusting resume-writing guidelines you come across online, make sure the site is reputable and the author is credible.

While some employers still like to see an objective, most can't tell you how it helps or hinders your job search. Some will say it's because they want to know if *you* know what you want. This happens a lot with employers who look to hire college graduates right out of school.

What they *don't* tell you is that if your job objective doesn't match what they have to offer, then you might be knocking yourself out of the ballgame. And why would you want to do that?

Writing the Right Objective

If you decide that you want to include an objective on your resume, we have a few guidelines to help you write a good objective.

An objective serves two key purposes:

1. It quickly tells the reader what it is you want to do. This is critical because most resumes get only 10–30 seconds of attention.

2. It helps you focus the content of your resume. Writing a resume is hard enough without trying to be all things to all employers.

An objective is simply a statement about the work you want to do and where you want to do it. Follow this formula to write your objective:

Position in (name the type of organization or company) where (skills you have) and (knowledge/experience) can be used to (purpose of job or organization).

We believe that most employers who still want to read an objective are those who hired people under the old paradigm, when a job with a company meant a lifetime commitment. Back then, the employer knew you would be with the company for a long time and wanted to make sure that you would be happy and that the company would match your personal and professional interests. He planned to invest a lot of training and money into getting you up to speed, which often took a few years, and he didn't want you to jump ship after he had made a major investment.

Careers are shorter now. Job contracts have an average range of a few years. Employers don't have the luxury of waiting months or years for you to get up to speed with your job.

Employers need people who can hit the ground running. If you don't believe this, take a look at the job postings on any Internet job site. Not only do the job listings indicate the needed skills, most detail the experience and education you must bring to the job. This means that the employer is not likely to train you—he wants you ready to go!

How do you do this? The Web is packed with tips and techniques of the resume writing business. If you know where to go, you can learn how to change your resume from a good resume to a powerful resume. We know where to go and we'll tell you how to get there! Although there is a lot of advice online, we've identified the sites offering strategies that work! Once you get the hang of it, it's not that difficult to do.

The Employer/Job Hunter Connection

You need to tailor each resume for each job, based on the employer's interests and needs. How? Research, my friend. Where? The Internet, of course!

Let's say that an employer needs someone who can communicate with executive-level staff and develop marketing campaigns for under-represented sales regions. You need to focus on the key skills and functions requested. Sometimes, the easiest way to do this is by using the same verbs used by the employer, such as communicate and develop. Next, use the key words of the duties with other work you have done, such as planned meetings for *executive level staff.*

Do you see what you're doing? You're connecting your experience to the needs of the employer. You're making it easy for the employer to say, "Here's somebody who's got the experience we're looking for! Let's bring him in for an interview."

Five Steps to Connecting Your Experience to Employers

1. Highlight the key action words in a job vacancy announcement.

2. Identify the company's buzzwords on its home page.

3. Identify company problems or issues related to the position that interests you.

4. Weave this language into your resume, if possible.

5. Review what you wrote to make sure that you don't misrepresent your experience and skills.

The Two Resume Formats: Chronological and Functional

Resume formats are quite diverse, but generally fall into two categories: chronological and functional. You'll find good and bad examples of both throughout cyberspace.

Chronological Resumes

A *chronological resume* presents your work experience in the reverse order of occurrence. For example, your current or most recent job is written first, followed by your prior job, followed by the job prior to that. You go all the way back to your first significant job, which is listed last.

Chronological resumes tend to be the format of choice among most employers—but certainly not by all. This format is especially effective if your present career field and your past and present work experience are relevant to your career objective.

A chronological resume usually has a heading such as Career Experience or Professional Experience instead of Work History. If you don't use the phrase Work History, you may include paid and unpaid experiences that support your job objective. Most employers will consider both paid and unpaid experience, so long as it is relevant.

Chronological Resumes

There are any number of possible titles that you can use to head the chronological section of work experience. Try one of these:

• Career Experience

• Professional Experience

• Professional Accomplishments

• Experience

You can also use a functional heading to help the reader focus on your skills or job functions. Try using this formula:

(Name Major Function), (Name Other Major Function), and Related Experience

For example, "Administration, Sales, and Related Experience" or "Accounting, Management, and Related Experience." Such a title helps the employer zero in on your accounting and management experience.

If you're in college, a recent college grad, or seeking entry-level work, you should check out the chronological resume sample and the resume templates at the College Grad site at *www. collegegrad.com/resumes/index.shtml*. The resume templates cover 28 different career fields and can be downloaded into your word-processing program.

For those with more work experience, Monster.com at *http:// content.monster.com/resume/samples/resumes* has excellent resume samples for various career fields. If your career field isn't represented there, check out the sample resume for financial analysts. This is a great model with which to develop your own resume.

Monster.com has some of the best examples of chronological resumes. Check them out at http://content. monster.com/ resume/samples/ resumes.

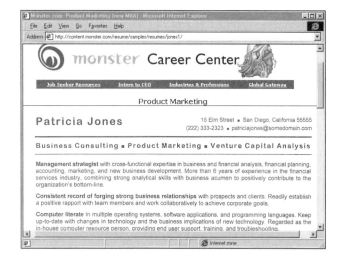

If you're looking for excellent examples of resumes, look no further than Monster.com:

▼ **Try It Yourself**

1. Go to *http://content.monster.com/resume/samples/resumes*.

2. Scroll down the page to the section called Sample Traditional
   Resumes.

3. Click the name of any profession that interests you. If you
   don't have a preference, click the sample for a financial
   analyst.

4. Note how the resume is well-organized, sharply designed,
   and focused on accomplishments and results. Also note that
   relevant training is included in the Education section.   ▲

Functional Resumes

A *functional resume* presents your experience according to your
areas of expertise and significant functional skills that demonstrate your qualifications for a job. For example, you might be
able to list all of your relevant experience under two or three
headings, such as Management and Administration,
Communication, and Project Planning and Implementation.

A functional style is often used by people changing career direction, by those who have held jobs in a number of different career
fields, by those who have had gaps in their work history, or by
those who have limited experience. However, this format can be
risky, since most employers know the reason why people use this
style!

The functional style works when the chronological format just
doesn't seem to do the trick. However, if you decide to use this
format, we strongly urge you to include a brief section detailing
your employment history. By including this information, you
hope to dispel the employer's suspicion by providing such details.
Some resume sites call this the combination style because it com-
bines elements of the chronological and functional styles.

You'll find great examples of a functional resume at JobStar at
http://jobsmart.org/tools/resume/res-fu1.htm and at Career
Experience at *http://careerexperience.com/resources/ resumes/
functional_prof.html*.

A functional resume has all employment experience under a heading such as Relevant Skills and Experiences, Skills and Abilities, or Areas of Expertise. Then, under this heading, describe your functional skills and experiences under specific skill headings such as Teaching and Training, Curriculum Development, and Program Management.

What Format Is Best for You?

We believe that the best style to use can be determined by assuming first that you will write a chronological resume. However, if you think the functional resume works best, then go ahead and use it. Then, develop a chronological resume with a focus on the functions and skills you outlined in the combination resume.

If the functional format still seems best for you, you need to go with what works, but be sure to include your work history and get plenty of feedback from your network and contacts with regard to employer preferences in your career field.

Resume Components: What Stays and What Goes

Generally speaking, there are four main components in a well-written, powerful resume:

- Your contact information

- Your qualifications

- Your skills and experiences

- Your education, training, and affiliations

As you can see, it's a simple framework that keeps the reader focused on what you want him to see in the short time he will spend reviewing your resume. We'll briefly define each of these four areas and then go into detail in the sections that follow.

Your *contact information* goes first. Some people place it to the right or left, but most place it in the center. Regardless of position, it goes first on your paper.

The *qualifications* summary replaces the outdated and overrated job objective and follows the contact information. This is a synopsis of your skills and experiences that relates to the job you are applying for. It's usually a short paragraph or a sentence or two with a bulleted list of your skills. We'll go into more detail about this later in this chapter.

The *experience* section can be presented in either the functional or combination format. If the combination format is used, then your career history should be inserted between the experience and education sections.

The *education, training, and affiliations* section is last. Most people who write resumes often put this information at the top. Unless your network tells you differently or you're in an academic field, or your education is more significant than your career experience, we strongly advise you to place it at the bottom. By placing it at the top, you're saying I don't have any experience that is as relevant as my education. And, again, what are most employers looking for? Experience! Show 'em what you've got and *then* tell 'em how you were trained!

What Contact Information to Include

The contact information you need to include is your name, street address, home phone number, day phone number, and dependable email address. If you have more than one residence (as do many college students), list your current address *and* your permanent address. Be sure to label them as such.

Employers still prefer to contact candidates by phone. You need to include your home phone number and day phone number. These two may be the same, but if not, be sure you can accept and retrieve messages at the phone numbers included on your resume. Also, if the employer is going to hear an answering machine, make sure the message is professional and includes your name. Lose the *Beverly Hillbillies* theme song in the background.

Your Resume Speaks!

Your resume says a lot about you:

1. Who you are.
2. How to find you.
3. What you've accomplished.
4. How you did it.
5. How you learned it.

What Does Your Email Address Say to Employers?

It's important to present a professional image, and your resume is often the first impression you make on an employer. When considering including your email address on your resume, make sure it appears professional, because your email is first identified and then archived by your name and the title you give to it. Avoid using email addresses that have unprofessional names in them such as *bigboy, skifan,* or *daydreamer*. People remember most what they read first and last!

Web-based AOL Email:

If you have an AOL account, you can access your AOL email through the company's Web-based server at http://www.aol.com/aolmail.

If you don't have a dependable number to leave and retrieve messages, we encourage you to either rent voicemail or consider getting a cell phone. Voicemail providers can be found in the phone directory. Most voicemail services offer features such as personal greetings and the ability to retrieve messages from anywhere. It's also fairly inexpensive (about $10 to $15 per month).

If you don't have an email account, now is the time to set one up. We recommend that you establish a free, Web-based email account so that you can access it from anywhere in the world where there is an Internet connection. What a deal! Rather than going home to check your email account several times a day, you can do so from wherever you are that day.

If you're looking for specific services, such as mail-forwarding, compare services at Email Addresses at *http://www. emailaddresses.com/email_web.htm*. If you're looking for a standard email service that allows you to send and receive messages, it might be just as easy to set up an account through Yahoo! at *www.yahoo.com*. Simply click the Mail link at the top of the page and follow the directions from there. Yahoo! is known for its ability to handle graphics, video, and sound.

Try It Yourself ▼

Are you ready to set up your own Web-based email account? Follow these steps, and you'll have one ready to go!

1. Go to Yahoo! at *www.yahoo.com*.

2. Just below the search box are two lines that have many of the Yahoo! services listed. Look for the word Mail (it's often on the left side). Click the Mail link.

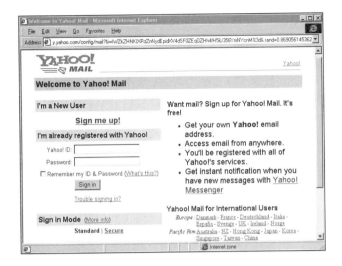

The free email you can sign up for through Yahoo! at www.yahoo.com is one of the more popular free email accounts you can find, because of its reliability and its capability to handle graphics, video, and sound.

3. You should now see a page that has a section called I'm a New User. Click the Sign Me Up! link to see a page that you fill out to set up your free account.

4. Select and type a name that you want to use for the first half of your email address. The second half will be *@yahoo.com.*

5. Select a password that you can remember easily and type it in (also write it down so that you can remember it when needed). Type your password again to confirm it.

6. From a pull-down menu of options, select a question that you can answer easily, such as your birthplace. In the event that you need to ask the Yahoo! staff for your password again, you will be asked this question.

7. If you have a current email address, fill that in next. If you don't, leave the line blank.

8. Fill in some information about you, such as your name, zip code, gender, and occupation. You may also choose to select areas of interest in the event that you want to hear about future events or promotions from Yahoo!

9. Click Submit, and you're on your way to communicating in the cyberworld!

What Makes a Powerful Career Summary

Your career summary serves as an overview of your resume. It highlights the most important elements of your background to catch the attention of a reader. Think about going into a bookstore to buy an interesting book. You might read the book jacket or the back cover to find a book that meets your interests. The career summary works in much the same way, to grab the employer's attention so that he will want to read your resume more closely.

The Difference Between Objective and Career Summary

As we mentioned earlier, a career summary—also called a *career profile* or a *qualifications summary*—is usually more relevant than an objective. On a piece of paper that the reader probably spends less than 30 seconds viewing, you need to select carefully what you want to include. Each word should serve some purpose that relates to your job objective and addresses the employer's needs. If it doesn't, then it doesn't belong there.

Simply put, objectives tell the employer what you want in the job market. Employers are less interested in what you want and more interested in what *they* want. A career summary provides a concise picture of what you have to offer. The career summary tells the employer *I have the experience you want.*

Keep in mind that you *do* need a job objective! You just don't need to put it on your resume.

How to Write a Career Summary

Imagine that we gave you a 3×5 index card and asked you to write in the lined spaces everything we need to know about you in order to make a decision as to whether or not to call you for an interview. It's not a lot of space. You need to be particular about the words you choose, and you need to be focused. What you write on this card is what you'll write for your career summary on your resume.

Yet, just like resumes, career summary styles vary significantly. You may have written your information as a paragraph, as a list, or as a combination of the two. There are no hard and fast rules, but there are some general guidelines. Fortunately, the Internet is teeming with resources and samples.

We strongly encourage you to take a look at the different models on the Internet, such as the samples at Distinctive Documents at

http://www.distinctiveweb.com/samples.htm. This site is designed
to sell resume-writing services, but it also offers outstanding
examples of resumes. Notice that each career summary is slightly
different to address the strengths of the job seeker and to address
the needs of the potential employer. In addition to these online
examples, we have some of our own models to help you on
your way.

Your career summary should include the following:

- Level of experience

- Area of experience (if relevant)

- Areas of expertise

- Skills and abilities

Some Career Summary Models

Following are some models for career summaries that consider
various kinds of experience you may have accumulated.

If you have less than three years of relevant experience:

> *Career Summary:* X years of (industry or setting) experi-
> ence in A, B, and C. Background also includes X, Y, and Z.
> Computer experience in _____. (Also add foreign
> languages, if relevant.)

If you have more than three years of relevant experience:

> *Career Profile:* X years of significant _____ expe-
> rience in A, B, and C. Expertise in the following:

• (list relevant skill)	• (list relevant skill)
• (list relevant skill)	• (list relevant skill)
• (list relevant skill)	• (list relevant skill)
• (list computer skills)	• (list languages you know)

These models list the number of years of experience to emphasize
that you have the length and level of experience the employer
wants. However, include this information only if you meet the
requirements of the employer.

Computer and Language Skills Count!

Remember to include computer and language skills in your career summary.

Following the number of years, include the industry or setting, if it is relevant to the employer's needs. For example, you might write *Fortune 100, financial industry*, or *education*.

A, B, and *C* relate to the top three areas of expertise you have that are relevant to the employer's needs. If it's not relevant, you don't need to include it here.

X, Y, and *Z* or *relevant skill* should be your skills and competencies, such as *budgeting, team-building*, and *written communications*. These skills are usually your transferable skills and should be specific to the employer's needs for the job. If the employer doesn't need for you to have these skills, don't include them. Also, if you don't want to use these skills (such as phone work), don't list them.

You might be wondering why we said to include computer skills in your career summary. It's because employers want to know that you *have* computer skills. Believe it or not, many people still don't. By letting the employer know what computer programs you know, you're removing a big concern of many employers.

There are different ways to list your computer skills. You can be either specific or generic. Your best bet is to find out what type of computer system your employer uses (PC or Macintosh) and then list your experience accordingly.

Let's say that you have experience on a Macintosh system with PageMaker, Microsoft Word, and Excel. You find out that the employer wants somebody with computer experience, but the company uses PC systems. Instead of writing *Computer: Macintosh programs, including PageMaker, Microsoft Word, and Excel*, simply eliminate *Macintosh programs*. However, if the employer uses the Macintosh system, then leave it.

The goal here is not to fool the employer, but to help the employer focus on what you *can* do and not what you *can't*. With computer systems being so similar today, the system doesn't matter as much as your experience with different programs.

This brings us to another point. What do you do if the employer wants experience on a software program that you are not familiar with? Your best bet is to list your software programs generically, such as *desktop publishing*, *spreadsheets*, and *word processing*. This will help the reader connect your experience to his computer needs, as opposed to connecting one software package to another.

If you have experience in a second language, it's a good idea to list the language. As the marketplace becomes more global, and as employers become more sensitive to the importance of managing diversity in the workplace, your language skills indicate some level of experience with diverse populations.

One caution with including language skills, however. We strongly discourage you from qualifying your language skills. For example, you may think you are fluent in French. But can you read, write, and speak using French business language?

If you are a native speaker or grew up speaking, writing, and reading the language, then you probably are fluent. We think it's enough just to write *Languages: French, English*. If the employer is interested in the second language, he will interview you in that language.

Remember the goal for your career summary: to pique the employer's interest enough that he reads your resume and, ultimately, calls you for an interview.

How to Write Your Experiences as Accomplishments and Results

Crafting your resume to include specific language that creates a picture of your accomplishments and results takes time.

You need to consider the main problems, needs, or requirements of the job for which you are applying. List the top three to five problems of your employer. If you don't know what they are, then go to the company's home page on the Web to learn more about what it does and potential challenges it faces. Also, connect with your network.

The Internet has a lot of information about how to write accomplishments and results. However, keep in mind that just because John Doe says he got a great job with his resume and wants to share his secret writing style with the world doesn't mean that his style is appropriate for most employers. We suggest a more conservative approach and strongly encourage you to stick with the online guidance from experts with more broad experience in the field, such as the sites we mention in this chapter.

Your accomplishments are what make you stand out from the crowd, give you a distinctive personality, and help identify your strengths.

What Have I Accomplished?

Can't think of specific accomplishments? Consider the following when brainstorming your list:

* Problems you addressed for an employer.
* System changes as a result of your involvement or ideas.
* Leadership roles you were assigned for projects.
* Successful teams you were involved with.
* Recommendations you made that were implemented.
* Budget reductions that resulted from your ideas or smart business practices.
* Materials you wrote that were distributed to the organization internally or externally.
* Increases in productivity because of your work systems.
* Promotions or appointments you received because of confidence in your ability to perform duties.
* Successful projects you designed and implemented.

Online, the best assistance in writing accomplishment statements is on the Career Lab Web site at *http://www.careerlab.com/ art_homeruns.htm*. Be sure to read both Part I and Part II of the article/tutorial on how to write accomplishment statements. This article offers excellent examples and shows you how to analyze a statement to determine what needs to be changed to make it more powerful. This article is a must-read!

Accomplishments are often the things about which you are most proud and may tend to hide because of a sense of modesty, such as successful projects or campaigns or competitions you entered and won. But, they are precisely what makes your resume interesting and can help your job search campaign immensely.

Think about your life, job by job, project by project, and event by event. Think about the problems you faced on the job. What did you do to address them? What resulted from this action? Start listing your accomplishments, no matter how large or small. Your list should be fairly long. Keep in mind that an accomplishment statement describes the results you obtained after taking action to solve a problem for an organization. The result should be described as a measurable outcome, if at all possible.

Get Up to PAR with Your Accomplishments!

Use the simple PAR formula to develop your accomplishment statement:

P = Problem (an issue, problem, or need in the organization, unit, or office)

A = Action (what you did about it)

R = Result (the result of what you did)

You need to list your experience in terms of accomplishments, skills, and results of your work. Avoid listing duties and responsibilities, because these weaken a resume. All employers know you have duties and responsibilities; what they really want to know is what you've done with them. Sometimes significant accomplishments come from events or duties that you spend very little time on—but you should include them if they are significant and relevant.

Often, a different perspective helps you to recognize accomplishments. If you're having a tough time determining your own accomplishments, ask a friend or former colleague or supervisor to help you.

Who Am I?

When you consider your achievements, it's critical to think of them in terms of what the employer needs. Look at the following profile and see if you can tell what this person's job is.

1. I am responsible for establishing the critical first impression that clients have of my organization.

2. I provide clients with information to assist them in making decisions.

3. I may be called on to make foreign-language translations.

4. To maintain the highest level of client satisfaction, I am expected to recognize key clients and to uphold their service expectations.

continues

continued

> **5.** I may be required to remember long lists of detailed items or to use a portable computing device.
>
> **6.** I transfer client requests to operational staff who produce and assemble final products.
>
> **7.** Sometimes, I make creative or artistic additions to produced items.
>
> **8.** I match orders to specific clients and provide quality control assurance.
>
> **9.** I use computational skills and may handle electronic funds transfers and cash accounts receivables.
>
> **10.** I am accountable for client satisfaction and receive incentive compensation based on client satisfaction.

> **I Am a Waiter/Waitress!**
>
> Did you guess right? Notice how waiters or waitresses can present achievements, skills, and responsibilities in a way that demonstrates their value to the company. Here is how the duties correspond to the achievements presented in the preceding exercise.
>
> **1.** Greet diners.
>
> **2.** Inform diners of daily specials.
>
> **3.** Translate foreign-name menu items.
>
> **4.** "I'll take the usual, please."
>
> **5.** Take food orders, by either remembering items or using a computer such as a Palm Pilot.
>
> **6.** Organize food orders for kitchen staff.
>
> **7.** Add garnishes.
>
> **8.** Serve correct order to right diner.
>
> **9.** Add up check, handle credit card or cash payments.
>
> **10.** Receive tips when service is good.

Now go back through your list and highlight the accomplishments that are relevant to the employers' needs or those that you think would elicit the most positive reactions from employers.

Keep in mind that this information may change from employer to employer, so keep all the information you've collected for future use. You may want or need to cut and paste different accomplishments into your resume for different jobs. Keep an ongoing list of accomplishments and pull what information you need to create a unique and tailored version for the specific job you are interested in.

How to Quantify and Qualify Your Accomplishments and Results

You need to quantify your achievements as much as possible. By *quantifying*, you describe the depth and the breadth of your experience. Quantification brings your work to life in the eyes of the reader.

The employer can't always relate to your work situation. However, employers relate well to dollars, numbers, percentages, and phrases that indicate positive change, such as *time saved* or *productivity increased*. Help the employer relate to your accomplishments and results by quantifying as much as possible.

You also may have some experience that you can qualify. This means you include language such as *significantly*, *successfully*, and *top-notch*. Use this language carefully. You don't want to come off as someone who thinks too highly of himself, because this may be interpreted as arrogance. Go back to Career Lab Web site at *http://www.careerlab.com/art_homeruns.htm* to see examples on how to qualify and quantify your experience.

What Types of Verbs Make Your Resume Powerful

Using the right action verbs not only helps you write accomplishment statements, they also make your resume more powerful! The verbs you select for each phrase affect the reaction of the reader regarding that specific accomplishment.

There are excellent lists on the Internet, but one of our favorites is on Monster.com at *http://content.monster.com/resume/resources/ phrases_verbs*. Monster.com not only lists hundreds of power verbs but also provides an outstanding list of action phrases to be used, depending on your resume's career emphasis.

Monster.com has
a great resume-
writing section.
You can find a list
of action phrases
to use in writing
your resume at
http://content.
monster.com/
resume/resources/
phrases_verbs.

If you scroll down
past the list of
action phrases,
you will see an
alphabetical list of
power verbs. Use
these verbs to
strengthen your
accomplishment
statements.

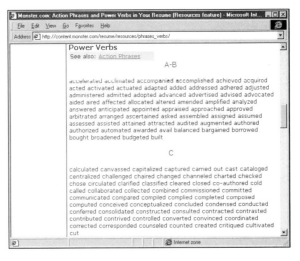

Power Verbs

Verb lists are crawling all over the Internet. Use them well! Make sure they show your successes, speak to the employer's needs, and reflect your job objective. We'll get you started with a sampling of our favorites:

General

Transformed

Achieved

Completed

Improved

Reduced

Management/Leadership Skills

Spearheaded

Hired

Strengthened

Streamlined

Initiated

Managed

Produced

Administered

Communication/People Skills

Authored

Communicated

Wrote

Edited

Persuaded

Resolved

Synthesized

Research Skills

Analyzed

Interpreted

Investigated

Researched

Reviewed

Technical Skills

Engineered

Repaired

Upgraded

Developed

Converted

Applied

Adapted

Financial/Data Skills

Assessed

Budgeted

Corrected

Forecasted

Reduced

Creative Skills

Composed

Conceptualized

Created

Designed

Performed

Revitalized

Integrated

Helping Skills

Advocated

Assessed

Coached

Encouraged

Facilitated

Motivated

Organization/Administration Skills

Updated

Standardized

Reviewed

Organized

Maintained

Monitored

How to Describe Your Education, Training, and Professional Affiliations

The Internet has more information than you'll ever need to help you develop your resume. However, most of the guidance offered on where to put your education information does not reflect the needs of employers in the current job market. Employers want to know you have relevant experience. By placing education at the top of your resume, you're sending the message that your education is more relevant than your experience—not exactly what you want with today's job market.

Your education is usually the last section on your resume. There are a few exceptions to this rule, such as if you're applying to education and academic institutions or if you are just graduating from school and don't have any relevant work experience. If you're not sure, now is the time to count on your network to give you some input.

If you are part of the majority who should place education last, remember to give just the basics: your degree, specialization (field), name of educational institution, and date you received your degree.

Don't include information on your fraternity, sorority, classes, title of thesis, clubs, scholarships, or relevant coursework unless specifically requested in a job announcement, if it is particularly relevant, or if you have very minimal work experience.

Also include any relevant training. If you're applying for a job in a hospital, you should include training in CPR as well as other relevant certificates or training.

Lastly, if you are affiliated with a relevant association, then include the name of the association, your position (member, president, and so on), and the years of membership. This information demonstrates your commitment to the field.

Curriculum Vitas (CV): Just the Facts

In the United States, a curriculum vitas (CV) is usually three to five pages long. Although the style varies, depending on who you ask, in general it is a resume that includes greater detail of your accomplishments, a list of published articles and books, speeches, and more detail on your dissertation or thesis, if you have one and if it's relevant.

Although we're not covering this information in this book, you can find some excellent guidance at the University of Virginia Web site at *http://minerva.acc.virginia.edu/~career/handouts/vita.html* as well as Berkeley's Web site at *http://career.berkeley.edu/Phds/PhDCVelements.stm*. The Quintessential Careers site at *http://www.quintcareers.com/curriculum_vitae.html* includes links to other good Web sites that have CV information as well as links to sample CVs.

A Resume for a Job Overseas

Did you know that resume styles vary country to country? In the United States, you would never include your birth date, marital status, or personal information on your resume. But if you apply for a job in Costa Rica, not only do they expect this information, they'll want a picture of you, too!

Regardless of whether you are applying for a job in Bangladesh or Botswana, the bottom line is, if you're applying for a job with a foreign firm based in another country (some are also based in the United States), you need to know the resume styles for that country. For example, in France, many employers frequently ask for hand-written cover letters so that they can do a handwriting analysis.

We suggest you use the Internet to surf around for resume postings from residents of that country or for sites that offer specific guidance on how to write a resume for that country.

One of our favorite sites is Eurograduate. This site has European-style resumes at *http://www.eurograduate.com/plan.html*.

Looking Good: The Elements of Resume Design

It's important that a resume look just as good as it reads. In an unpredictable world of greater competition for jobs and frequent job and career changes, it's in your best interest to make a lasting first impression—you may not get a second chance. Often, your resume is the first thing an employer sees, so it better be well written, and it better look good!

There are some good Web sites that incorporate good design elements. We suggest taking a look at Superior Staffing's site at *http://www.superiorstaffing.com/newpages/resumebody.html*. This site has great design tips to help you make sure that your resume is up to snuff! Scroll down a bit until you see the Resume Appearance section and review the tips on paper color, texture, and text style. This page also provides links to good examples of both chronological and functional resume layouts. Scroll down to Resume Layouts and click View Sample Format. Notice that the sample resume is easy to read, with bullets pulling you into the key accomplishments. Additional samples of good resume layout are at Monster.com at *http://content.monster.com/resume/samples/resumes*.

Use the checklist below to keep yourself on track with the design:

Matching Envelopes and Cover Letters:

When you buy paper to print your resume, also purchase matching envelopes and additional sheets for your cover letters. You will find more information on cover letters in Chapter 9, "Writing Letters for the Information Age."

- Use high quality white, cream, or gray bond paper. These colors look professional and fax best. You can find this paper in any office supply store or on Web sites that sell paper supplies.

- Don't use graphics or lines if you expect to fax your resume or if you think it will be scanned. The lines on a fax machine come out crooked, thus ruining the sharp design intended.

- You don't need to print your resume at a print shop, but make sure that the print is letter quality—a laser printer works well.

- A resume should rarely exceed two pages. If you go over one page, write *continued* at the bottom of the first page, and write your last name with *page 2* at the top of the second page. A good example can be found at Monster.com at *http://content.monster.com/resume/samples/resumes/jones2*. This URL shows the second page of a resume. Notice that the words *Page Two* are in the upper-right corner of the page. If the second page is inadvertently separated from the first page, the reader will know which pages go together. Also, if you use two pages, it's best to fill both pages to give the resume a finished and polished look.

- The best type size to use is 10, 11, or 12 point. You might vary the size to fit your text to the page or to create a different look. For example, you may want to use 12-point for headings and 10-point for the content.

- The best font type to use is a serif font, which is designed to keep the eye traveling across the page. A serif font is one that has the curlicues on the ends of the letters, such as Roman Times, Palatino, or New York. Sans-serif fonts such as Helvetica are designed for headlines or short phrases. You might mix the styles, but never use more than one serif and one sans-serif per resume. Try using a sans-serif for headings and a serif for the content. This looks sharp and reads well.

- Use bold type for your name, but not for your address or other contact information. Also use bold for the section headings and your job titles.

- Your resume should have breathing room. In other words, it needs lots of white space so that it doesn't look too dense with words. If it has enough white space around the edges and between sections, it is easier on the eyes of the reader.

- Make sure that at the end of a sentence you hit the spacebar only once and not twice. Hitting it once keeps the spaces evenly distributed throughout the resume and avoids rivers of white space traveling down a page.

- A skimming eye looks at a resume from top to bottom, gradually moving from left to right. Therefore, be sure that your information is designed so the reader catches the verbs and buzzwords on the left side.

What to Do with Your List of References

Don't include a list of references with your resume unless an employer specifically requests it. In the same vein, don't include the language *References Available on Request* on your resume.

Why? Employers who want references will ask for them and will expect you to produce them. Your resume needs to be focused on what the employer needs to know immediately. Therefore, use your space and words carefully—don't write meaningless phrases on the resume.

continues

continued

However, do keep in mind that you will need to bring a list of references to job interviews. Prepare a list and print it on the same paper on which you printed your resume.

For each reference you list, include the person's name, title, address, phone number, email address, and fax number and a brief description of his relationship to you (former boss, colleague, client, and so on).

We suggest that you include at least two professional references and one personal reference (someone who can speak to your character). If possible, include up to five references— three professional and two personal references. This mixture gives the employer options to contact others if the initial references aren't available.

Ten Tips on the Nuts and Bolts

Here are some tips to help you power up your resume:

1. Devote more space to recent work than to earlier work.

2. Include only the information that supports your objective for this specific resume.

3. Use words and phrases appropriate to your prospective employer.

4. Be consistent with format.

5. Use bullets, bold, italics, or dashes for emphasis—but don't overdo it.

6. Be sure the final product is free of spelling, punctuation, grammatical, and typographical errors.

7. Keep your potential employer in mind. Ask yourself: If I were the employer, would I interview this person?

8. Avoid using technical jargon unless it's relevant to the position you are applying for.

9. Don't include salary information.

10. Don't use odd-size paper, overly fancy stock, color, or style, or anything that could be considered eccentric. If you are in a creative arts field, you should ask those in your network about what style is appropriate. Some employers may want a more stylish resume, while others may expect a more conservative approach.

Putting It All Together

You now know how to write a powerful resume. You understand the four components and the techniques for developing them. Also, you have probably visited several sites that offer great information to guide you through this process.

Your resume is your key marketing tool. You will leave copies of it with people you meet in informational meetings and at networking events and with potential employers. Your resume makes your first impression, so make it a powerful one!

To make your resume powerful, you need to determine the format in which you will present your experience (chronological or functional), and you must focus on accomplishment statements. You also know that it's important that your resume looks as good as it can. It must have plenty of white space and be easy to read.

Next stop: exploring the world of electronic resumes. You've heard about them and maybe you've even tried out some of the online resume databases. We'll take you on a virtual tour of these groundbreaking job search techniques. Learning how to find the right systems and present the right products will help ensure your success in entering the cyberworld of job applications.

CHAPTER 8

Sending Resumes: The Electronic Word

The job-hunting cybernaut knows that the online opportunities for posting a resume are skyrocketing! Savvy job hunters are preparing their resumes for the electronic job search market. This includes

- Posting the resume on job bank or resume bank sites

- Sending the resume directly to employers via email

- Preparing the resume in a form that is most likely to be accepted by a resume scan

Resume banks are quickly becoming popular with (and confusing to) job seekers. Most resume banks allow you to post your resume and allow employers to explore and identify potential candidates for jobs. Some resume banks even offer to market your resume to employers. Still others try to match your qualifications with job opportunities. It sounds almost too good to be true. Maybe it is; maybe it isn't.

Many employers now request that resumes be sent to them *online* or via *email*. This is particularly true for employers that have an urgent need to fill a position or that are conducting a full-scale nationwide or global job search for candidates. Be careful with this approach. Many people think they can simply attach their resume to an email message. Wrong. We'll show you how to do it right!

There is also a growing interest by employers and job search sites to *scan* resumes for specific content. This is done mostly by large employers that either receive thousands of resumes or are streamlining their human resource review process. This hurdle can be tricky to navigate but, with a little knowledge, you'll do just fine.

What You'll Learn in This Chapter:

▶ How electronic resumes are different from paper ones.

▶ How to develop a resume to post at an online resume database.

▶ How to identify the resume databases to use.

▶ How to prepare and send a resume to employers using email.

▶ How to change your resume so that it can be scanned.

How Electronic Resumes Are Different

Just like the printed resumes we discussed in the previous chapter, the electronic resume is simply a marketing tool in your job search. Like the paper version, the electronic resume focuses on what skills and abilities you have to offer an employer. Also, its purpose is to pique the interest of a potential employer.

The differences, however, are significant. Not only does your electronic resume's format change, but the style in which you highlight your accomplishments is also slightly different.

The major difference between the electronic and the paper resume is in the ability to customize your resume for each job opening. A paper resume is usually submitted for a specific job opening or sent to a specific employer. You have a lot of control with a paper resume. You decide who receives it, who views it, and what specific skills and abilities you think those people need to see. You lose much of this control when it comes to using an electronic resume, because you usually submit only one, which is reviewed for various opportunities. Your electronic resume risks not connecting your experience to a specific job.

Nonetheless, there are great advantages in posting your resume online. The key to making the job banks work for you is strategic focus. Let's see how you do this.

The Who, What, Why, and How of Online Resumes

The purpose of developing an online resume is to provide information about your skills and abilities. The reason employers access your online resume is to see if your skills and abilities match what they are looking for.

In general, there are two types of Web sites that accept online resumes. The first is an employer Web site that allows you to submit your resume directly to the employer. If you go to the job-listing site of some particular employer, you may be asked to apply for a specific job by submitting your resume electronically. You also may be offered the option of submitting your resume to the employer's database for general consideration. Sometimes a specific format will be outlined for you. Think of this type of online resume simply as an online job application. At other times the employer will provide the space for you to cut and paste your own resume version and to send it electronically. Before you do so, check out our guidance on how to prepare your online resume, later in this chapter.

The second type of Web site is more popular with job seekers and is commonly referred to as an *online resume databank* or *resume database*. It focuses on placing electronic resumes of job seekers into a database and then allows employers to access the resumes—usually for a fee.

Some Web sites that offer resume databases charge the job seeker to post a resume. Buyer beware! Unless the company is specifically marketing your resume to employers with positions that you can't access by other means, it's probably best to bypass them.

JobTrak, at *http://www.jobtrak.com*, is one of several excellent sites that focus on jobs for graduating college students. The educational institution must pay for students to access the database of jobs and to post their resumes to the database. This service is rated highly by students.

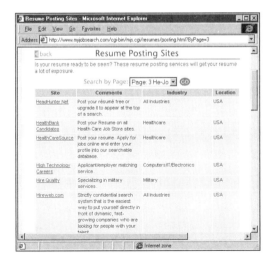

My Job Search at http://www. myjobsearch.com/ cgibin/mjs.cgi/ resumes/posting. html *has links to more than 100 resume posting sites.*

Considerations for Posting Your Resume Online

Before posting your resume online, you need to know a few things. We know that you want a job but, as we mentioned in the previous chapter, your resume is not going to connect you directly with a job offer. Instead, your resume will hopefully spark interest in a potential employer.

Since you rarely have the opportunity to target specific employers or specific job openings, the goal with your electronic resume is to connect to certain *types* of jobs or employers that interest you.

To connect with these employers effectively, you need to understand what happens to your resume after you click the Submit button and send your resume off into cyberspace. Although the process varies from site to site, most of the larger resume databases will store your resume in memory until an employer decides to search through the resume database. The employer enters criteria, or qualifications, into the computer. The computer searches for key words or phrases and identifies the resumes that meet the criteria. If you're interested in reading more about how the computer scans your resume, check out the Job Choices Online article on this topic at *www.jobweb.org/jconline/resumes/ resumes/Resmatch.shtml.*

Pick the Posting Site with Care:
If you post your electronic resume on a site that doesn't help you connect to your career interests, then it's not worth your time or effort in posting it.

To meet the criteria established by an employer, your resume must clearly present your skills, abilities, and knowledge in a particular field and must have the same or similar language that the employer uses. You can best develop this information on your resume by following the guidelines in Chapter 7, "Writing Resumes: The Printed Word," on how to write a career summary and accomplishment statements.

Preparing Your Resume to Post Online

Just when you think you've got the writing and design down for developing a powerful resume, the rules change. Well, not for a paper resume, but they do for an online resume.

Many job seekers are confused about how to prepare online resumes because they are usually written in different formats and are often scanned by computers for employers. Because of this, the rules don't change completely, but they are dramatically modified when you're working with online resumes. It will be easier for you to develop an online resume if you understand who will receive it and how they will use it.

To do this, go to the Web site where you plan to post it, such as Career Mosaic at *http://www.careermosaic.com*, and find out what you can about the types of employers that access resumes at that site. Take a look at the Web site's guidelines for writing the resume. Note, however, that most sites don't offer guidelines, but they may link you to other sites that provide this information. If you don't see guidelines on how to write or post your resume, check out the Proven Resumes Web site at *http://www. provenresumes.com/reswkshps/electronic/electrespg1.html* to find excellent guidance for developing and posting your electronic resume.

Here are the steps to follow if you're interested in posting your resume on any of the online resume databases:

▼ **Try It Yourself**

1. **Read the Rules**   Go to the site where you plan to post your resume and follow its guidelines, if there are any. If not, go to step 2.

2. **Develop a Text-Only Document**   Open the file that contains the resume you developed in Chapter 7. Make a copy of the file so that you have two different versions of your resume: one for printing to paper and one for sending electronically. Change all the text from its current format to plain text, also known as *simple text*, *ASCII text*, or *text only* format. This conversion removes all formatting, bullets, italics, bold, tabs, and any other design elements you created. When you save your text-only document as a file, give it a new name and the extension *.txt*. The *.txt* extension will help others who receive it as an entire document to identify the program that created the file.

3. **Delete Your Street Address**   It can be a wacky world, and the Internet offers minimal protection from those in search of trouble online. Although many resume banks may ensure confidentiality, you still don't want to take the chance of a someone finding out where you live. It's doubtful that any employer would need your address up front. If he is finding

Changing Text to Text Only:

If you are using a standard word processing program such as Microsoft Works or Word, it's easy to change a file to text-only format. Select File, Save As. In the dialog box that appears, select the format, type in the new filename and extension, and then click OK to save the text as another document.

your information online, he probably has email access, so be sure to include an email address. Our sense is that employers still prefer to contact job candidates by phone, so include a phone number. However, if you don't want your phone number lost in space, consider renting a voice mail system. They are usually inexpensive ($10 to $15 per month) and can be found in your local phone directory.

4. **Give It Eye Appeal**   Changing your document to plain text can make it dull and lacking in eye appeal. It's tough to do much about this, but there are a few tricks of the trade. Try the following:

   • Leave the material in the same order you had it on your other resume.

   • Emphasize phrases or words that were previously italic or bold by changing them to ALL CAPS.

   • You may need to create a little extra whitespace by double-spacing the lines between accomplishment statements. That way you are giving the reader an "eye break" between statements and helping him not to see a mass of gray type, which can be a visual turnoff.

   • You can use asterisks for bullets. Some people like to use the small letter *o*. This can work if you are careful to include two or three spaces after the bullet, before you begin a sentence.

   • Use blank lines to separate pieces of information that were previously separated by tabs. For example, you may have placed your job title to the left and included the years you held that position on the same line but to the far right. With plain text, the tabs are gone and the words become crowded. Try separating the information by using a comma between topics, subjects, or word groups; alternatively, list your title on one line and the years you held that title immediately below it.

- Consider listing specific skills in the Career Summary section at the top of your resume. List only one skill per line and don't skip lines between entries.

5. **Review and Edit**   Review your final plain-text resume to make sure that you adjusted any text that may have been squashed together when tabs were eliminated when you made the file text only. Also, proofread and edit your document *very* carefully. You've made changes, which means that you may have misspellings or grammatical errors. Read it, give it to a friend to read, and then read it again.

6. **Do a Trial Run**   Although you can't do a trial run with a resume bank, you can probably edit your posted resume if needed. A quick check is to try emailing your resume to yourself by copying and pasting it into the body of an email message. Then open your email message to see how it looks. This will give you a good idea of how the resume will be received electronically. Also, send it to two or three friends and ask for their opinions of its format.

Congratulations! You now have an electronic resume ready to go!

> **Six Steps to Change a Paper Resume to an Electronic Resume**
> 1. Read the rules of the resume posting site you plan to use.
> 2. Develop a text-only document.
> 3. Delete your street address.
> 4. Give the resume as much eye appeal as possible in the text-only format.
> 5. Review and edit the resume.
> 6. Do a trial run online.

Developing Your Electronic Resume Posting Strategy

The good news is that you've done the lion's share of work already! If you went through each of the chapters in Part II, "Establishing Personal Goals," you have established a career or

job goal, and you have a sense of which employers interest you
most. In Chapter 7 you developed a powerful resume. You are
now ready to hit the ground running in the job market! But don't
tie your running shoes too tight yet. You've got a few things to do
to develop your strategy if you want to plug into the online
resume banks. Follow these four steps, and you'll save yourself
lots of time, effort, and frustration.

1. **Review your career or job goal**   This is your guiding light
   throughout the job search process. Don't fall victim to
   cyber-hype that promises that top employers will find you.
   The site's definition of *top employer* may be very different
   from yours.

2. **Make sure that your online resume stands out from the
   rest**   This is tough to do because your design and fonts are
   limited, and sometimes even your word choices are limited
   (for example, when you are required to select from a list of
   pre-identified skills). Also, you're stuck with only one
   resume, which means it may not have the specific language
   that might otherwise grab a specific employer's attention if
   you had the chance to research that employer's needs. Check
   out the guidance in this chapter on how to prepare and format
   your resume. Pay close attention to the strategies you can use
   to power it up!

3. **Find the sites that list jobs or employers that interest you**
   If you're an accountant and want to post your resume for
   employers in the finance industry, you probably don't want a
   site that lists only engineering jobs. Instead, you'll want to
   find a site that lists a number of jobs in the human resource
   arena, such as Headhunter.net at *www.headhunter.net/
   123res.htm*. Or you might take a look at sites that connect
   your resume to employers that you like. If you're in an international field, you will want to look at sites such as Vacancies in International Organizations at *http://missions.itu.int/
   ~italy/vacancor.htm*. The best way to find out about sites that
   accept resumes for your career field is to check out the
   resume posting sites on My Job Search at *www.myjobsearch.
   com/cgi-bin/mjs.cgi/resumes/posting.html* and at the Riley

Guide at *www.dbm.com/jobguide/ resumes.html.* Remember: To be effective, be selective!

4. **Be discreet!**   After you find the sites that increase your chance for appropriate exposure, be sure that your resume isn't advertising your job search to your current employer! In other words, if your current boss doesn't know that you are job hunting, and you don't want her to know, you may want to rethink posting your resume if your employer uses such resume banks to identify candidates. If you're not sure, try to find out through your Human Resources office.

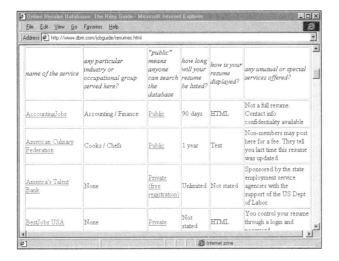

The Riley Guide's list of resume posting sites at http://www.dbm. com/jobguide/ resumes.html provides basic information to help you decide the site on which you want to post your resume.

Are you ready to check out a few sites to post your resume? Follow these steps to start your list!

▼ **Try It Yourself**

1. Go to the Riley Guide's list of resume databases at *http://www.dbm.com/jobguide/resumes.html.*

2. Scroll down until you see the section called Free Resume Databases.

3. Read through the descriptions until you find one that would be a good fit for your career field, such as HotJobs.com. Click that link.

4. Review the resume posting site to find out who accesses the resumes, when and how to make changes to your resume, and how long your resume will be posted.

5. Identify how to submit your resume information. Some sites, such as HotJobs.com, allow you to paste your entire resume into their sites; you may also have the option of submitting this information in a standard format. We suggest that you read Job Star's article on how to evaluate resume banks at *http://jobstar.org/internet/reseval.htm*. This article offers practical suggestions and questions you should answer before signing up to join a resume bank.

6. Record the database site in this book or in a separate notebook with your own comments about whether or not it is a site where you want to post your resume.

Read the Fine Print:

Some sites require you to register. Rarely does this involve a fee, but be sure to read the fine print and look for those magic words *no charge* or *free*.

Resume Bank Checklist

Use this checklist to help you determine which resume bank sites have the greatest potential for targeting your resume:

1. **Relevance to Your Needs**   First and foremost, you want to post your resume where you will gain exposure to employers and jobs that interest you. If the Web site doesn't clearly indicate that it's for a particular career field, such as health-related careers or high tech careers, look at some of the resumes already posted. Try to get a sense of the level of experience and the types of career fields of other job hunters at that site. Also, find out which employers are accessing the resumes. If the site doesn't list them, send an email to the Web developer (this email address is often at the bottom of the home page).

2. **Number of Resumes Versus Number of Employer Visits** This information is important to know before getting involved with any resume bank. If a resume bank has 100,000 resumes but only a few dozen employers looking at them, your chance of exposure isn't great. However, if the resume bank has 100,000 resumes with thousands of employers visiting to review them regularly, now you're talking

about favorable exposure! One of our favorites for college students is JOBTRAK.COM at *http://www.jobtrak.com*, where there are usually more employers interested in the resume bank than the total number of posted resumes. Another favorite is Career Mosaic at *www.careermosaic.com*, a site where there are actually more employers who visit the resume bank than there are posted resumes.

3. **Resume Time Online**   Although it might seem like a pain to resubmit or update your resume or renew your membership every one, two, or three months, it actually is to your benefit to do so. Employers prefer to review resumes that they know are current, so these sites are often more popular with employers.

4. **Cost**   As we mentioned earlier, there are tons of resume banks that charge no cost to the job seeker but do cost the employer. It's worth your time to find out the cost to both you and the employer. Why? Because if there is no fee to the employer (some of the larger resume banks charge nothing to employers or to job seekers), chances are that employers will return to these resume banks frequently. One such resume bank is America's Talent Bank at *http://www.ajb.org/ html/atb_home.html*. At this site, there is no fee to you or the employer, which increases the chance that employers with smaller budgets will get online and search for candidates.

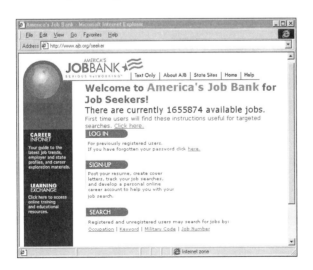

America's Talent Bank is part of America's Job Bank. ATB, at http://www.ajb. org/seeker, allows you to submit your resume to its database.

5. **Interactivity Between the Site and You and the Site and the Employer**   Find out what information the site automatically sends to you and to registered employers. Does the Web site tell you when employers access your resume? Does it let you know whether your resume meets the qualifications for jobs listed in its database? (The My Job Finder feature at the America's Employers site at *http://www.americasemployers. com/resume.html* lets you do so.) Does the site let employers know when new resumes with qualifications relevant to their needs are added? (Monster.com at *www.monster.com* does this.) If the site lists jobs, does it let you know when new jobs are posted if they match the interests you noted on your profile? (Career Builder at *www.careerbuilder.com* does so.) Resume bank sites that offer more information help you track whether or not your resume is getting the necessary exposure. If it's not, you may need to revise your resume or find another site.

International Resume Banks

If you're looking for employment outside the United States, you'll find some pretty good resume banks on the Web. Some of the international resume banks are part of job sites that list international jobs, such as Career Mosaic at *http://www.careermosaic.com/cm/gateway*. Simply click the country or region of interest and then go to the resume posting section. Also, Monster.com at *http://international.monster.com* allows you to post your resume for employers that have job opportunities in Africa, Central and South America, Canada, Asia, and the Middle East.

The Who, What, Why, and How of Emailed Resumes

If you've been job hunting recently, you've probably noticed that many employers are now requesting that you apply for jobs by sending them your resume via email. If you've been networking a lot, you've probably had requests from your contacts to send your resume to them via email as well.

Emailed resume requests are quickly replacing the fax requests, overnight deliveries, and the old envelope and stamp. Lucky you! You've just created an electronic resume for the resume banks, and this same resume can be used for email requests.

Rules of the Road for Emailing Resumes

There are only a few things you need to know to master the art of making an impression with an emailed resume:

- Make sure the employer wants to receive your resume via email. Many employers request them that way, but there are others who don't.

- Edit your electronic resume to reflect the employer's needs. If you need a refresher course on how to do this, review Chapter 7.

- Always include your cover letter and resume in the *body* of the same email message. Check out Chapter 9, "Writing Letters for the Information Age," for guidance on writing cover letters. By pasting your resume into the body of the email message, you are ensuring that it is read immediately. When employers have to download attachments, they often put off reviewing them until later.

- Send your resume in several formats. In your cover letter, tell the employer that you have included your resume in the message and that you have attached two copies of your resume (your original resume, the one with formatting). But let the employer know what program your original is in, so he doesn't waste time trying to open it only to find out that he doesn't have the right program. Also, ask the employer to provide an address to which you can send a hard copy of your resume. Yes, all bases are covered now.

The Who, What, Why, and How of Scannable Resumes

More and more companies are turning toward electronic resume scanners and related software to review and assess resumes and other job application forms. In these cases, your resume is read by a computer, not by a person. However your resume is transmitted to a prospective employer, you need to prepare it—and yourself—for potential scanning.

The scanner takes an electronic picture of your resume and feeds it to a sophisticated computer program that quickly and automatically looks for specific words and phrases that the employer has identified as key information. This develops a profile of who you are and often links you to specific job categories within a company, eliminates you from further consideration, or creates a searchable profile of you for future opportunities.

Two of the largest and best-known systems for scanning resumes are Resumix™ and Webhire (formerly known as Restrac). You can get a lot more information about this process by visiting their Web sites at *http://www.resumix.com* and *http://www.webhire. com*, respectively. These sites are not gateways to employers, but they will give you more information about how the process works.

Webhire's site at www.webhire. com offers software for recruiters to mine resume databases in search of appropriate candidates.

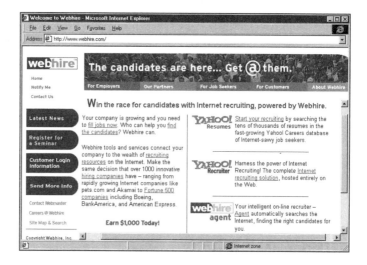

Try It Yourself ▼

Do you want the inside scoop on how to write a scannable resume? One of the best ways to get it is to go to the sites that offer guidance to recruiters on how to find candidates online:

1. Go to Webhire's site at *www.webhire.com*.

2. Look in the right column and click the Webhire Agent icon. This link takes you to a menu of information about how the site works.

3. Click the What It Is link to read about how a scannable resume is used in the recruitment industry. This information will help you put into perspective how a recruiter may come into contact with a resume you post in a database.

4. Click the How It Works link to learn more about how the database software selects and qualifies candidates and delivers results to employers.

5. At the top of the page, click For Job Seekers. This link leads you to a page of helpful information on how to post your resume online.

6. At the bottom of the page, click Resume Workshop. In the right column is a menu of several articles and links to online resume databases and job boards. We suggest that you check out the article "How to Write a Scannable Resume." This article provides detailed information on how Webhire's system scans job seekers' resumes. This article also provides a checklist of Do's and Don'ts as well as sample scannable resumes.

Now you've got the inside scoop!

How to Prepare and Submit a Scannable Resume

Fortunately, you already did most of the work when you developed your text-only resume. Here is what you need to do to transform your electronic resume into a scannable one.

1. **Use Key Words**   Your goal in developing a scannable resume is to include a variety of words and phrases that define your skills and abilities. For a great listing of keywords, check out eResumes at *http://www.eresumes.com/ tut_keyresume.html*. Scroll down until you see a link to skill keywords; click this link to find a list of keywords by job category and keywords for personal traits. For example, keywords for a civil engineer include *land development projects* and *public works*; keywords for personal traits include *problem-solving* and *safety conscious*.

2. **Use Industry Jargon** Include the industry buzzwords, including the names of software packages with which you are familiar.

3. **Start Phrases with Action Verbs** Include accomplishment statements beginning with strong, active verbs. There's a great list of verbs in Chapter 7.

4. **Make It a Plain Design** Just as you did for the electronic resume for emails and resume banks, it's critical you keep your resume in text-only format. However, avoid using asterisks, all caps, or other highlighting tricks. Remember that it's a computer that will review your resume at first, and it's important that you make it easy for the computer to identify the key words.

5. **Hard Copy Tips** If you're submitting your resume on paper to be scanned, use only white paper and print on one side only. Don't fold or staple the resume. Don't include any italics, bold text, underlines, or graphics.

6. **Prepare for the Human Scan, Too** Chances are that your resume will eventually be reviewed by some*body*. So be sure that your resume is presentable, well written, well edited, and easy to read.

Putting It All Together

Congratulations! You now have your electronic resume ready to go! You've learned that electronic resumes are basically the same as paper resumes, but formatted differently.

You know now how to develop and post resumes in online resume posting sites. You also know how and where to find these sites.

By now, you're ready to email a resume when asked for one, and you know just what to do to create a scannable resume as well!

Next stop: Learning how to write letters to accompany your resume.

CHAPTER 9

Writing Letters for the Information Age

The letters you write are key communication and job search marketing tools. You will write several types of letters, including letters to ask for information or a meeting, to apply for jobs, to follow up on different events, to accept or reject job offers, and to maintain your network. It's clear that you'll be doing a lot of writing, and now is as good a time as any to nail down the basics and beyond.

Tips for Letter Writing

There are different styles and different needs that are addressed, but here are the basic things to consider when writing a letter.

- Keep it simple and uncluttered. Be direct and use a business-like format. Plan and organize what you will say by outlining your letter. Use short paragraphs and sentences[md]avoid complex sentences!

- Know your purpose and plan the elements of the letter accordingly. Communicate your message in a logical, sequential manner.

- Individualize letters, adapting your model. Be original; allow your style to show.

- Punctuate properly and use correct grammar and spelling. Did you know that many employers use cover letters as a writing sample?

- End your letter by stating what your reader can expect from you next.

- Always send a letter with a resume.

- Carefully check all correspondence. Keep copies and records.

What You'll Learn in This Chapter:

- How to write good letters for the job search.

- How to write cover letters for job applications.

- How to write thank-you letters to employers.

Strong Letters:

A letter's strength comes from what it says, not how long the letter is. Keep it short and to the point!

For more tips on writing letters, check out the MSN Careers Web site at *http://content.careers.msn.com/gh_cl_htg_intro.html.* Here you will find a guide on how to develop content and format as well as tips for writing these kinds of letters. If you're looking for sample letters, one of the best sites we've seen is Career Lab at *http://www.careerlab.com/letters/default.htm.* You'll not only find information on how to write job search letters, but you'll find excellent examples.

Career Lab at www.careerlab. com/letters/ default.htm is a great Web site to find information on how to write professional job search letters that grab attention.

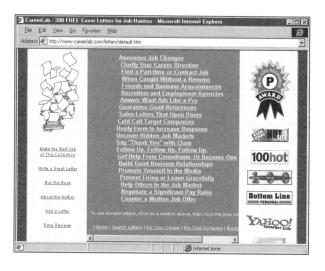

Try It Yourself ▼ Are you ready to take a look at good job search letters? To find a sample that fits your needs, follow these steps:

1. Go to Career Lab at *http://www.careerlab.com/letters/ default.htm,* where you will find a list of more than 20 categories of job search letters. For this example, click Answer Want Ads Like a Pro, since job openings you might find on the Internet can be considered "want ads."

2. Read the text, which offers general guidance and statistics about applying for jobs found through job listings that resemble want ads.

3. Take a look at the left column, where you'll see a list of situations you may find yourself in. Scroll down and click the example for the one-page generic letter for a senior management position.

4. Notice how the letter immediately grabs the employer's attention, because it directly connects the experience of the job seeker with the qualifications sought by the employer for this position. The bullets are effectively used to highlight this job seeker's experience.

5. Just below the bulleted achievements, 'notice that this job seeker included personal information such as age, marital status, and information about his children. We strongly discourage you from including such information in your letters.

Approach Letters to Request an Informational Meeting

Approach letters are used to gain access to individuals who may provide you with contacts, leads, and information that will assist you in career decision making or job hunting. These kinds of letters are used to obtain informational meetings and to build a network of contacts. You can view an excellent example of an approach letter at the University of Virginia's Web site at *http://minerva.acc.virginia.edu/~career/handouts/cover.html#sample6.* Note that in the last paragraph, the job seeker indicates that she will take action by following up with the individual the next week. This takes some pressure off the reader to do the follow-up and also ensures the job seeker an opportunity to connect with the individual.

Why Write an Approach letter?

Approach letters help you connect with others who may be able to help you out with your job search.

Follow these guidelines in writing your approach letters:

- Start with a personal statement that connects you to the reader. If you have a referral, you might start with: "Dr. Jones suggested I contact you..." If you lack a personal referral, you might open with: "I am writing to you because of your position as..." or "Because of your experience in..." or "Because we are both alumni of State College, I thought..."

- Orient the reader to your purpose. Explain that you do not expect the reader to know of any current job openings, but you would like his or her help, advice, suggestions, or guidance regarding your career plans, future work possibilities, and in obtaining occupational information. Explain your current situation.

- Close your letter with a request for a brief meeting at a mutually convenient time. Indicate that you will call in a few days to arrange a meeting.

- Always address the letter to a name, not to a position or title.

- Be brief.

- Make your letter warm and personal. Avoid language that is stereotyped or too jargony.

A Sample Approach Letter

1212 Boogey Avenue
Phoenix, AZ 01134
April 18, 2000

Ms. Janet L. Cooper
RT Associates
621 21st Street
New York, NY 10015

Dear Ms. Cooper:

Julie Sayres suggested that I write to you about my interest in project development. She thought you would be a good person to give me some career advice.

I am interested in a position with a firm specializing in education issues in developing countries. Having studied human resources and education, I want to put that knowledge to work where it will do the most good. I am particularly interested in projects involving the education of women.

Ms. Sayres mentioned you as one of the leading experts in this field. Would it be possible for us to meet briefly?

I will call your office next week to see if your schedule permits such a meeting.

Sincerely,

Maria Lopez
(202) 992-1234
mlopez@aol.com

Cover Letters for Job Applications

The *cover letter* serves to market you and explain why the reader should consider your resume. If you want the reader to examine your resume, your cover letter must have impact. The letter should advertise your resume; not just regurgitate it. It must capture the reader's attention, stress the employer's needs and what you have to contribute, and invite the employer to read your resume in depth. As mentioned earlier in this chapter, Career Lab has outstanding examples of cover letters. You can also find great examples of cover letters on the Quintessential Careers Web site at *http://www.quintcareers.com/cover_letter_samples.html.* Try clicking the link to the referral letter. Notice how the letter starts out by immediately mentioning the person who referred the job seeker to the reader. Follow these guidelines in writing your cover letters:

Cover Letters Are Important:
Your cover letter had better be well written and look great! Many employers use cover letters as writing samples.

- Address it to a particular person by name and title. If you are uncertain to whom to address the letter, look on the Internet for the appropriate name or call the company and tell the receptionist: "I'm sending some important papers (or correspondence) to the head of the department. I'm not sure, however, if I have the correct name and address. Could you please tell me to whom I should address these documents?" Then ask for the correct spelling and title.

- Communicate something personal. In your opening line, write something that is uniquely associated with the person, department, or organization that will communicate your interest. For example, you might say, "When I read your ad for a graphic designer, I was thrilled because I have long held an interest in how your firm operates and how my skills fit your project needs."

- Answer the employer's question, "Why should I see you?" This establishes your value.

- Make sure your writing style is direct, powerful, and error free. Eliminate extraneous words.

- Keep the letter short and to the point. Cover these three points:

  1. State your interest and purpose.

  2. Highlight your enclosed resume by stressing what you will do for the employer.

  3. Request an interview and indicate that you will call for an appointment.

- Use appropriate, active language.

- Always be positive. Stress your accomplishments and skills as well as your future value.

- Print on good quality bond paper. Use the same paper for your cover letter and your resume.

- Note that some employers discard cover letters. Don't say something important that is not included on your resume.

- Keep copies of your letter in a filing system for follow-up purposes.

The Components of a Cover Letter

                                                        Your address
                                                        Date

    Name (addressed to a person)
    Title
    Organization Name
    Address

    Dear Mr./Ms. _____:

    Opening paragraph. Arouse interest. Explain why you are writing; name the position or type of work for which you are applying. If writing in response to an advertised vacancy, mention how you learned of this opening. If someone referred you, mention his name.

    Middle paragraph(s). Create desire and market yourself. Explain why you are interested in working for this employer and specify your qualifications for this type of work. Highlight your particular achievements or other experiences in this field, and particularly those that address the job requirements. Refer to your enclosed resume, highlighting key points that illustrate how your skills, abilities, and experience match selection criteria.

Closing paragraph. Prompt action. Encourage follow-up by requesting an appointment or interview. Offer to call, specifying a time, for example "on Tuesday" or some similar suggestion to facilitate a favorable reply. State your interest or enthusiasm for meeting with the individual.

Sincerely,

Your signature
Your name
Your phone number
Your email address

A Sample Cover Letter

100 Any Street
Anytown, IL 60001
January 14, 2000

Mr. David Myers
Vice President
Fulton Corporation
1243 Madison Street
Chicago, IL 60616

Dear Mr. Myers:

John Bird, the Director of Research at the Ottings Company, informed me that you are looking for analysts in your newly re-engineered economic consulting division.

I have enclosed my resume for your consideration. During the past two summers I have had internships doing economic research and analyses. Having worked in a consulting firm, I know how to collaborate on teams to serve client needs.

I would appreciate an opportunity to discuss my candidacy. If requested, I could provide you with writing samples before an interview. I will call you next week to make arrangements for a visit. Thank you for your consideration.

Sincerely,

Gary S. Yamimoto
(302) 908-3241
gyamimoto@aol.com

Thank-You Letters After an Interview

Sincere Thanks: Although it seems obvious that you'd send a thank-you letter to an employer, most job seekers never do so. Employers often remember this genuine gesture of professionalism.

Professionals in the field of career counseling are unanimous in stressing the importance of sending thank-you letters to almost everyone who helps you in the process of getting a job. The person you talk with at the job interview or informational meeting, the receptionist who helped you get in to see the boss, the human resources worker who gave you a job lead; all those people should be thanked. In addition to basic courtesy, a thank-you letter is an opportunity to present yourself as a person with good interpersonal skills.

Thoughtful people are remembered. A thank-you letter helps you stand out from other job seekers. Write your thank-you letters within 24 hours of your interview. Highlight your interview discussion and reiterate your qualifications and continuing interest, expressing your gratitude for assistance. Write thank-you letters after job interviews, after informational meetings (even if they are conducted by phone), after being rejected for a job, and after accepting a job. The Career Lab site mentioned earlier in this chapter has outstanding samples of letters that match these situations.

A Sample Thank-You Letter

1234 56th Avenue
Gary, IN 00987
May 2, 2000

Mr. Mark Price
Planning & Development Associates
1818 J Street, N.W.
Washington, D.C. 20433

Dear Mr. Price:

It was a pleasure to meet you and talk with you at the recent Careers 2000 Job Fair in Daytona Beach. How surprised I was to learn that your organization is looking for candidates with exactly the background I have.

I certainly enjoyed informing you about my academic background in economics, as well as my internships on Capitol Hill. However, I realize that I did not have a chance to elaborate on my senior research project, which was a study of the variable rate charges that investment funds have utilized during the last three years. Using statistical analyses and econometric models, I was able to identify key elements that have caused a strengthening of investment opportunities.

Because this study was so similar to the kind of work we discussed, I believe that my qualifications are a perfect match for your Economic Analyst position. I look forward to hearing from you about an office visit. Again, thank you for the material you gave me in Daytona.

Sincerely,

Leslie Faye
(987) 234-5678
lfaye@hotmail.com

A Sample Post Informational Meeting Thank-You Letter

9876 54ᵗʰ Street, NW
Blair, OH 05026
March 22, 2000

Mr. Scott Dobbs, President
Food for the World, Inc.
6189 Rice Avenue
Dallas, TX 75648

Dear Mr. Dobbs:

Jan Winkle was right when she said you would be most helpful in advising me on a career in nutrition.

I appreciate that you took time from your busy schedule to meet with me. Your advice was most helpful, and I have incorporated your suggestions into my resume. I will send you a copy next week so that you can see the changes I made based on our meeting. Please feel free to pass it along should you know of anybody who might be interested in reading it.

Again, thank you so much for your assistance.

Sincerely,

Allen Klee
(793) 678-9876
aklee@compuserv.com

A Sample Post-Interview Thank-You Letter

9987 So. Weber Way
Minneapolis, MN 31345
April 22, 2000

Dr. Alvin Z. Tolleson
Human Resources Department
Myrtle Corporation
17 Hatfield Dr.
Syracuse, NY 12291

Dear Mr. Tolleson:

Thank you for the opportunity to interview with you yesterday for the Management Trainee position. I enjoyed meeting you and learning about Myrtle Corporation. I was especially impressed with your progressive stance regarding personnel issues.

Your organization appears to be moving in a direction that parallels my interests and career goals. The interview confirmed my initial positive impression of Myrtle Corporation, and I want to reiterate my strong interest in working with you. My experience in managing a small-business cooperative in the Dominican Republic, plus my training in communications, would enable me to progress steadily through your training program and become a productive member of your management team.

Again, thank you for your consideration. If you need any additional information from me, please feel free to call.

Sincerely,

Al Garrett
(543) 123-4567
agarrett@mindspring.com

Putting It All Together

Congratulations! You now know that, to write a powerful letter for the job search, you need to keep it simple and to the point while expressing your enthusiasm or other sentiments (depending on the topic of the letter).

You can now write approach letters for informational meetings, cover letters for job applications, and thank-you letters to follow up after an interview. Good job!

Next step: Learning how to network both online and offline!

PART IV
e-Job Search Strategies

CHAPTER 10

Networking: Online and Offline

Fewer than 15% of all jobs are found in newspapers. The majority of jobs are obtained through contacts and *networking*. But networking is not about collecting business cards or asking people you don't know if they have a job for you. Rather, it is about building and maintaining mutually beneficial relationships with others for the purpose of sharing information and resources to learn about business and professional trends and opportunities.

The Internet has expanded the already wide range of opportunities to meet others so that you may begin or continue building and nurturing such relationships. We'll show you how to effectively build a professional network to help you in your job search and in your career.

The Difference Between Networking and Information Meetings

Many job seekers don't understand the difference between networking and *information meetings*. This confusion and the unintentional misuse of these techniques have landed many job seekers in the hot seat with potential contacts. It's important to know the difference so that you know what you're doing and you know you're doing it right.

Why You Network or Schedule an Information Meeting

When you network, you need to make contacts and meet people in your career field to stay connected for the purposes of sharing professional information, helping each other succeed and thrive, and helping each other with job transitions. You also network to

What You'll Learn in This Chapter:

► What is meant by networking?

► How to become an expert in networking.

► How to make contacts effectively.

► How to develop your 30-second verbal resume.

► How to network electronically.

► How to build and sustain your network.

let people know that you are actively seeking employment so that they will let you know if they hear of any job openings.

In an information meeting, you meet with those in and out of your network for the specific purpose of gathering information related to your career or career field. These meetings do not involve asking for job placement assistance, but they do help to expand your network. Because of the specific information you gather, this process helps you make well-informed job and career decisions.

Who Is Involved in a Network or an Information Meeting?

In your network, you can include parents, friends, friends of parents and friends, members of professional associations related to your interests, workers in your past, current, or future career field of interest, people who are doing the job you want to do, college professors and alumni, neighbors and colleagues, people you meet at social events—to name just a few.

In an information meeting, you meet with the contacts you already have, those you made through networking, those you identified to be relevant sources of job search information, and those you are told about when asking others for assistance.

What You Do with a Network or an Information Meeting

In a network, your role is to seek out and develop relationships with people who may be able to help you with your job search or in your career.

In an information meeting, your role is to gather information to get a clearer idea of the kind of job or career you want and where you want to work.

When to Network or Schedule an Information Meeting

You must network now and always! Maintain relationships with these contacts even after you are employed. Remember that part of the process of networking is giving back.

Usually, you conduct information meetings when you are exploring career opportunities. Remember that the purpose of an information meeting is to gather professional information to help you make career decisions.

Where to Network or Have an Information Meeting

You should network continually throughout your professional life: in meetings, conferences, referrals, conventions, and some social gatherings.

It's usually best to request that an information meeting take place in the office of the person you want to speak with. If this isn't possible, ask if the person will meet you near her workplace for a cup of coffee or tea.

Becoming an Expert in Networking

People search for jobs in many different ways. The traditional approaches—responding to newspaper employment ads, mailing resumes to employers without applying for a specific job, and using employment agencies—yield minimal results. What's working these days is networking—both online and offline. Networking is nontraditional as far as job search approaches go, but in the changing world of work, it's networking that is keeping people alive and thriving in their career growth and job changes. Learning how to network now will serve you well in the future.

Networking has been a dirty word in the job search world in the last decade. Even now, many online job hunters are wearing out a potential welcome for others because of the inappropriate way they conduct their electronic networking. Unfortunately, it's because many job seekers just don't learn how to network professionally.

To maximize networking opportunities in person, you need to be confident, self-assured, respectful, and gracious with the contacts you make. You should be ready to introduce yourself to any individual, regardless of position or rank. You should be confident about your approach, your needs, your goals, and your value to a potential employer. You should always be committed to the individuals who help you out. Send them thank-you notes, notes of congratulations, articles of interest to them, and invitations for professional events.

You'll find some excellent guidance on electronic networking at the University of California at Los Angeles site at *http://dlis.gseis. ucla.edu/people/pagre/network.html*, in the article, "Networking on the Network." Although the purpose of this article is to assist doctoral students, the steps in learning how to network effectively can serve as a primer for any job hunter today. The author of this article turns an intimidating concept into an easy-to-understand aspect of life as a working professional. Pay close attention to the advice offered on electronic networking, such as avoiding the temptation to treat people like machines. These tips will save you great pain from potentially costly mistakes.

Try It Yourself ▼   If you're feeling too timid to step up to the networking plate, check out some of the articles on the *Wall Street Journal* site by following these steps:

1. Go to *The Wall Street Journal* site at *http://www.careers.wsj.com*.

2. Click the Job Hunting Advice link in the left column.

3. Click the Networking Effectively link to display a list of articles on this topic.

4. Scroll through the article titles and find one that fits your situation, such as "Networking Tips for Shy Job Seekers" or "Networking for Introverts." These articles address the concerns of many people who feel extremely uncomfortable introducing themselves to others.

▲

Where to Begin Networking

If you're not sure where to begin the process of networking, we have some proven strategies that will get you going immediately. You can probably come up with more ideas as well, but here are some tried-and-true strategies.

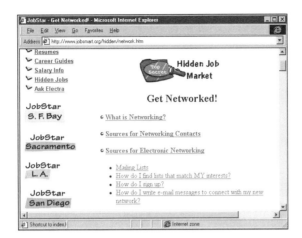

California's JobStar site has an excellent section called Get Networked! that explains how to network both online and offline, including some great ideas on how to develop a list of contacts and sources for electronic networking.

Family and Friends

Most of us don't necessarily think of our siblings, friends, neighbors, and family in terms of being professionals in the workplace. We know they work, and we know they're probably very good at what they do, but we don't see them in that environment day to day. Stop a minute and let them know you recognize that they might know somebody either where they work or elsewhere who might be a good contact for you. You'll be surprised at the number of contacts you will find in this circle of family and friends.

Also consider family and friends with whom you haven't maintained contact. They'll probably be happy to hear from you again—just make sure you let them know you'll repay the favor someday. If you don't have their contact information, you can easily find just about anybody these days through one of the multitude of electronic directories. You can link to a number of online directories through Telephone Directories on the Web at *http://www.teldir.com/eng*. This site will link you to more than 350 directories for businesses, individuals, fax numbers, and email addresses in the United States and more than 150 countries. The site is well organized by country and region and provides its own rating system for helping you determine how helpful an online directory may be.

Friends:

More than just a bunch of folks you spend your off hours with, your friends can supply valuable contact information in your search for a better job. It's said that any person is just seven people away from knowing everyone else in the world—and your friends are the first step in your networking process.

Telephone Directories on the Web at www.teldir. com/eng is the best set of online directories to help locate lost contacts and find new ones.

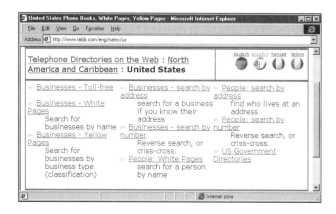

Try It Yourself ▼

Are you ready to search for somebody you've lost contact with? It's easy to search on one of the many online directories that offer this service.

1. Go to Telephone Directories on the Web at *http://www.teldir.com/eng.*

2. Click the link for the country you think the person lives in. If you're looking for an email address, scroll down the page and click Email Addresses in the left column. For this exercise, click the link for the United States in the top-left column.

3. Suppose that you knew this person in college, but don't know where he now works. Click the White Pages link to access People listings.

4. Because the AnyWho directory seems to have a good three-star rating, click that link to go to the AnyWho Web site.

5. Follow the simple directions on the page that appears, which include typing the first and last name of the person you're looking for. Note that when you use many online directories, it's not necessary to fill in all the blanks, but filling in all you know about a person will definitely help narrow your search. If you're not successful in finding the person you're looking for by using one directory, try another directory; there are many other places to search, and it only takes a cyber-minute to do so!

Congratulations! You've just completed your first online search for someone you want to find!

▲

Professional Associations

Jump in feet first and join a professional association. These organizations are overflowing with opportunities to network and build your career. Associations are designed to support the worker in his trade by offering professional growth opportunities, lobbying on behalf of the field, providing career information, and a lot more.

If you don't know what association to join, check out Associations Unlimited at *http://www.galenet.com/servlet/AU* for a comprehensive listing of associations. You will need to connect to this site from a library, university, career center, or business that has leased access, because this site is a fee-for-service. Finding a place with access to this site is well worth the time you spend, because this is the best online listing we've found. Although it's always worth double-checking, there is usually no cost to the user to access this site if the institution has a user license. You can search by keywords, titles, and locations. Most associations are based in Washington, D.C., New York City, Boston, or Chicago. However, the larger associations have local branches nationwide and some even worldwide.

If Galenet is not accessible to you, you can search more than 6,500 associations through the American Society of Association Executives Web site at *http://info.asaenet.org/gateway/ OnlineAssocSlist.html*. Although this is not a comprehensive database of all associations, it's one of the largest collections online. The limitation of this database, however, is that you can only search by selecting a word you think is in the formal title of the association, or you can search by category. The site provides about 100 different categories from which to select. Unfortunately, the list of names returned to you contains only the name of the associations and not descriptions. You have to click the link and go to the site directly to find out what the association's mission is.

Where to Find Galenet Access:

You can usually find access to the Galenet database through universities, community colleges, larger nonprofit organizations, associations, and some public libraries.

Associations Unlimited at www.galenet.com /servlet/AU offers the most comprehensive listing of associations and societies in the United States.

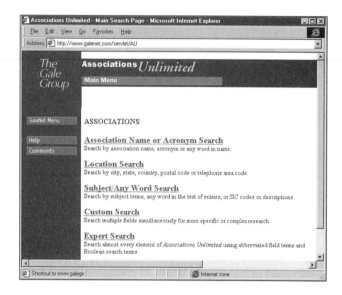

We also suggest that you check into regional and local associations. Although the Galenet database will help you identify local associations, you'll find a limited listing on the ASAE site. However, you can find a selection of local and regional associations through Yahoo's Guide to Professional Associations at *http://dir.yahoo.com/business_and_economy/organizations/ professional*. Yahoo! categorizes the associations by industry but also has a search function that allows you to limit the search by selecting Just This Category.

After you link to the association's Web site, check to see if there are events or meetings in your area. Ask for a copy of the membership directory and connect with others near you. If no members live nearby, consider traveling to the closest meeting. Attend annual conferences and meet with other professionals in your career field.

Keep in mind that, of all the associations that have Web sites, most offer a page of links to related Web sites. Check those links out! You might find a conference, training session, or workshop nearby that you can attend to meet others.

Many associations are also now putting their bulletins and trade magazines online. You can use this information to identify the key players in a career field. Make a note of those you want to connect with at a future meeting or conference. If you haven't seen an online newsletter for a particular association, check out the American Society for Training and Development at *www.astd.org* and click the T&D Magazine link under the Products and Services heading in the left column. Note that this is the link to the official trade magazine of the association. As you will note in the table of contents, some of the contents are not available online; however, you still can read the major articles that discuss trends in the training industry and announce key players in different areas of interest.

Fellow Alumni and Your Alma Mater

Become an active alumnus. The students you met in college may be key contacts for your next job. If you are still a student, make those contacts now and stay in touch. Also, connect with professors in your field, because they may have broad networks in their specialized fields.

Check to see if your alma mater has a Web site by going to My Job Search at *www.myjobsearch.com/network/associations.html* and clicking the Alumni Associations link. This link will take you to a U.S. map on which you can click the state where you went to college and see a list of links to online alumni Web sites. This site has links to nearly 500 alumni associations.

Many colleges are now posting their alumni activities and directories online for the purpose of expanding the alumni network. Make sure your information is current and connect with others in your field. Many directories offer great information to help you network, such as career title, organization, and additional degrees. The alumni page of Northern Arizona University at *http://www.nau.edu/~alumni/index.html* is an excellent example of a helpful networking tool for alumni. This site lists the alumni chapters around the country and even allows alumni to update their information online.

Alumni associations nationwide offer great opportunities for alumni to network with each other. Here is Northern Arizona University's alumni page.

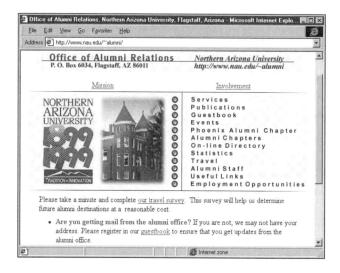

Try It Yourself ▼ Are you ready to find your alumni association to see what networking opportunities await you? Follow these steps:

1. Go to My Job Search at *www.myjobsearch.com/network/associations.html* and click Alumni Associations. This link will take you to the U.S. map.

2. Click the state where you went to school. This action turns up a list of universities and colleges in that state that have Web pages for their alumni associations.

3. Click the name of the school you attended. The link will take you to the alumni Web page.

4. Look at the contents of the Web site to see if there are links to online directories of alumni, links to alumni chapters in your area, listings of events to meet up with other alumni, and other services that allow for networking opportunities.

Congratulations! You've found your alumni association. Time to
▲ start networking!

Contacts at Work

Your current boss and colleagues can be your connection to your future. Maintain those relationships, because they may serve you well tomorrow. Be helpful and honest with your co-workers and give help when needed. Also remember to ask for help when you need it. Give credit where credit is due—and share credit when you can. If you have many years of experience, offer to mentor others. If you don't, ask somebody to mentor you. Maintain your visibility at work by offering to train, teach, write, speak, and lead whenever possible.

Ten Steps to Making Contacts Effectively

1. Determine your goals and decide who you want to contact and why.
2. Make a list of people you know: family, friends, faculty, former employers, fellow students, neighbors, colleagues, and so on.
3. Determine what you want to gain from each contact.
4. Select the best method for contacting each person. You have many options: by phone, by mail, by email, by fax, in person, or through somebody you know. If you have been referred, say so.
5. Initiate the contact and assert yourself positively. Be honest about your intentions.
6. When you meet with people, keep to your original goals.
7. Present yourself professionally and be viewed as knowledgeable or skillful in a particular area.
8. Follow up immediately on information you offer to send.
9. Continue to use your contacts and offer assistance to others in your network.
10. Show interest in empowering others.

Some Possible Situations in Making Contacts

You may feel uncomfortable at first with initiating contact with someone you've identified as a potential node in your network. But the more often you make contacts, the easier it gets.

Here are six situations in which perhaps you can envision yourself. Imagine yourself in each situation and experiment with and modify the suggested responses we've provided. The goal of this exercise is to help you develop your skills in approaching others in varied situations.

▼ **Try It Yourself**

1. A friend arranges a meeting between you and his boss, who works in your field of interest. You arrive in her office. After some initial conversation, she says, "So tell me, what are you interested in?" You respond

Well, I've been working in (name your field and specialty). I really have enjoyed it and I feel I've made some very effective contributions. (Perhaps give a brief example or two). But now I want to move into (an area you are interested in). (Name of your good friend) tells me that you have a lot of expertise in this area. I would really value your advice. Given my experience, what direction or area do you think I would be most marketable in?

2. You attend a meeting of the local chapter of a professional association. You are told that the first half-hour will be devoted to "networking." People are talking in small groups. You walk up to one group and introduce yourself. You're asked, "What do you do?" You respond:

Right now, I am working for (name of your organization). I do (describe what you do, not your job title). How about you? (He tells you what he does.) You know, I've been thinking about moving to (name an organization or type of organization you are interested in OR another area of your field). Do you know anything about them? (He says no). I haven't been a member of (name the association) long; maybe you know another member who might have some experience in this area?

3. You have identified several individuals you want to contact because they work and have hiring authority for organizations you have targeted. You call first and say

Mr. Jones, my name is Nedra Blair and I've worked for several years in (name your career field and region of employment if overseas), specifically on projects dealing with (name one or two projects). I understand that your organization is currently working on these types of projects in (name city or country). I'm calling to see if we could meet to discuss whether there may be an opportunity for me to work in these projects. I have extensive experience in the region and have managed several projects myself. When would be a good time for us to get together?

4. At a social event, you are introduced to someone who works for an organization you have targeted in your job search. You say to this person

It's nice to meet you. I've always been interested in (name of organization). How long have you worked there? Do you enjoy it? You know, I've worked for about six years in (your field), and I particularly enjoy (a certain aspect of your work). Would there be anyone in your organization who might be interested in someone with my background?

Response #1: *Ideally, he says yes and names an individual. You respond: "Do you think he would be willing to talk to me?" He says yes. You respond "I'd really like to talk with him. Would you mind making an introduction?"*

Response #2: *Not so ideally, he says no, he doesn't know of anyone. You can probe a bit by asking, "Well, is there a part of the organization that does that kind of work?" He says something like, "Well maybe in X department." You ask if he knows who heads the department.*

5. You are studying in your dorm. The phone rings. The caller introduces herself as a recruiter and then says, "I understand from (a friend of yours) that you are interested in working in (your career field). I am interviewing candidates for current vacancies. Tell me about yourself." You say

Thanks for thinking of me. I've done a lot of work in that area, serving as a task manager (or other position), working in (name one or two areas). I'd be very interested in talking to you about your project. When could we get together?

or

Thanks for calling. Your project sounds like something that would be a good fit for me. Unfortunately, I'm right in the middle of something that I need to finish. When would be a good time for me to call you back?

6. Your contract has not been renewed or your position has been downsized. You have made a list of all the people you have worked for or with in the past who might be able to help you locate other opportunities. One of the people on your list is an official from another organization who you met and worked with briefly on a work-related project. You call her and say

Is this Ms. Little? (She says yes.) Hello, my name is Helen Haddad. I don't know if you remember me, but we worked together in 1994 on a project in (name the location). (She says she does remember you.) Well, the reason I'm calling is to see if you might have some advice for me. I am getting ready to leave my job at (name of your organization) and I am exploring possibilities in other similar organizations. I want very much to work in (name of location, organization, or career field) again, and I remember that you have worked with that extensively. Would it be possible to have a short meeting sometime next week?

▲

The 30-Second Resume

When to Use a Verbal Resume:

A verbal resume is an introductory statement to be used when contacting others for information (networking), introducing yourself to prospective employers, and answering the question, "Tell me about yourself."

The most uncomfortable piece about networking is introducing yourself properly without stumbling and fumbling and talking on forever. To remedy this, you need to develop your 30-second resume. It should articulate succinctly your work search goal and create a positive first impression. When developed well and delivered with a natural tone, this verbal resume will help you soar past the introduction as well as respond to the one question you can count on hearing over and over again: "Tell me about yourself."

Considerations in Preparing Your Verbal Resume

As you approach the task of formulating your verbal resume, you should take into account several questions. When you can answer these questions with some surety, you'll be well on your way to crafting an effective message:

• What point are you trying to make?

• What impression do you want to create?

- Who is the audience?

- What are they likely to be interested in?

- What core skills or areas of competence match the needs of your audience?

Formula for Your Verbal Resume

Here's a template you can start with when you're trying to craft an effective verbal resume:

My name is (state name). I have (#) years experience in (industry/sector/function). Most recently, I have (mention general career field). Before that, I did (mention previous related experience). My area of expertise is (mention your key job-specific skills). My particular strengths are (relate them to the specific position you are inquiring about or applying for). I would be interested in (learning more about opportunities in this area, speaking with others in the field, talking with you about how I might contribute to your organization, and so on).

Some Examples of 30-Second Verbal Resumes

You can and *should* vary the presentation of the formula given in the preceding sidebar to meet your particular situation. Here are three examples of great verbal resumes.

For someone whose job target is corporate training "For the past eight years, I've worked in adult education and training. I've designed and implemented in-house training centers at three organizations and done a lot of work developing job aids and computer-based training. I've also taught a variety of courses. What I enjoy most is teaching performance management and communication skills. I'm interested in talking to you because your organization runs a top-notch training function."

For someone whose job target is project management in an agricultural or health project "I have more than six years of experience managing complex field projects. I've supervised both health and agricultural development projects, most recently in Kenya, where I managed a large project on AIDS. My strengths are supervising field staff working in remote locations and working with local governments and nongovernmental organizations. What I would like to do next is work on another health project in Africa. What organizations might offer these types of assignments?"

For someone who just graduated from college and whose job target is marketing   "During the past four years, I've intensely studied and put to the test marketing skills and creative promotions. I served as the president of our university's student marketing association, which included promoting campus events to newspapers and radio and TV stations around the state. I led a team of students on one project to market the new cafeteria on campus, which increased its number of patrons significantly within three months. I would be interested in talking with you about how I might apply my skills to your needs in this organization."

Your 30-Second Verbal Resume

What would you say in answer to the question, "Tell me about yourself"? Write your answer below.

Electronic Networking: It's Time to Plug In

Although you won't find coffee bars, wine and cheese parties, and other such social events online, you will find incredible networking opportunities that are helping job hunters develop a network that leads to job search and career successes.

Online networking opportunities can be found in numerous formats, from simple email to listservs, chat rooms, bulletin boards, Usenet or newsgroups, virtual communities, and other forums.

Email

If you already have an email account, you probably know the power of sending and receiving messages directly. You can break communication barriers and avoid answering machines and voice mail simply by writing and sending an electronic message. Also, if somebody refers you to somebody else and gives you that person's email address, you've got a direct link to a potential contact who might be able to help you.

If you have email, you should know that you no longer have to be at your home computer to access your email. Now you can sign up for free email and access it and send messages from it from virtually any place that has an Internet connection.

If you don't have email and want to set up a free email account, go back to Chapter 7, "Writing Resumes: The Printed Word," where we offer step-by-step instructions on how to set up a free Web-based account.

Get Email

If you don't have an email address where you can check your messages daily, we strongly suggest that you get one.

Listservs

If you have an email address, you can participate on a listserv. Listservs are basically groups of people or businesses that communicate by email with all group members simultaneously. This means that you send one message to a certain email address your message is then distributed to everyone on the list.

Hundreds of special topic listservs are popping up on the Internet every month. All you have to do to participate is subscribe, although there is no charge. *Subscribing* means that you send an email to an address to request to be added to the list. One individual or one business usually maintains a listserv. Occasionally, the list of participants is limited to certain individuals, such as association members or people in a specific career field.

Listservs serve any number of needs for the participants. If the listserv is for professionals in the field, the list may host discussions on different topics, issues, organizations, or other areas relevant to the field. The great strength of listservs is that you can use them to communicate with professionals in your field any time of day, and others on the list can communicate with you. Many people who hear of jobs related to the listserv content will send announcements to the listserv.

Once you've been on a listserv for a few weeks and have participated in the varied discussions, you may identify a few individuals who might be of interest to you. Since you'll find out about the participants by reading the information they post to the list, you should save their messages, which contain the email addresses of the correspondents, and contact these people directly by email to discuss your job search.

We strongly caution you not to participate in a listserv discussion the first week or so after you subscribe. You need to read through the instructions that are sent to you, which describe the purpose of the listserv and the appropriate reasons and ways to communicate with the list. Remember that even though nobody can see you, your communication style speaks volumes about you.

One of the best Web sites to visit to identify listservs in your field is The Liszt at *www.liszt.com*. You can search the database by words or phrases or you can search the different lists by topic, such as business or science. After you find a list that interests you, simply read the instructions on how to subscribe, and you're on your way!

The Liszt is the Web's best compilation of listservs. There are more than 90,000 listservs in its database.

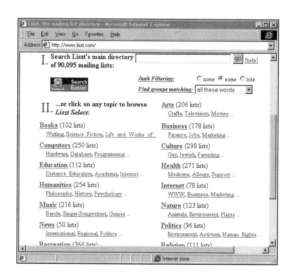

Chat Rooms

You can meet others online by connecting to a chat room that is hosted by a specific site, such as Monster.com at *www.monster.com* (click the Today's Chats link), or by a specific Internet provider, such as America Online (AOL) at *www.aol.com*. Note that AOL allows access to some of its chat rooms to nonsubscribers. If you are a subscriber, AOL has a wide range of workplace topics; it's worth your time to take a look at what's available. After you find the Web page that lists the chat rooms, you can choose which one to enter and participate in a typed discussion or request that an individual have a private discussion with you.

Chat rooms have been very popular and are used for socializing, sharing information, networking, and more. The difference between a chat room and a listserv is that chat rooms are temporary and anyone can jump into the chat room at any time. Take a look at the chat rooms on CareerPath.com at *http://chat.careerpath.com*. When you scroll down the page, you'll see a list of topics and dates and times for the chat. CareerPath.com has an impressive list of hosts for the chats. For example, CareerPath.com held a chat about translating old media skills to the new digital world. The host was the president of *USA Today*.

Chats, Chit-Chats, and Bad Chats

Although chat rooms offer great opportunities to network with others, they also pose potential problems if you're caught in the wrong chat room.

Chat rooms are infamous for careless talk and inappropriate proposals. They offer a disguise to those who wouldn't be caught in person holding such tasteless conversations.

You can reduce your chances of getting caught in such conversations by being selective about the chat rooms in which you participate. For example, chats that have a moderator or host, such as those found on CareerPath.com and other job search sites, offer some degree of assurance that the topic proposed will be addressed and that nonconformers will be forced to leave the chat.

You can also search for specific chat rooms through Yahoo! Net Events at *http://events.yahoo.com*. When we typed *career chat* in the search box, we got a list of more than 60 chats going on today. However, this list isn't comprehensive. We suggest that you also check Yack.com at *www.yack.com*, which also allows you to search for current chats on varied topics.

It's time to check out some of the chat rooms that may offer networking opportunities.

1. Go to Yack.com at *www.yack.com* and scroll down until you see the search box in the left column.

2. Type *career* and click Go.

3. You will see a list of events, mostly chats, taking place around the Net for the day. Chances are you will have several pages of events to review.

4. You can find similar chat events about careers by clicking the Money link in the top-left column that lists the events that are "Now Playing."

5. After clicking the Money link, you will see several options for events. Click Careers.

6. In the middle of the page is a list of special events. Note, however, that there are several tabbed options from which you can choose career events. Click the Selected Chatrooms option to see a list of today's chats on career topics.

7. You then have the option to get more information about the chat topic, or you can click the link that takes you directly to the chat room on another Web site.

8. Click a chat that interests you and try it out!

Congratulations! You've just participated in an online chat and networking event.

Newsgroups

Newsgroups (a.k.a. *bulletin boards* and *Usenet*) are forums that allow you to have a discussion with others by posting messages and waiting for someone to respond directly to you or to respond by leaving a message on the board for all to read. This approach, however, tends to be a bit passive, and the discussion groups tend to be made up of much larger groups with more diverse interests than is true of listservs. We encourage you to try some of the other ways to connect with potential nodes in your network.

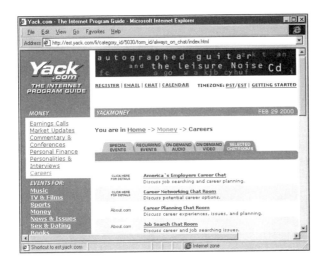

Yack.com is a great site for finding today's chat events on the Internet.

Virtual Communities

More and more special-interest communities are popping up online. You can now find numerous communities, such as those for college students, women, minorities, techies, and other professions and groups. Usually, the virtual community is a Web site itself, such as WomenConnect.com at *www.womenconnect.com.* You can find links to thousands of virtual communities, including minority groups, women, 30-somethings, and others on Yahoo! at *http://dir.yahoo.com/Society_and_Culture/Cultures_and_Groups.*

More on Newsgroups:

If you are still interested in checking out how newsgroups work and whether they may be helpful in your networking efforts, go to Synapse at *www.synapse.net/~radio/finding.htm* for links to newsgroup search engines.

Ten Networking Tips

1. Use every opportunity to make contacts; plan on meeting your contacts regularly (weekly, monthly, every other month, twice a year, or whatever works for both of you).

2. Contribute articles to journals and newsletters of trade and professional organizations. Connect with the editors, staff, and readers.

3. Follow up when you receive information or advice. Inform your network of your results.

4. Stay on top of the job market in your field. As you come across jobs that might suit somebody in your network, pass that lead along with a note saying "I don't know if you're looking for another job, but I came across this and it seemed to fit you and your expertise well."

5. Create a system for keeping track of your network contacts. Use a Rolodex or some other file system to keep track of pertinent information.

continues

continued

6. Say thank you. Show appreciation to those who help you.

7. Create your own business card. Many of the larger office supply stores sell business cards for as little as $15 for 1,000 cards.

8. Develop a solid verbal resume. Practice. Practice. Practice.

9. Give back. Networking is a two-way street. Send relevant articles or information to those you think would be interested in them.

10. Stay in touch with those in your network. Try to connect by letter, email, phone, or in person at least once a year.

Putting It All Together

Congratulations! You now know how to effectively network both online and offline. If you followed the guidance in this chapter, you learned that who you know and who knows you are the keys to a successful job search. You also now know that developing a 30-second verbal resume will help you make great first impressions and reduce your anxiety.

You've now nailed down the difference between networking and information meetings, and you know that electronic networking is alive and thriving on the Internet. You also know how to use the different communication options such as listservs, chat rooms, and email.

Next stop: Finding the jobs online!

CHAPTER 11

Finding the Perfect Job on the Net

With hundreds of Web sites devoted to job listings, job hunting on the Internet seems to be getting easier each year. At the same time, with more variety comes more analysis and more decisions, so it also seems to be increasingly overwhelming for job hunters. The bottom line is that there are thousands of sites that are waiting for you to click and search through their job offerings. This chapter will help you zero in on what it is you're looking for.

When seeking a job or an employer, you must focus, focus, focus. Otherwise, the job lists are no more than mega databases of classified ads—and we know how few job offers result from such listings. If you don't know what you're looking for, then you're not ready for this chapter. If this is the case, we suggest that you go back to Chapter 3, "e-Career Mapping and Job Search Planning," and take it from there. If you *are* ready to use the job banks, this chapter will teach you how to use them to your best advantage.

How Effective the Job Sites *Really* Are

It's next to impossible to track how many people are hired through the job listings on the Internet. Our findings indicate that fewer than 2 percent of individuals who apply for noncomputer jobs listed on the Internet are offered jobs. Although this percentage seems to be minimal, it appears to be slowly increasing each year.

As employers increasingly take to the Net to advertise their vacancies, our sense is that the 2 percent will increase further. However, it will never replace the human dimension of the job search, and you know what that means: networking!

What You'll Learn in This Chapter:

▶ How effective job sites are.

▶ How to *really* find the perfect job.

▶ Values of a job posting.

▶ Where to find the jobs.

If this is the case, you're probably wondering why employers are posting millions of jobs into cyberspace. Well, there are many reasons, and several of them have to do with broadening their reach to attract the best talent. However, it's important to remember that if you are able to access these jobs, so is everybody else. Hence, your competition skyrockets, your uniqueness diminishes, and the employer becomes inundated with applications from both qualified and unqualified candidates.

Why Employers Post Jobs Online:

There are lots of reasons employers post jobs online. Here are just a few:

- **Broader reach**   More job seekers will see the online postings.
- **Convenience**   Many job sites save the employer time by creating easy-to-use systems they can use to drop in ads.
- **Deadlines**   Employers can make a job announcement immediately on the Internet, as opposed to waiting for the Sunday want ads or a monthly job bulletin.
- **Cost savings**   Some Web sites reach a larger audience for less than it costs to post in some newspapers or magazines.
- **Exposure**   Employers can make their jobs available for as long as they want rather than a one-day ad. Many sites also offer links directly to an employer's Web site, which gives job seekers a chance to check out the employer and determine if it's a good fit before applying.

Should you be counting on the effectiveness of these job listings? The answer is, at best, "maybe." Online job listings are effective enough that you should include them as a resource in your job search, but not effective enough to count on them as your sole source for job vacancies.

How to Find the Perfect Job

If you've been reading this book chapter by chapter, you already know that to find the perfect job, you need to know who you are, how you fit, what you need, what you've got, and what you want. Once you have this focus, you are ready to tap your network and apply for jobs.

There are numerous benefits to using the Internet to find job postings. However, we have two golden rules for job surfing:

- **Focus your search** As we've said before, if you don't know what you're looking for, you'll end up somewhere—but who knows where.

- **Limit your time online** Limit the amount of time you spend searching through the job banks. We suggest that you search for jobs online no more than 10% of the time you devote each week to your job search. (Of course, you will need to spend more time online if you're networking and researching.)

If you can stick to these two rules, you'll save yourself a great deal of lost time and more quickly reach your job search goal.

As we already mentioned, the majority of jobs are found through some form of contact and networking. Quite frankly, this doesn't change for online job searches—even though you'll find millions of jobs on the Internet.

Although more employers are posting their announcements online, it has yet to be proven that the Internet has dramatically changed the way employers hire. The fact is that job listings are simply electronic want ads. You still need to spend the majority of your job search time networking. The job banks can help you do just that!

Beyond the Job: Five Values of a Job Posting

Just when you think it's a waste of time to surf the job lists—think again! A job opening posted online can be dissected to help you peek through the doors of job search success. You can find job market data, which employers are using the Internet to hire what types of employees, what current salary levels are out there in different regions for different jobs, what language to incorporate into your resume, and who you can connect with for future networking. Let's take a look at each of these:

- **Job Market Data** Look for information such as what types of jobs are out there, what qualifications you need, and where different career fields tend to be located. Also look for information regarding responsibility at different job levels.

Golden Rules for Online Job Hunters:

- Focus your search.
- Limit your time at the online job banks.

Cast Your Net Online!

Most jobs are found through networking. This fact doesn't change for online job hunters—even though you'll find millions of jobs on the Internet.

- **Who's Hiring Online Versus Offline**   Although there are millions of jobs posted to the Internet, there are millions more that will never see a Web page. You can find out which employers are using the Internet to find employees or to advertise their jobs. You can find out which jobs they are advertising online. They may be posting only entry-level or executive-level jobs, or they may post only technical, sales, or administrative jobs.

  Similar to help wanted ads, the jobs that are tougher to fill or less popular are often the ones you'll find online. Think about it. If an employer can fill a job without paying to post it, or if the employer already knows who he wants for a job, then there is no reason to post it to a job bank that will reap hundreds or thousands of resumes that will need to be handled.

  Remember that finding only certain jobs from certain employers doesn't mean that these are the only jobs open. Instead, the employer may be selective about which jobs are posted.

  Of course there are other employers who may never post jobs online. The majority of the employment opportunities in the United States are with small and mid-size companies. However, the majority of the jobs you'll find online seem to be with the larger companies. Why? For several reasons: First, the online job banks can be costly to employers with smaller recruitment budgets. Second, smaller employers tend to count heavily on their networks—not a big surprise for the savvy job seeker.

- **Salary Levels**   You can find some excellent information on salaries at different Web sites. We'll cover this in Chapter 13, "Job Offers: E-valuating and Net-gotiating." However, you can find a wealth of salary information for specific employers that may interest you. Look for what salary ranges they are offering and then look at their competitors. Also take a look at the benefits pages on their Web sites. You can arm yourself with a lot of negotiating power by seeing what employers are offering in posted positions online.

- **Resume Language**   Use the job banks to find the buzz-words in your career field. You'll be able to pull out the verbs you can use to create a powerful resume. You can also get a sense of what words are most commonly used by different employers. By tracking their word use, you'll most likely come up with a list of words that are critical on a resume that will be scanned.

- **Contacts**   You're back in the networking saddle if you can find out the name of the person or persons who are hiring for the positions that interest you. Follow your networking strategies to connect with these individuals rather than just zipping them your resume. Remember: These contacts are your passport to employment.

Words Matter:

A job listing often gives you words that are important to the employer. For example, if an employer is looking for a "financial analyst for a position that entails accounts/receiving analysis, revenue recognition, and reconciliations," you've just found the keywords to include on your resume that will grab the employer's attention.

Types of Sites That List Jobs

There are tens of thousands of Web sites that offer job listings in one form or another. You can find jobs posted on association Web sites, employer recruiting sites, university career center sites, large and small job bank sites, listservs, newsgroups, bulletin boards...and the list goes on.

Your goal is to nail the sites that contain the jobs you want or the employers that interest you. The listings and information in this chapter and in Appendix A, "Web Directory," will help you do just that.

Because job sites change regularly, we think that the best way to stay on top of what's hot and what's not is to count on the online reviews from a few experts in the field.

Richard Bolles has a site called the Job Hunter's Bible at *www.jobhuntersbible.com*. Bolles, the author of *What Color Is Your Parachute?*, is highly regarded in the job search field, and his reviews of the different job search sites will send you clicking in the right direction.

                CHAPTER 11

The Job Hunter's Bible is an excellent guide to the different job sites on the Web. You can check it out at www.jobhuntersbible.com.

Another great guide for updates on job sites is Margaret Dikel's Riley Guide at *www.rileyguide.com.* Dikel provides extensive listings of links to job listings. Her site has minimal graphics, so it uploads quickly, and it is updated regularly. She provides commentary on the different sites.

As for links to career-specific and regional job listing sites, My Job Search at *www.myjobsearch.com* takes the prize. For regional job listings, this site allows you to pick a state and then lists the job search sites that focus on job listings in that state. If you're looking for a career-specific site, such as job listings in the engineering/science field, simply click the appropriate category, and the site presents a listing of job sites for that field. This site also does an excellent job of rating the different general job sites by ease of use, quality of the job search function, and user services. It also provides a detailed review of the different job sites, including the number of job postings and resume postings and details on how the site operates.

Types of Job Sites

Job listings generally can be found in any of these types of Web sites:

- Mega Job Sites
- Targeted and Recruiter Job Sites
- Regional Job Sites
- Virtual Career Fair Sites
- University Career Pages
- Association, Alumni, Nonprofit, and Other Special Interest Group Sites
- Organization Recruitment Pages
- Email, Listservs, Newsgroups, and Bulletin Boards
- Online Newspapers, Magazines, and other Reading Materials
- Government Job Assistance Pages

Mega Job Sites

These sites are usually more popular with job hunters because they contain hundreds of thousands of listings in all career fields. These sites usually offer assistance on writing resumes, guidance for the job search, and information on employers. Most of the larger sites are free to the job hunter. However, the employer pays a fee to post a job.

One of the more popular mega job search sites is Monster.com at *www.monster.com*. This site has thousands of new job listings each week. They keep their job bank freshly updated and provide excellent assistance in identifying specific jobs. This wonderfully organized site also allows you to search for jobs based on job category, location, salary, and more. It lists more than 300,000 current job listings for employment around the world.

We suggest that you check out The Job-Search-Engine at *www.job-search-engine.com*. This site is not a job bank, nor does it offer reviews of the different job sites. Instead, it actually searches many of the more popular job sites and returns a listing of jobs from these sites that match your query.

More Job Sites:

For a comprehensive list of Web sites that list job vacancies, check out our Web Directory in the appendix section at the end of this book.

The Job-Search-Engine serves as a one-stop service that simultaneously scans for jobs at many major job sites. You can check it out at www.job-search-engine.com.

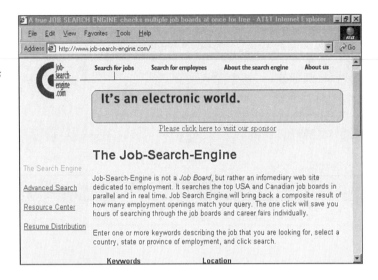

Targeted and Recruiter Job Sites

These sites offer job listings in specific career fields, such as accounting and finance, education, biology, computer technology, and others. You will also find job sites targeting specific groups, such as executives, international workers, or Hispanics. Most of these sites are free to use, but occasionally you will come across a site that charges for access to its jobs. Our advice on this: Don't pay unless you know that there are jobs there that meet your career goals. If you decide to pay for these sites, request a trial-period of two to four weeks.

ExecSearches.com at *www.execsearches.com* is a free access site that posts executive-level jobs from around the country. Most of the jobs we've seen on this site are in the nonprofit arena.

Training and Development—Human Resource Job Mart at *www.tcm.com/hr-careers/career* lists jobs organized by area of HR specialization, such as employment and recruitment, management, training and development, and so on.

The Chronicle of Higher Education at *http://chronicle.com/jobs* is a top choice for those seeking employment in academia and related organizations. The access to jobs is free, and the jobs are updated weekly.

The Internet is a gold mine for recruiters, recruitment firms, and temporary agencies. Recruiters continually frequent the resume banks in search of viable candidates. They post the jobs they are hired to fill in the job banks that will reap them the best results. And now, many recruiters and temporary agencies are establishing their own Web pages to post their jobs and attract talent.

Job Hunters and Headhunters: Who's Hunting Whom?

Both job hunters and headhunters are scouring the career Web sites to see if opportunity is knocking—or clicking. While headhunters—more professionally known as *recruiters*—scour the resume banks in search of talent, they are mostly looking for specific career profiles of seasoned workers, often in management or technical fields.

Lots of job seekers have the mistaken idea that recruiters exist to find the job seeker a job. Quite the contrary: Recruiters are in business to fill jobs for a company or other organization that pays them for this service.

If a recruiter approaches you by email or by phone, or if you send a recruiter your resume and he accepts it, this does not guarantee that he will place you in a position. Usually recruiters will call you only if and when an employer has reviewed your resume and expressed interest in interviewing you.

Many recruiters operate on a "Don't call us, we'll call you" basis. However, if you have executive-level experience, are an expert in your field, have a specialized or technical skill in a field such as nursing, information management, or telecommunications, or are fairly well-known in your field, you may want to contact a recruiter to see if this is a relationship you both want to explore.

Regional Sites

Regional sites focus on a city, county, neighborhood, state, country, or region. These sites are gaining online attention because of their focus on a specific job market. Therefore, more and more jobs are being posted to attract local talent to local employers. We suggest that before you go to the national or global job banks, you should first try some regional sites for the area where you plan to live.

CareerPath.com at *www.careerpath.com* compiles the daily classified want ads from more than 90 major newspapers around the country. With more than 350,000 job listings, it's an outstanding source to check out the general job market in other regions. It allows you to search by job category, location, or newspaper.

America's Job Bank at *www.ajb.dni.us* is a compilation of jobs from 1,800 state employment service offices. There are more than 1,000,000 jobs in both the public sector and the private sector. Because employers don't pay to list the jobs, you can find many job openings at small and medium-size businesses, which is where the job market is expanding significantly.

Duke University's Job Resources by U.S. Region at *http://cdc. stuaff.duke.edu/stualum/employment/JobResources/jregion.html* is one of the Net's best collections of job resources by region.

The Riley Guide at *www.dbm.com/jobguide/internat.html* is a fabulous site that provides links to sites that contain job listings in nearly every country around the world. This is a great site if you're looking for a job outside the United States.

Virtual Career Fairs

Many sites are creating what they refer to as a *Virtual Career Fair*. However, we've found that many of these fairs tend to be little more than advertising links to employer Web pages or links to profiles about the employer. Even so, that means the employer may be looking to hire or wants the word to get out about its career opportunities. The better Virtual Career Fairs work similarly to career fairs that you visit at a convention center, hotel, or university. These sites invite employers to join a virtual community to share employment opportunities, career information, and job search advice with job seekers. One company, College Central at *www.collegecentral.com*, appears to be announcing career fairs for colleges and entry-level job seekers. You can check out its site to see which colleges are sponsoring these virtual fairs. Just click Job Fairs Online and then select the area of interest, such as Health, fill in some data, and you'll be given a list of participating institutions. Although you might need to belong to the organization or university to access the event, you should check out your options thoroughly. You may be able to attend a job fair as an alumnus of a college or university, or you might be able to attend if it's an open fair.

In general, we find these fairs to be great networking events—if someone from the company is actively involved. If not, then the fair is really no better than searching the job banks.

University Career Center Sites

Universities and colleges have been by far the most impressive when it comes to serving client needs for the job search. Most university and college career centers have at least one person who works full-time at developing contacts with employers to hire their students. More and more of these job opportunities are becoming available to students and alumni online.

The institutions that don't post their jobs tend to have another online method for offering job opportunities, such as a subscription to one of the many Web sites that list jobs for students. One such site is JobTrak at *www.jobtrak.com.* Job Trak works with hundreds of universities and thousands of employers to connect students to entry-level positions. Students rate its value as high; academic institutions are increasingly turning to this service because of its ability to expand the reach to employers. Check out your university to see what it has.

Association, Alumni, Nonprofit, and Other Special Interest Group Sites

You can often find job postings at sites that have a focus on a particular career, industry, or special interest. These sites have increasingly stepped up to the plate to meet the needs of the populations they serve or the populations that support them.

Many alumni groups are developing Web sites and Web communities. You can find a listing of online alumni communities at WiredAlumni.com at *http://wiredalumni.com.*

Other sites are devoted to jobs in associations or nonprofit organizations, such as ACTION's IdeaList site at *www.idealist.org* and Opportunity Nocs at *www.opportunitynocs.org.* These sites are two of the best we've seen for finding employment opportunities with nonprofit organizations.

Web sites that serve special interest groups or represent associations usually have links to sites of interest, such as relevant job search sites. For example, the American Society of Agricultural Engineers at *www.asae.org* has job listings for agricultural engineering and related careers.

Professional associations and related organizations usually publish trade magazines and newsletters. These magazines and bulletins include industry information, political issues, career
development articles and, often, job postings. As more and more
associations develop their online presence, they are also beginning to upload their publications to their Web sites. Although
some organizations may print only a Table of Contents or highlights from their publications, many others include the full text, as
well as job listings. Check out your professional association's
Web site to see if the online publications include job listings. You
can search and link to thousands of association sites through the
Web site of the American Society of Association Executives at
www.asaenet.org.

Organization Recruitment Pages

Human resource offices are finding the Web to be a great tool for
posting and updating their job listings. Many Fortune 500 companies now have their jobs posted somewhere on their Web sites.
Many smaller companies are also plugging into this recruitment
strategy. However, we've found that many companies don't have
all their jobs listed. For example, if you go to a high-tech company, you'll probably find listings for high-tech vacancies, but
you might not find jobs in the Communications or Human
Resources offices.

However, there are still many organizations that list all of their
job vacancies. This is also true for just about every federal organization that has a Web site, such as the Peace Corps at
www.peacecorps.gov and the Environmental Protection Agency at
www.epa.gov. If you go to their internal job-listing pages, you'll
find a current list of job vacancies, including the duties and qualifications for a given position and instructions on how to apply.

If you are interested in a particular organization, your best bet
would be to go to its home page and see where it posts its job
openings. Keep in mind, however, that larger companies—
particularly the Fortune 500 companies—have offices nationwide
and around the globe. If you're interested in a position in a particular location, you need to find out if that office has its own Web
site, where it might post vacancies for that particular location. For

example, if you go to the Human Resources pages of Deloitte & Touche at *www.us.deloitte.com,* you'll find job openings for positions at its central office. However, if you want to work with Deloitte & Touche in Costa Rica, you will find these jobs only at the company's Costa Rica Web site at *www.dtcr.com.* Once you get to the job listing, find out when the information is updated and whether it is comprehensive. If you have questions, look for a contact number or email address. Our best advice is to call the Human Resources department at either office if you're not clear about what information is available.

Email, Listservs, Newsgroups, and Bulletin Boards

Many listservs devoted to special interests include occasional job postings from participating members. However, if you missed out on the last few months of communication, you can probably still access these messages by tapping the listserv's archives. If the listserv is sponsored by a professional association or related organization, you can probably find the archives at the organization's Web site. If you don't know where to find the archives, you can send an email to the listserv's administrator to ask if this option is available.

Other listservs are devoted exclusively to job listings. The My Great Jobs listserv includes jobs at international resorts, summer employment, unusual jobs, and other nontraditional employment opportunities. To subscribe to this listserv, send a blank message to *greatjobs-subscribe@onelist.com.* You can also find regional listservs such as NW Jobs, which posts jobs in the Pacific Northwest region. To join NW Jobs, send a blank message to *nwjobs-subscribe@onelist.com.* NW Jobs Wanted, on the other hand, is a list where job seekers can post their resumes or job queries for recruiters and potential employers. All postings are archived for recruiters to access at any time.

If you are interested in the job listings on a listserv, check out Topica.com at *www.topica.com.* To find links to nearly 200 job listservs, click the More Categories link; then click the Employment link under the Business section, and finally click Jobs. Although it is not a comprehensive listing, this site makes it easy to identify listservs that may post jobs relevant to your career.

To search more than 90,000 listservs, go to The Liszt at
www.liszt.comwww.liszt.com.

*The Liszt is the
most comprehen-
sive database for
more than 90,000
listservs and news-
groups. You can
check it out at
www.liszt.com.*

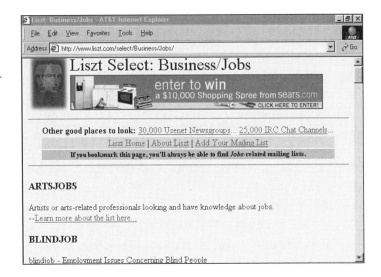

Online Newspapers, Trade Magazines, and Other Electronic Publications

It was once thought that the Internet would replace newspapers
and magazines. Instead, it appears that the Internet has not
replaced them but has created a new dimension of reading
material.

These days, you can find most major newspapers online.
Although you won't find the online paper to be as complete as the
paper version, you will find the major articles and often the classified ad section. Career Path at *www.careerpath.com* is an outstanding site that compiles the help wanted ads from more than
90 U.S. newspapers. It continues to add more papers regularly.
However, if you're interested in a newspaper that is not part of
Career Path's broad network, you can search for it at the
American Journal Review site at *http://ajr.newslink.org.* This site
has links to more than 9,000 newspapers, magazines, broadcasters, and news services in the United States. Between these two
sites, you've covered just about every major online news service
in the United States. However, if you're looking overseas, try All
Newspapers at *www.allnewspapers.com,* where you will find

thousands of links to newspapers and other media around the world. This site is well organized by region and country.

Government Job Search Assistance Pages

The government has picked up the pace with regard to helping job seekers around the country. State employment services now compile all their job listings and offer the list through one easy-to-use Web site called America's Job Bank at *www.ajb.dni.us*. The Department of Labor has led the effort to deploy what is called "America's One-Stop Career Center System." This initiative involves more than 600 sites around the country that offer job search services in varied formats. These services range from actual career centers in most major cities to virtual services in many rural areas.

It might be difficult to identify the service, since each has its own unique name. To find out what services are available in your area, you can link to it at the main Web site at *www.ttrc.doleta.gov/ onestop*.

You can also find job assistance and job listings at the Web site of the State's Occupational Information Coordinating Committee (SOICC). Link to your state's site through the National Committee's page at *www.noicc.gov*.

How to Evaluate a Job Site

If you're not sure if you should bookmark a job site so that you can return to it frequently, use this checklist to determine its value to you.

- **Variety of Employers** Does the site list jobs with the employers that interest you most? If not, does it list employers that you may want to research further? Who knows, you might find an employer that you never thought about—you just need to make sure they are offering the type of job you are looking for. For example, HotJobs.com at *www.hotjobs. com* lists employers by career field, as well as by location and keyword. If you want to find a marketing job in Texas, this site can help you find such jobs.

- **Number of New Jobs Posted Monthly**   Does the site keep its jobs updated, or will you be sorting through the same announcements next week? You want to find a site that updates its job listings at least once a week. If it doesn't, then you're probably losing time at that site. For example, USA Jobs at *www.usajobs.opm.gov* lists U.S. federal government jobs and allows you to limit your review of jobs posted within the last one to seven days.

- **Cost to You to Find Jobs**   If you have to pay to access job listings, then you need to know how much and how often. You need to know if there is a trial period to find out if the jobs listed are what you are looking for (such as salary level, qualifications, industry, and employer). Finally, you need to decide if the cost is worth the benefit. Sometimes it will be and other times it won't. For example, Netshare at *www.netshare.com* charges a membership fee (approximately $200 for 6 months) for access to over 1,000 executive-level jobs (most over $100,000) that have been posted in the last 30 days. This site also offers confidentiality to the job seeker and provides direct contact to the employer. This site also offers a 90-day trial for a reduced rate.

- **Cost to Employer to Post Jobs**   How much does the employer have to pay to post its job openings? If it's a significant amount (over $100 per job), then you're probably missing out on jobs with smaller employers who can't afford to pay such high premiums. On the other hand, if the site offers the exposure needed by an employer, the employer may post a position at this site, but not at others. America's Job Bank at *www.ajb.dni.us* does not charge employers for job listings and has more than one million jobs posted to its site—many more than just about every other job bank that charges employers a fee.

- **Types of Jobs Posted**   This is an easy one: If the site doesn't list the type of jobs you are looking for, there is no need to return. If you're looking for a job as a nurse, for example, you don't want to waste your time at Dice (*www.dice.com*), which is touted as a great job site—but which lists only high-tech jobs.

- **How Long a Job Is Posted**   Do jobs stay on the site for one week, two weeks, one month? Do they stay up even if the deadline has passed? You want to return to a job listing only if the information stays current. A job listing may stay up for as long as a month but, unless the employer is continuously recruiting for that position, beyond a month is too long.

- **Type of Information Included in the Job Listings**   You want as much information as possible. The absolute minimum is the position's title, location, duties and responsibilities, qualifications, name of the employer, and application procedure. However, you should look beyond that. Look for information on salary, benefits, start date, and other pertinent data. Headhunter.net at *www.headhunter.net* provides great details to jobs, including salary ranges, title and company, job type (such as contractor, part-time, or full-time), required education, required travel, relocation expenses included, required experience, and additional details on the posted position.

- **Information Made Available to Job Seeker**   Does the site give you guidance on the job search process? You might not necessarily need the information at this site, but if the site is working with employers from a particular industry, it might be helpful if some guidance is offered regarding the job search nuances of the industry. Monster.com at *www.monster.com* does an outstanding job of providing information on how to write a resume, how to prepare for an interview, and other relevant information.

- **Application Process**   What options are available to apply for the jobs posted? Does the site allow you to email your resume directly to the employer? You want to know what options are available. Some sites offer immediate email options, and you may find yourself competing with others who are mass emailing their resumes. You also need to prepare an appropriate electronic version of your resume if you plan to use this option. Check out Chapter 8, "Sending Resumes: The Electronic Word." Check out JobOptions.com at *www.joboptions.com* to choose between sending your resume by email or through its application process.

- **Search Options**   Some of the easiest sites to maneuver are those that allow you to search for jobs using keywords, identifying preferred locations, specifying salary ranges, and limiting responses with other factors. These sites will definitely save you time if you return to them weekly. However, these sites don't necessarily secure employment any better than another site with fewer features. Nation Job at *www. nationjob.com* has excellent search features that allow you to specify location, salary range, and education level.

Top Job Sites

Literally thousands of new jobs are posted daily to hundreds of job sites. These sites have become virtual listings of classified ads. As you know, there are sites for specific careers, such as business jobs, environmental jobs, and nonprofit jobs. There are sites for specific locations, such as jobs overseas, jobs in the midwest, and jobs in Seattle. And there are sites for specific employers, such as jobs with the government, jobs with Microsoft, jobs at universities, and jobs with the United Nations. There are so many different kinds of job sites that you could never visit them all and still search for employment.

The following is a list of some of the best sites on the Web. This list is far from comprehensive, but it will quickly get you where you need to be.

Top Job Listing Mega-Sites for All Career Fields

Monster.com (*www.monster.com*)   Offers hundreds of thousands of job listings in diverse fields from employers around the world. It's easy and fast to search the jobs without having to fill out a profile form first. You select a location and a job category. You may also add a keyword. Monster.com also allows you to browse all jobs in a particular city, state, country, or by employer. Although you can't always link directly to the employer, the site usually provides a contact's email address. Although you can apply online, you must register first (at no cost). You can also store up to five resumes and cover letters on the site. This site has a nice, free feature called a "search agent." After you sign up for it, it sends emails to you when a job listing matches your criteria.

CareerPath.com (*www.careerpath.com*)   This site offers a
unique search feature to scan want ads from nearly 90 major
newspapers nationwide, plus one international paper. You can
search by choosing up to 10 job categories, adding keywords, and
selecting up to 10 newspapers to search (although the site doesn't
tell you about this limitation unless you exceed it).
CareerPath.com has a nice feature that allows you to narrow down
the results (it allows a maximum of 200 returned results) by
adding additional keywords after your initial search. This site
allows you to choose from the recent Sunday want ads, the current day's ads, or the previous Sunday's ads. The only drawback
with this site is that you usually can't search the current Sunday
on the same day because ads aren't posted until later. There is no
link to the employer through email or a Web site and no way to
apply for the job online. Basically, you're reading the ad as it
appears in the paper. CareerPath.com also has a feature to search
through jobs gathered directly from the Web sites of employers.
We noted that nearly 100,000 jobs were collected and can be
searched using job categories; the jobs also can be sorted by
employer and location.

CareerPath is the best site on the Web for searching the want ads from more than 90 U.S. newspapers. You can check it out at www.careerpath.com.

America's Job Bank (*www.ajb.dni.us*)   This is one of the
largest job databases, with more than one million jobs posted
nationwide. You can search only by job title and state. After the

results are provided, you can sort your search by salary, city, state, title, and the age of the posting. You can also limit the job category to a subcategory, or you can search for jobs that fit the entire category. The search is quick and easy, but rarely provides a link to the employer's Web site. However, because the employers enter their data directly, not all of the fields of information are filled, and the job seeker has more research to do to fill in the gaps.

America's Job Bank is an excellent site for finding jobs with the smaller employers around the country. You can check it out at www.ajb. dni.us.

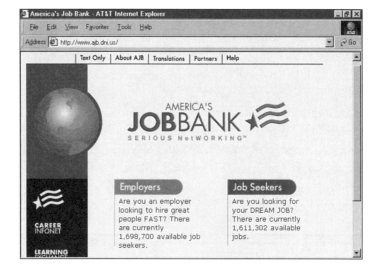

Career Builder (*www.careerbuilder.com*)   With more than 50 job sites participating in the Career Builder network, you can identify which sites you want to include in your search and can access millions of jobs through one search. The search is quick and easy: You select a job category and location, and the results usually take you directly to the job posted on the employer's site.

Career Builder is one of the best job listing sites on the Web. You can check it out at www.careerbuilder.com.

Career Mosaic (*www.careermosaic.com*)   You can search by keyword, job title, company name, and location. You can also search jobs in other countries by selecting a specific country. You can apply for most jobs directly to the employer by clicking the handy link that takes you to the employer's Web site application page. Career Mosaic also has a great feature that allows you to search through newsgroup postings (Usenet) by keyword and location. It searches through more than 70,000 postings and returns the results quickly.

Headhunter.net (*www.headhunter.net*)   Although half of the nearly 200,000 jobs are usually computer related, this site still has an impressive listing of jobs in all fields and is easy to search. The search options on this site are outstanding. You can narrow your search by specifying full-time or part-time jobs, you can specify education level or a minimum salary range, and you can request to see only recent postings. You will also find links to the employers' Web sites, as well as direct email links to apply for the jobs listed.

Hot Jobs (*www.hotjobs.com*)   You can quickly find jobs by searching through the thousands of jobs offered here by keyword and location. The job descriptions offer links to company profiles, which include a list of all jobs posted by the company. You can also store jobs in a folder for an hour, or you can create a free account for longer storage. You can apply online by using a resume you have stored in this site's database, or you have the option to cut and paste a cover letter and resume—a nice feature!

Job Options (*www.joboptions.com*)   This site offers an outstanding selection of diverse jobs at all experience levels in cities across the country. It is easy to search the job listings by keyword, location, or career category. One drawback is that many jobs appear in career categories that don't seem to fit. You can apply for jobs by email or submit a resume you have in the site's resume bank. You can also sign up for a weekly email that includes new jobs that match your criteria.

Job Bank USA (*www.jobbankusa.com*)   The variety of options you have to search for jobs makes this a great job site, even though it has fewer job listings than some of the other sites listed in this section. You can opt to search through Fortune 500 employers, or you can search through the job bank identifying a job by location, keyword, and position type (contract, permanent, summer, and so on). Results are nicely organized by date posted, title, location, years of experience required, and salary range (the listing notes whether citizenship is required). The best feature on this site is the page of links to newspapers in all 50 states. This is one of the best compilations of local newspapers that you'll find on a job site. You can also link to different job boards that list jobs nationwide or only in specific regions. You can also link to industry-specific job sites and a few international job sites. You also have the option of signing up for a daily email that contains new job postings that match your criteria.

6-Figure Jobs (*www.6figurejobs.com*)   This is our favorite site for executive-level jobs. This site provides current listings, and 85% of the jobs offer salaries of more than $100,000. You are given an email link to the employer, but no link to the employer's Web site. Most jobs are accessible from the home page, but some jobs are available only to executive members, which means that you must first be screened to make sure that you qualify for the salary levels posted.

My Job Search (*www.myjobsearch.com*)   Rather than actual job postings, this site does an excellent job of linking you directly to the jobs posted on Fortune 500 Web sites. You can also find direct links to regional job openings by clicking on a state and selecting a job board or by clicking on a local newspaper and linking directly to the help wanted ads. My Job Search also provides links and details about hundreds of general and specialty job boards.

Top Sites Listing Jobs for Students and Recent Graduates

JOBTRAK (*www.jobtrak.com*)   More than 950 colleges, universities, alumni associations, and MBA programs participate in the JOBTRAK network. Only students and alumni from the participating network can access these jobs. The jobs are diverse and target entry-level and college graduates. All Fortune 500 companies post their jobs here, and students have rated this site highly.

Job Direct (*www.jobdirect.com*)Job hunters take a more passive approach to finding jobs at this site. You are required to register and fill out a resume. The information you provide is matched against the criteria set by employers, which you cannot access. Then, you wait for an email notifying you of any matches between your resume and employers in their database.

Career/Industry-Specific Jobs

There are literally hundreds of job Web sites that list openings for specific careers. Fortunately, you can find your specific career field by looking it up on the following Web sites that provide links to career-specific job sites.

My Job Search (*www.myjobsearch.com/cgi-bin/mjs.cgi/ specialty.html*)   This site has one of the largest selections for finding industry-specific job sites. This is the site to go if you're looking for sites in any of the following fields: administrative support, healthcare, aerospace, hospitality, agribusiness, human

resources, legal, amusement/recreation, library, arts and entertainment, athletics, military, automotive, communications/media, non-
profit/membership organizations, computers/IT/electronics,
personal services, construction, protective services, raw materials,
extraction and processing, distribution/transportation, real estate,
education/consulting/training, retail, engineering/science, sales
and marketing, environmental, social science, finance, food and
beverage, and government.

You will also find links to sites that list jobs specifically for man-
agers/executives, MBAs, minorities and women, contract and
part-time jobs, and students and entry-level jobs.

Duke University
(*http://cdc.stuaff.duke.edu/stualum/employment/JobResources/
jregion.html*)   Here you will find links to excellent job sites for
the following career fields: archaeology, museums and preserva-
tion, arts and entertainment, business, education, government and
law, healthcare, mass media and communications, nonprofit and
social services, religious, science, engineering and technology,
sports, and travel and hospitality.

The Riley Guide (*www.dbm.com/jobguide/jobs.html#spec*)
Although this site provides links to general career information in
different career fields, it also offers great descriptions about what
you find in the sites that it links to, including whether there are
jobs listed. This is a must-visit site if you're looking for jobs in
any of the following career fields: agriculture/forestry/animal
science, art/humanities/recreation/hospitality, business/finance,
sales/marketing, natural sciences, healthcare/medical, engineer-
ing/mathematics, computing/technology, education/information,
legal/protective services, nonprofits/social sciences, public ser-
vice/government, personal/commercial services, building/
construction/mining, manufacturing/maintenance/repair/plant
operations, and transportation/utilities.

Yahoo! (*http://dir.yahoo.com/Business_and_Economy/
Employment_and_Work/Jobs/Career_Fields*)   We suggest that
you check out job sites in the Yahoo! directory for career fields.
Here you will find links to job sites in the following fields:
accounting, advertising and marketing, aerospace, agriculture, arts

and design, automotive, aviation, biomedical, casinos, computers, construction, cruise lines, dental, education, engineering, entertainment, environment, financial services, fire protection, food service, graphic design, health, hospitality, human resources, insurance, journalism, law, law enforcement, library and information science, management consulting, mining and mineral exploration, news and media, nursing, office and administrative support, physical therapy, physicians, physics, public interest, real estate, religion, retail management, science, social science, sports, technology, trucking, and U.S. government.

Snap.com (*www.snap.com/directory/category/ 0,16,-65686,00.html*)   Similar to the career fields listed above in Yahoo!, this site is an excellent resource for job sites for the following career fields: administrative and clerical, advertising and marketing, arts and design, automotive, aviation, banking and finance, broadcasting and publishing, business and entrepreneurship, construction, entertainment, environment, freelance writing, government and public service, healthcare, human resources, insurance, library and information science, nonprofit, real estate, retail sales, science and technology, service industries, sports, transportation, and travel.

Top Sites Listing Region-Specific Jobs

Duke University (*http://cdc.stuaff.duke.edu/stualum/ employment/JobResources/jregion.html*)   The Career Center at Duke has a well-organized listing of job resources by region. The site includes a clickable map that takes you to one of five U.S. regions. You then select a state and scroll through the many links that help you search for job listings for that state.

My Job Search (*www.myjobsearch.com/career/regional.html*) This site has a great compilation of job sources for all 50 states. Click the state on the map and select from a comprehensive list of links to local jobs.

The Riley Guide   You will find links to job listings by state at *www.dbm.com/jobguide/local.html*, and you will find an excellent listing of links to international job sites at *www.dbm.com/jobguide/internat.html*.

Association Sites Can Hook You Up!
Many professional associations offer links to job sites that are related to the association members' interests. Be sure to check out the associations in your career field. You can search more than 6,000 associations through the American Society of Association Executives' Web site at www.asaenet.org/ find (register for free and go to Gateway to Associations).

Top Sites Listing Jobs for Minorities, Women, and Special Interest Populations

The Black Collegian (*www.blackcollegian.com*) The jobs listed here are for students of color and are posted by employers who are committed to recruiting a diverse work force. You can quickly search for jobs by keyword and state.

Women in Technology International (*www.witi4hire.com/ candidates/search_frm.phtml*) Although most of the jobs listed for women are high tech, this site also includes jobs in other industries, such as accounting and finance, education and training, and human resources.

Hispanic Online (*www.hisp.com*) Although this site lists fewer than 1,000 jobs, the jobs that are listed are excellent and geared toward Latin-Americans. You can search by location, salary level, and keyword and can apply for the jobs directly from the job description by pasting in your resume.

Saludos (*www.saludos.com*) This site lists a lot of retail and government jobs, but it is still a good place for Latin-Americans to check out opportunities by employers who are seeking to diversify their workforce.

Latin Professional (*www.latpro.com*) If you are bilingual and speak either Spanish or Portuguese in addition to English, this is the site for you! Hundreds of jobs are listed in the United States, Spain, Portugal, and Latin America. Most jobs are for professionals, and the descriptions include salary levels. You can search for jobs by country, by language requirements, or by keyword.

Bilingual Jobs (*www.bilingual-jobs.com*) This is a great site if you're bilingual in English and an Asian language. You will sometimes find jobs for European languages as well.

Minorities' Job Bank (*www.minorities-jb.com/search_page.htm*) Here's another great site for finding jobs with employers who are looking to diversify their staffs. This site covers all minorities, including Asian-Americans, African-Americans, Native Americans, Latin-Americans, women, and others.

DiversiLink (*www.diversilink.com*)   Organized by the Society of Hispanic Professional Engineers, this site lists mostly engineering-related positions, but has a few jobs in other fields as well. All jobs are in the United States and can be searched by region or by keyword.

Gaywork.com (*www.gaywork.com*)   This is one of the few sites that offer jobs with employers that have been identified as gay friendly.

Putting It All Together

Congratulations! You should now feel quite comfortable maneuvering to and through the job sites and using them to your best advantage. If you followed the guidance in this chapter, you learned that the job sites are most effective as a resource for networking.

You can find a job in the job banks, but you need to do more than just send in your resume. You need to research, network, and build a relationship with the employer.

Different types of sites provide job listings—not just the mega career sites. Regardless, you should spend no more than 20% of your job search time looking at the job sites.

Lastly, you can assess the value of a site to determine whether or not you want to return to it each week.

Next stop: Interviewing for jobs!

CHAPTER 12

Interview Techniques Online

If you've made it to a job interview, the lights are on! The interview is an opportunity to present your worth to the employer. In today's competitive job market, you need to be prepared to convince the employer that you can make a significant contribution. Equally important, the interview gives you another opportunity to assess your prospective employer. This is a good time to ask appropriate questions to decide if the job meets your career needs and interests and whether the employer is a good fit for you.

Each interview is different, and it may take you a while to develop your own style and level of comfort with the process. However, whether you feel comfortable with interviewing or are terrified of the process, there is a lot you can learn online that can help you prepare yourself for this critical juncture.

Interview Styles: Know Them and Nail Them!

There are at least six different styles of interviews. The more familiar you become with each, the more relaxed you'll be come Interview Day. We will discuss each style briefly, but we strongly suggest that you take a look at some of the great Web sites that will take you through the interview process to prepare and feel confident! The six general types of interviews are

- Screening
- Non-directed
- Behavioral
- Panel
- Directed
- Stress

What You'll Learn in This Chapter:

▶ What you must know about different interview styles.

▶ How to prepare for the interview.

▶ What to know about pre-interview details, such as attire and directions.

▶ What to say and do at the beginning, middle, and end of the interview.

▶ How to follow-up after an interview.

There is great information online regarding these interview styles at both Capital University's site at *www.capital.edu/services/ career/csintypes.htm* and Western Illinois University's Career Services site at *http://wiuadm1.wiu.edu/mioip/interview/ i_type.asp*. If you're interviewing with third-party recruiters at a career fair or in a Human Resources office, check out the guidance for this interview style at JobWeb at *www.jobweb.org/ catapult/student.htm*. *The Wall Street Journal*'s career site is also an excellent reference for finding information on how to prepare for job interviews. Go to *http://careers.wsj.com*. In the left column, click Job Hunting Advice. Then click the Interviewing Guidance button in the middle of the page. You should see a list of great articles.

The Wall Street Journal's career site is an excellent reference for finding information on how to prepare for the job interview.

Screening Interviews

Many large businesses use *screening interviews* to determine who should be invited to interview for actual job vacancies. Screening interviews are common on college campuses, at career fairs, and in Human Resource departments. Often, Human Resources staff members conduct these interviews.

The focus of these interviews is to reduce a number of potential candidates to a small number who will fit the organization's culture. This means that attitude, enthusiasm, professionalism, maturity, and communication skills are critical to convey positively to the interviewer. Additionally, the interviewers will always check to ensure that you meet the minimum qualifications for the job or jobs you are being considered for.

Behavioral Interviews

Behavioral interviews are quickly becoming more popular with interviewers. The purpose of this interview style is to force you to provide specific examples of how you handled yourself or your work in previous situations. The philosophy behind this style is that previous performance is the best indication of future performance.

You can read a great article on how to plan for behavioral interviews at *Career Magazine*'s site at *www.careermag.com/newsarts/ interviewing/1050.html*.

Directed Interviews

A *directed interview* is one in which the interviewer has a list of questions that are asked of each person being interviewed. Rarely does the interviewer probe the interviewee's answers because the objective is to get through the predetermined list of questions. Also, many interviewers use this style to maintain a level of fairness to the interviewees by asking the same questions of each person.

Non-Directed Interviews

The *non-directed interview* style allows the interviewer to carry on more of a conversation with the subject. The interviewer often asks questions based on the candidate's resume and his answers to other questions. The interviewer might have some predetermined questions but will often take great liberties at expounding on both questions and answers. The interviewer does this to probe candidates' backgrounds further to find out why they performed or behaved the way they did, as well as to find out how the candidates have matured or learned from the experience described.

Panel Interviews

When there is more than one interviewer, you may feel a bit more stressed. However, keep in mind that the interviewers may be interested in seeing how you handle such stress. Generally, *panel interviews* bring together the people that will be involved with the position. They may come from all different levels of responsibility and may include people from other departments. You can learn more about how to handle group interviews and telephone interviews at the Online Career and Management Consulting site at *www.dnai.com/~career/ccpan.htm.*

Stress Interviews

Although this style has been met with mixed reviews by both interviewers and interviewees, the *stress interview* elicits a candidate's reactions to a stressful situation so that the interviewer can see how he works under stress. This type of interview is more often used for positions that will involve competition, such as sales. For example, if you are interviewing for a sales job, the interviewer may hold up a pen or a paperclip and ask you to "sell" the object. You can find some great examples of stress interview questions at the Knock 'Em Dead site at *www. knockemdead.com/interview/#Stress.*

Before the Interview: Prep Work

After you have been invited to an interview, you've got a lot to do before you arrive at the interviewer's door. Always remember, however, to confirm the date, time, and location of the interview at least one or two days before. We provide some guidance in this chapter, but we think you can get some excellent advice online at several different Web sites, depending on the type of information you need.

If you're looking for guidance on general communication styles and speaking tips, we suggest you take a look at NACE's site at *www.jobweb.org/jconline/quick/tips/tips6-13.shtml.* You'll find great tips on how to deal with silence, how to maintain eye contact, and how to speak clearly and confidently. This site also offers great information on how to prepare, in general, before an interview.

To be thoroughly prepared for the interview, you must prepare and be able to articulate your knowledge in the following areas:

- Your strengths and weaknesses

- Your greatest accomplishments

- Your skills, abilities, and needs

- The organization and your value to it

- Questions you may have about the job or the company

How you put this information together can either make or break your chance at a job offer. Let's take a look at each of these topics.

Your Strengths and Weaknesses

If you've been following this book chapter by chapter, you're probably in great shape with regard to knowing who you are and what you bring to the employer's table. This information is an asset at this stage, because if you're going to be ready to wow them in the interview, you'd better be prepared to analyze and discuss your strengths and weaknesses.

In discussing your strengths, you want to convey your value to the employer by sharing the traits you have that have made you successful to date, while also mentioning your main areas of expertise. For example, you might say, "I've consistently progressed in my career as an accountant at a Big Five firm. I attribute this to my enthusiasm and commitment to teamwork, the creative analyses of my work, and my ability to meet tight deadlines while exceeding the goals during the last three years within our department. Because of this, I was formally acknowledged by the manager each of the three years and given the opportunity to take on increasingly challenging assignments."

Although you probably don't want to think about your weaknesses, let alone discuss them with a potential employer, employers know you've got them and they want to know that *you* know what they are and how to manage them. This concept is crucial to a successful interview. If you can articulate to an employer what you've done to overcome your weaknesses, such as additional

Formula to Discuss Your Weaknesses

Weakness
+ What You Did to Improve or Overcome It

= Ability to Self-Manage and Succeed!

training or behavioral modification, you are demonstrating your ability to balance your self analysis, thus giving credence to the subsequent positive aspects you present about yourself.

Got it? In other words, most employers have greater respect for someone who can say, "I've had a tough time managing my projects at my current position. So I discussed this with my supervisor to see what I could do to become more efficient and effective. We decided that I should go to a two-day workshop on time management. I've been applying a lot of what I learned in that workshop, and since then I've been meeting all my deadlines as well as getting home at a decent hour."

As you can see in the formula, you should state a weakness that you have overcome and tell the interviewer what you did to manage it. Avoid weaknesses that reveal personal issues that are not related to your work performance. In other words, don't discuss family issues, drug or alcohol abuse, battles with bosses or colleagues, or other issues that might demonstrate personal or personality deficits.

Your Greatest Accomplishments

The next step in preparing for the interview is to think about the five greatest problems you solved on the job, at school, at home, or as a community member. Clearly and concisely, describe the results you obtained. Include what you learned and how you would do it differently. You've already done this with your resume, so this part should come easy to you!

Your Experience, Skills, Abilities, Values, and Needs

You need to convey to the employer how your experience, skills, and abilities meet the employer's needs. Also, you need to know how the job fits your values and needs. Here are some strategies to address these issues:

- Read the job description (if you don't have it, ask to have it faxed to you).

- Review the work experience and education you included on your resume. Prepare to speak about the skills and abilities you have developed and how they relate to this job.

- If you have been fired from a job, be prepared to state the reasons. Have something positive to say about the experience.

- Think through your career goals. How would this job contribute to your overall career goal or to your personal needs?

- Review your values. Will your personal values conflict in any way with those of the organization? Go back to the needs assessments you did in Chapter 4, "Finding Yourself in the e-World." Review what you identified as personal and professional needs and values. Does this organization match up? If not, you may want to find out what you can before the interview or consider asking a related question at the end of your interview.

- Lastly, even though the interview is not the time to discuss salary, know your basic salary requirements. The next chapter covers this important topic in greater detail.

The Organization

Without a doubt, you must know something about the organization with which you are interviewing. If you can't match what you have to offer with the needs of the employer, then you've missed the boat. To brush up on the organization, you simply need to research it via the Web, in print, and through contacts with other people.

Go to the employer's Web site and find out as much as possible about the organization and the particular position for which you are applying. If you can't find anything about the position or if the position is new, research the department in which it will exist. Look for annual reports and general information about the company's goals and mission. If the information is available on the Human Resources pages, check out the company's salary scale, benefits, and promotional opportunities.

You can find links to thousands of companies by using many of the online search engines and directories. Yahoo! is a great search engine to start with, at *http://dir.yahoo.com/business_and_ economy/companies*. When you find the industry you're interested in, click it to see direct links to companies as well as links to online directories of companies.

Yahoo! is a great tool for finding information about a company you are interviewing with.

Also, take a look at other Web sites that offer information about the organization. Look for recent articles on some of the newspaper and magazine Web sites. Check out the *American Journal Review* at *http://ajr.newslink.org*. This site links you to more than 3,000 U.S. newspapers as well as Web sites for more than 6,000 radio and television stations. You should be able to find some information about both large and small companies. If you can't, check out the Better Business Bureau site at *www.bbb.com* to look into any complaints that have been filed against the company or to get company and charity reports for some areas around the country.

If possible and appropriate, visit the building where the job will be located and talk with some of the employees. In this way, you can obtain personal information about the work situation and what the employer is really looking for. To meet an employee, try sitting on a nearby park bench during the lunch hour or request to visit the office and meet briefly with some of your future colleagues. Try inviting somebody to lunch to get to know each other better.

You might also be able to find out inside information by visiting Vault.com's message boards at *www.vault.com/forums/ messageintro.cfm*, which offers information about hundreds of companies at its Electronic Watercooler. Most companies on the site are in the high-tech, human resources, consulting, investment banking, and law industries. However, you will find some interesting topics that are relevant to most career fields. A word of caution: Try to remain completely anonymous if you begin a dialog online.

The Internet now offers its own form of "getting the scoop" on what's happening at thousands of different companies. You can read about hundreds of companies at Vault.com's Electronic Watercooler at www.vault.com/ forums/ messageintro.cfm.

Of course, our preferred surefire method is to speak with people in your network. By now, you should have established a decent sized network. Now is the time to call on some of them to learn what they know about the organization, its management, and the company's reputation.

Carefully analyze all the information you now have about yourself and the organization. Be able to state clearly how your skills, experience, education, and values fit the needs and expectations of the employer and the goals of the company.

Questions, Questions, Questions: Be Prepared!

You never know what kinds of questions the interviewer will ask you. There are some strategies to help you prepare for whatever is tossed your way.

- In general, you can expect a seasoned interviewer, but be prepared for someone who is not. Guide the interview if necessary to make your key points. You can ask "Would it be helpful if I told you about my experience with…?"

- Plan to talk about what you have done, but emphasize what you have to offer.

- Be prepared to answer questions about your personal characteristics or work values such as "What are your weaknesses?," "How would co-workers describe you?," and "What do you want to contribute to this organization?"

- Always speak positively about former employers, supervisors, and co-workers. If you speak negatively about others, your interviewers will assume that you will speak negatively about them as well.

Not unlike a seasoned politician, you need to have talking points—the key pieces of information about yourself that you know will leave a favorable impression. The idea here is that you want to assure the interviewer who you are and what you have to offer before the interview is over. If there isn't an appropriate time to insert these points during the interview, you will usually have the opportunity at the end of the interview to add any information that you want to share.

Never Diss a Former Employer!

COne of the biggest mistakes a job candidate can make is to make disparaging comments about a former boss, employer, or colleague. The rule is: Don't do it!

We strongly suggest that you spend time developing answers to the following frequently asked interview questions. Verbalize the answers—even better, role-play your responses with a friend acting as an employer. Even if you are an accomplished speaker, the practice will help you project a knowledgeable and confident image. You can find some excellent practice interviews online at Monster.com at *http://content.monster.com/jobinfo/interview*. This site offers separate interactive practice sessions for college students and mid-career job hunters. The program presents a list of questions for which you choose an answer. Then you are told why your answer was right or why it was wrong, or why another answer would have been better.

Although creating a practice interview videotape may seem dramatic, watching yourself in a mock interview is very helpful. You'll be both pleased and shocked with how you come across.

The best interactive practice Web site we've found is at Monster.com. Go to http://content.monster.com/jobinfo/interview.

You can gear up for interviews by going online and practicing with the questions that you might face in the real interview.

▼ **Try It Yourself**

1. Go to Monster.com at *http://content.monster.com/jobinfo/interview*.

2. Click The Virtual Interview.

3. Click Start the Interview.

4. Read the first question and select your best answer from the options given.

5. Click the Did I Choose the Best Answer? button and see what it says!

You've done it! Now, continue through the rest of your virtual interview. Good luck!

Question Categories

Most interview questions will fall under the following categories:

- General questions about you
- Your career goals
- Your qualifications
- Your work experience
- What you know about the company
- Your interpersonal style
- Your motivation
- Your work style

Here are some typical questions you should be prepared to field in an interview. The questions generally fall into several categories.

General Focus (*expect* these questions!)

- Tell me about yourself.

- Why do you want this position?

- Why are you leaving your current job?

Your Career Goals

- What are your short-range objectives? Long-range?

- What are you looking for in a job?

- Where do you see yourself in five years? In ten years?

- How much money do you expect to be earning in five years? In ten years?

- How would you describe success for you?

- Why have you chosen to enter your particular field of work?

Your Qualifications

- What can you do for us that someone else cannot?

- What are your three greatest accomplishments?

- Are you creative? Analytical? A good team member? Give examples.

- What qualifications do you have that will make you a success in your field?

- How has your education and training prepared you for this position?

About Past Work Experiences

- Tell me about your last job. What did you like most about it? What did you like least about it?

- What was your favorite job and why? Least favorite and why?

About Your Knowledge of the Organization

- What do you know about our organization?

- How did you learn about us?

- Why do you want to work for us?

- How will you make the transition from your current job to this one?

About Your Interpersonal Style

- Tell me about yourself.

- Describe a situation in which your work was criticized. How did you handle it?

- What type of person rubs you the wrong way?

- How have you dealt with difficult customers? Difficult bosses?

About Your Motivation for the Job

- What interests you most about this job? Least?

- What other types of jobs are you considering? With which organizations?

- How long do you think you would stay in this job?

- How does this job fit with your career plans?

About Your Work Style

**More Practice
Questions Online:**
There is a great list
of interview ques-
tions at Job-
Interview.net at
www.job-interview.
net.

- How have you worked under pressure? Under deadlines? Alone? With others?

- How do you feel about routine work? Regular hours?

- How have you taken criticism without feeling upset?

- What have you done that shows your initiative and willingness to work?

- What type of supervisor do you prefer?

You can expect difficult questions from experienced interviewers. Check out Career City's site at *www.careercity.com/careercity/ content/interview/during/13quest.asp* for great advice on how to handle stressful and difficult interview questions. Also, take a look at Bio Online's interview articles at *www.bio.com/hr/search.* You will find the list of articles in the left column.

*Help prepare your-
self for questions
that may make
you nervous or
stressed. Check out
Career City's site at
www. careercity.
com/careercity/
content/interview/
during/13quest.asp
for a list of stress-
inducing questions
and answers.*

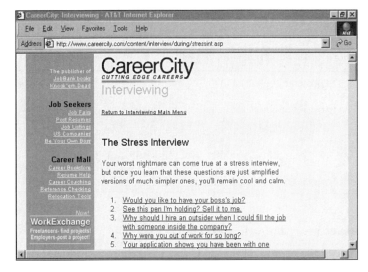

The Devil's in the Details

When your focus is on the stress of the interview itself, it's easy to lose sight of the details that can make a difference on interview day. However, if you keep these details in mind, such as what you

will wear, what time you will arrive, and what you will bring to
the interview, you'll lower your stress, be better prepared, and be
ready to conquer the interview!

How to Dress for the Interview

Prepare your interview outfit and dress for success! For most
hourly or temporary clerical jobs, it is appropriate to wear clean
and ironed casual slacks with a sport shirt and tie or a skirt and
blouse or dress. For salaried, administrative, technical, management trainee, supervisory, or managerial positions, wear a suit and
tie or a dress or business suit to the interview.

Always try to dress with the most conservative attire appropriate
for that organization. Wearing such items as jeans, running shoes,
sandals, very short or floor-length skirts or dresses, large or
clanking jewelry, or loud ties may send a negative message or dis-
tract the interviewer, even if you may be able to dress in such a
manner once you are working there.

No matter what job you are applying for, if you look professional
or business-like, you will make a better first impression. Don't
make your first impression your last one!

Wondering What to Wear?

If you're not sure what to wear to the interview, scout the work place by standing in front of the building (preferably on the other side of the street) and look at staff as they go in or out of the building. You can also check out the company's Web site or publications for photos of staff members.

What to Bring to the Interview

Depending on the job for which you are interviewing, you'll need
to bring some materials to be prepared for whatever requests are
made on the spot. In general, you should bring the following:

- Several copies of your resume and copies of work samples, if
  appropriate.

- Original reference letters and school transcripts, if appropriate. You should also bring extra copies of your resume or
  original application materials.

- A typed list of names, addresses, phone numbers, and fax
  numbers of your professional references. Include a brief note
  on your relationship to each and their knowledge about your
  work.

- Depending on the job, you may need to bring your portfolio of photos, art, and published articles. Trainers often bring copies of courses and manuals they have written. Bring writing samples; these are often requested by employers for many different positions.

- A pen and a notepad for taking notes during the interview. By having the notepad on your lap or on the desk in front of you and the pen in hand, you will be less likely to fidget. You can also take notes for future reference.

The Sure and Steady Path:
The day of your interview is not the time to try new commuter routes. Stick with routes you know will take you where you need to go.

Final Preparations Before the Interview

Being on time is important; don't be late. On the other hand, arriving too early could give the impression of over-anxiety or desperation. Plan to arrive 15 minutes early to relax and to rehearse your selling points. If sitting around makes you nervous, just go to a nearby café to wait.

If you are kept waiting more than 30 minutes, ask if it would be more convenient to reschedule the appointment and then excuse yourself.

The Interview

There is a beginning, middle, and end to an interview. Each of these periods involves different skills and techniques. The following sections explain what they are and how to prepare for them. In addition, there is always follow-up after an interview. This is critical if you want to leave a positive and lasting impression, review your effectiveness, and determine what you should do differently in future interviews.

The Beginning of the Interview: It's Only Just Begun

You are probably starting to sweat a little as you walk into the company's offices and prepare to say your first words to the receptionist. Take a deep breath, and simply show confidence and enthusiasm from the moment you walk into the organization. Do not brush past the receptionists or secretaries. Their perceptions of candidates are sometimes used in making hiring decisions.

As soon as you are introduced to the interviewer, give the person a firm handshake. Try to establish a rapport with the interviewer from the beginning. Determine if you and the interviewer share anything in common that you can chat about for a few minutes. Look at photos, paintings, artwork, or book titles in his office.

Be aware of your body language. Face the interviewer and sit slightly forward. Don't slouch! Maintain eye contact. Be professional, moderately animated, and continue to display enthusiasm.

Try to listen during the interview and avoid dominating the discussion. Don't ramble. The interviewer will ask you to elaborate if he wants more information. You can also ask "Am I answering your question?" or "I would be happy to provide more detail if you wish."

Remember to ask about the duties of the job and the qualities wanted in the individual to be hired. You want to uncover as much information as possible about the position and match your responses to the employer's needs. This will also help you evaluate a potential offer.

For more information on preparing for the first few minutes of the interview, check out Management Recruiters of Scottsdale's guidance at *www.mriscottsdale.com/candidate/interview.asp*.

The Middle of the Interview: You're Getting There!

Remember to tell the interviewer why you want to work for the organization and what you can contribute to the success of the specific department. In fact, all your responses to questions should focus on working for their organization.

Chances are that you will be asked about former employment. Remember to make only positive or neutral comments about any of your past employers, jobs, bosses, schools, or teachers. An interview is not the time to vent or air grievances. It sends an unprofessional message to the employer and can quickly lead to trouble during the interview, forcing you to doubletalk.

Keep your conversation to job-related information. Don't philosophize or tell your favorite stories about your favorite travels.

Discuss the company's services or products positively. This is not the time to complain about services or products.

Be prepared to describe your future plans (1 to 5 years from now).

You can find some great articles on how to handle yourself during the interview. Gary Will is a marketing consultant; his Web site, Work Search, has one of the best compilations of top-notch articles about interviewing. The site rates and reviews the articles to help you quickly find the ones that will meet your needs. You can check it out at *http://members.xoom.com/worksearch/intres.htm*.

Check out Gary Will's Work Search site. You'll find a selection of excellent articles that are rated to help you determine which ones to read.

The End of the Interview: It's Not Over Yet!

Never raise the issue of compensation. Some employers may mention it and ask you about it. However, discussions of salary should occur only after you have been chosen as the top candidate. You don't want to discuss salary until you have some leverage. If pressed for a salary range, state that you are confident that an agreement can be reached. If the interviewer continues to press, ask politely if he has any concerns about the salary level the company plans to offer—the company may be a bargain hunter.

In screening interviews with Human Resource representatives, the topic of salary is frequently mentioned. The next chapter covers this in greater detail and gives tips on how to respond to an employer who raises this topic during your first interview.

If it's true, tell the interviewer that you want the job. End the interview by asking, "I really want this job; when may I expect to hear from you?"

Smile and thank the interviewer for taking time to discuss this opportunity with you. Shake the person's hand and say "Goodbye. I look forward to hearing from you."

Have some thoughtful questions ready for when the interviewer asks if you have any questions. Use judgment in this area. A lack of questions may indicate to the interviewer that you are unprepared or uninterested. Too many questions might prove to be an annoyance. Some examples of good questions are

- What challenges do you anticipate needing immediate attention in this position?

- What are some of the difficulties others have faced in this position?

- What happened to the person who was previously in this position?

- What specific criteria will you use to make a hiring decision?

- Where do you see this position/division/department heading in the next five years?

- Do you have a training program? What specific responsibilities are trainees given?

- What are the possibilities of promotion within your firm?

- How does your employee turnover rate compare to that of other companies? (If there is a high turnover rate, you may want to inquire whether there is a specific reason. This can be a sign of poor management.)

- There must be some negative or less desirable aspects of the job you are offering. What are they?

- Can you tell me more about the management style and the relationship between the manager and the person in the position you are filling?

- What is the next step in this interview process, and when can I expect to hear from you again?

Opportunity Knocks—And Opens Doors:
Your questions to the interviewer should focus on *opportunity*—not on *security* (such as salary and benefits). Your questions should reassure the interviewer that you are interested in the work and the company.

After the Interview: Just when You Thought It Was Over

Congratulations! You made it through the interview and you're still alive! Your heart may be pounding, but you should be feeling pretty good if you prepared in advance.

Now, debrief yourself immediately, before you forget what just occurred. Go to a nearby coffee shop or McDonalds restaurant. Replay the whole interview in your mind. Review your answers to questions. On a separate piece of paper, write down the most difficult questions you were asked. Write down the answers you thought the interviewer liked the most and the least. Remember to refer to these notes before any future interviews.

Send thank-you correspondence to the interviewer and anyone else you met. Use a tone consistent with the tone of the interview. Mention the positives about yourself and the key issues discussed during the interview. Address points you forgot to mention in the interview, if needed. Say that you are very interested in the job and hope to hear from them soon.

If you haven't heard anything in a week or whenever the interviewer told you should be hearing from them, call to find out what the employer's decision was. If you wind up leaving messages or getting a vague answer, assume that you did not get the job. If you call more than once or twice, the employer may feel that you are a nuisance, which can hurt your chances. For jobs in the public sector, on the other hand, it pays to be persistent.

Lastly, carefully review the next chapter on accepting job offers and salary negotiations.

What to Avoid when Interviewing: A List of Don'ts

You've read the "Do's"; here are a few "Don'ts" for the interview process:

- Don't be late! If you aren't sure of the location or your means of transportation, allocate extra time.
- Don't fumble with a heavy coat or packages. Ask if you may put your coat in a closet.
- Don't smoke or chew gum.
- If interviewing during lunch, don't select sloppy or hard-to-manage foods. Take your cue on drinks from the interviewer. Let him or her pick up the tab.

- Don't drum your fingers nervously. Don't look at your watch. Don't exhibit other signs of nervousness or boredom.
- Don't mention your pet peeves about your last boss, job, or organization.
- Don't talk about race, religion, or politics.
- Don't imply that you can do everything or that you are a miracle worker. People won't believe you.
- Don't be a "yes" person and don't interrupt. Don't lose your temper.
- Don't brag and don't drop names. That trick usually backfires.
- Don't linger after the interview is finished.
- Don't accept the offer of a job during the interview. Ask for some time to think over any offer, even if it seems to be just what you want. Take at least a day to think it over to give yourself the opportunity to weigh your other job options as well as to consider whether or not you should negotiate for a higher salary or more benefits based on the additional information you gathered about the job during the interview. Remember that once the offer is made, the ball is in your court. You now have leverage with which to negotiate further.

Putting It All Together

You should be feeling confident to interview and ready to show 'em what you've got! If you followed the guidance in this chapter, you learned that although there are, at a minimum, six different interview styles, the behavioral interview is becoming more and more popular with interviewers. You need to prepare for each style, and the Web can help you do this!

You have to prepare for the interview rather than expecting to show up and simply answer questions. You need to analyze your strengths and weaknesses and be prepared to articulate your value to the company.

There are thousands of possible questions that can be asked in an interview, but you can prepare for the most commonly asked questions by taking a look at our list and by checking out some sites online.

An interview is a business meeting. You need to dress for the occasion. You never get a second chance to make a first impression!

You need to bring extra copies of your resume, a list of references, and your portfolio, if appropriate. You must prepare yourself to communicate at the beginning, middle, and end of the interview. Your communication style will tell the interviewer more than you think, so be prepared!

You must follow up after the interview with a thank-you letter and possibly a phone call. The Internet has plenty of valuable information to help you do this, so do it well!

Next stop: Negotiating job offers!

CHAPTER 13

Job Offers: E-valuating and Net-gotiating

Congratulations! The interview was a success, and the employer is calling to offer you the job. You've reached that critical juncture of negotiating and accepting or rejecting the job offer. It's time to make some serious decisions. Depending on how you negotiate your job offer, you could be determining your financial and professional status for years to come.

This is not a game to play, nor is this a chapter to skip. This chapter will show you how to negotiate a job offer and how the Internet can turn your decisions and negotiations into win-win situations for both you and the employer.

I Just Can't Decide

Most job seekers have a difficult time making a decision once a job offer is on the table. You might feel like you have to make a quick decision before the employer retracts the offer, or you might feel like you've been on the job search wagon long enough and now it's time to settle down. But before you have this knee-jerk reaction and accept the job without further discussion, some simple strategies can help you make a thoughtful decision and steer you in a direction of being in charge, instead of incapacitated.

Once an offer has been made, you are in the driver's seat—a great place to be! Don't give up the wheel before you've had a chance to drive around the block a few times.

Before you begin any discussion regarding an acceptance, rejection, or negotiation, simply and graciously let the employer know that you are happy to hear of his interest in you and that you will certainly consider his offer.

What You'll Learn in This Chapter:

▶ What to consider when evaluating job offers.

▶ How to negotiate salaries.

Confirm the position title and duties and ask for the starting date. Also ask what salary and benefits the company is offering. Tell him that you would like a few days to think about it and that you would like to meet in person to discuss it further. Usually, the employer will accommodate such a request but if not, ask for at least a day and a follow-up phone call. If he is concerned that you are not interested in the position, make it clear that you still have great interest but want to think it through carefully.

Some employers may get nervous with a confident job seeker who asks for some time to think it over. Why? The ball is in your court, and that's enough to make any employer uncomfortable. Your role is to stay calm, make sure you know what you can negotiate, and plan your next step.

Salary History Requests: To Tell or Not to Tell

Most job hunters don't know how to respond to an employer's request for their salary history. This request can happen at the application process, during the interview, or at the job offer stage. We have some guidance for each of these stages.

If a request is made at the application stage, during the interview, or during the job offer stage, it's not a good idea to ignore the request. Many employers want a salary history as part of an application—as another piece of information to consider about the applicant. Employers sometimes use this information to screen out candidates who make too much and sometimes those who make too little. Usually, employers use this information to gauge the salary level at which you would enter the organization.

Don't be intimidated by a request for a salary history and don't misrepresent your earnings. Savvy employers will double-check your information.

Often, a short narrative within your cover letter or at the interview is all that is needed for a salary history. Something like "As an entry-level accountant with a local firm, my salary, including benefits, started in the upper 30s. However, I progressed quickly and within six months was given an increase of 15%, followed by another increase of 10% by the end of my first year."

Show Me the Money! Find Out Online What You're Worth

By now, you've invested a lot of time in researching what you have to offer an employer. There's a price tag attached to that experience, and you need to know what it is.

Most likely, you have already done a bit of research regarding salary, or you might already know what the salary range is for the job you've been offered. However, we encourage you to take a closer look at what you're worth in the current job market. Four to eight hours invested in researching your worth could make a difference of thousands of dollars—not bad for a day's work. The best part about this is that you can do virtually all your research online.

To find out the going rate or salary range for somebody with your level of experience, you will get a lot of help from the online salary calculators. The best Web site for identifying salary ranges is at JobStar, a California-based career site. This site includes more than 300 different salary guides, calculators, and surveys. It's the largest and most comprehensive online collection we've found, and we think it's definitely worth a visit. Try it yourself by looking for average salaries of professionals working in public relations:

▼ **Try It Yourself**

1. Go to JobStar at *http://jobstar.org/tools/salary/index.htm* and click the Salary Surveys link.

2. Click the Profession-Specific Salary Surveys link.

3. Click Public Relations as the profession you want to investigate.

4. Click Average Salaries in PR. Note how the article indicates that public relations salaries are higher in the West than elsewhere in the United States. Also note that salaries are much higher in firms that gross higher revenues. The salary ranges give you a sense of what the average salaries are for the different levels of a public relations specialist, from entry-level to executive level.

JobStar is the largest and most comprehensive Web site for accessing salary guides, calculators, and surveys.

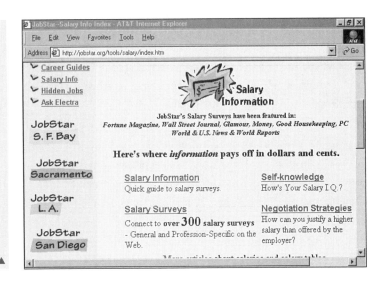

Abbott, Langer & Associates, Inc., at *www.abbott-langer.com* has outstanding salary and benefits survey reports for jobs in information technology, marketing, accounting, engineering, human resources, manufacturing, legal work, nonprofit work, consulting, and a few other fields. These reports are designed to be sold to businesses, but the Web site allows you to find the information on salaries or benefits for a particular field. Once you're at that page, you can also view a list of employers that contributed to the survey. The site indicates that information was collected from more than 7,000 organizations. We think it's definitely worth a visit if you're working in one of these career fields. Keep in mind, however, that the figures don't take location into account.

The Wall Street Journal's career site at *www.careers.wsj.com* is an outstanding resource for articles and data on more than 30 industries.

Economic Research Institute at *www.erieri.com/ cgi-bin/intsurvy.cgi* has an excellent compilation of nearly 100 international salary surveys.

If you are looking for work with the federal government, you can check out its pay scales and wage system at the Office of Personnel Management's Web site at *www.opm.gov/oca/payrates/ index.htm*.

Executives can find excellent information at Forbes, Inc., Online at *www.forbes.com/forbes/Section/Executiv.htm.*

Show Me the Benefits! What Perks Can You Count On?

Many of these salary surveys focus mostly on the salary itself. However, most full-time, permanent positions include benefits. You need to know what these "bennies" are because this information will help you determine if the salary range meets your needs. Take into account the following:

• Insurance, such as health, dental, life, and disability

• Retirement benefits, such as pension, 401K, percentage of employer contributions

• Leave benefits, such as sick leave, vacation leave, holiday leave, maternity or adoption leave (for fathers, too)

• Family benefits, such as on-site daycare, flexible work schedule, family career and transition assistance, work/life balance programs, sports club memberships or discounts, and relocation reimbursement or supplement

• Financial perks, such as annual salary reviews, cost of living increases, performance bonuses, retirement account contributions, holiday bonuses, and stock options and profit sharing

• Professional perks, such as education reimbursement, training programs, professional association memberships, and conference and workshop expenses

• Company perks, such as a clothing account, company car, expense account, club memberships, and concierge service

Benefits + Perks = Real Money!
Dollars aren't the only thing you should consider when looking at a salary offer. Often benefits and perks can equal 30% to 50% or more of the total salary. This is real money and demands real consideration when evaluating your compensation package.

Personal Finances

Now that you have a sense of the salary range for your job, you need to take into account your own financial needs. Maybe the salary range is just what you're looking for—maybe not. The only way to find out is to do the math. We suggest that you take into account this list of items. You may need to add your own as well.

Monthly Expenses = $_____

$_____	Rent or mortgage, phone, cable, utilities
$_____	Food and personal items
$_____	Education/school
$_____	Entertainment, gym, membership fees
$_____	Credit cards and other monthly bills
$_____	Car (payment, lease, maintenance, gas, insurance)
$_____	Medical and dental care not covered by insurance
$_____	Miscellaneous
$_____	Other:_____
$_____	Other:_____

Annual Expenses = $_____

$_____	Taxes (property, car, other)
$_____	Association and membership fees
$_____	Housing repairs
$_____	Vacation
$_____	Holidays, gifts, birthdays, special events
$_____	Computer/technology upgrades
$_____	Other:_____
$_____	Other:_____

Financial Desires = $_____

$_____	Investments/Retirement
$_____	Savings
$_____	College fund for children
$_____	Other:_____
$_____	Other:_____

Whew! It's a lot to think about. Next, add it up and see what you must have to meet your minimum expenses. Does it equal the salary range you're considering? If not, are your desires reasonable for your level of experience and the position you are being offered? Is there some way you can work toward these financial goals in the future or after a promotion?

Location, Location, Location!

If you accept the job offer, will you have to move now or in the future? The location of the position may affect your decision to accept or reject the job offer. If your job is going to send you packing, you should know if your new location fits your plan and your lifestyle.

Fortunately, the Internet is bursting with great information on relocation issues. There is a host of sites that can give you current economic, housing, education, entertainment, and recreation information. For example, check out the relocation resources at My Job Search at *www.myjobsearch.com/relocation.html*. With this information at your fingertips, there's no excuse to *not* find out what you're getting yourself into.

If you go to the Riley Guide, check out the links under I'm Considering Moving at *www.dbm.com/jobguide/relocate.html*. Here you can find great links to other relocation guides, local newspapers, cost of living, demographics, real estate information, telephone directories, maps, postal directories, education information, health care information, and weather. Also take a look at Best Jobs USA at *www.bestjobsusa.com/careerguide/ relocation/relocation.asp*, which has an excellent relocation guide.

Salary Negotiations: Where Confidence, Practice, and Research Meet

Congratulations! You've done the research and you're primed to negotiate your job offer.

Most salaries are negotiable—even many of those that seem non-negotiable, such as government salaries or businesses that have set pay scales. This section addresses the general principles and actions you may choose to incorporate into your job search strategy to be effective in determining your value and to negotiate a salary you deserve. There is a lot of online assistance in this area as well. My Job Search has excellent links to information on how to negotiate a better offer at

www.myjobsearch.com/negotiating.html. For example, if you want to know if you have gathered enough information about a salary to negotiate effectively, you will find a link to an article called "Are You a Salary Savvy Job Seeker?" This article explains what you should know and asks questions so that you can assess your level of knowledge about your salary know-how. If you're nervous about negotiating, you'll find a link to an article called, "Dealing with Difficult Negotiators."

Although it may be more difficult to negotiate some salaries, with research and practice you can learn to approach a salary negotiation with confidence. The Internet will be a great ally in preparing for this process. If you negotiate well, you can satisfy the hiring and salary needs of both you and your potential employer. Both sides win!

Try It Yourself ▼

Career Perfect's Interview Smart™ is an excellent site for brushing up on your salary negotiation skills. It also offers great interview information, but the salary information will help you understand the process and prepare appropriately.

1. Go to *www.careerperfect.com/ISOnline/OPEN.HTM.*

2. Click the Salary Discussion & Negotiation link.

3. Read through the page of instructions on how the program works and click the Start Salary Discussion & Negotiations button. This action displays the index for this section.

4. Click Salary Discussion and read the two-page article. Click the Back button to return to the index.

5. Click the Timing link and read that article. Follow this section by reading through the next two sections on risk evaluation and strategy. When you read the risk evaluation section, be sure to answer the questions completely and honestly. If your answers reflect that you are not ready for the salary negotiation, you should go back to the beginning of the salary research process and fill in the gaps.

▲

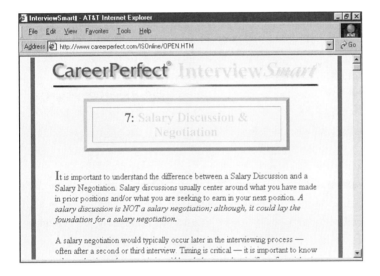

Career Perfect's Interview Smart™ at www.careerperfect.com/ISOnline/OPEN. HTM *is an outstanding online tutorial to help you learn and practice salary negotiation.*

Successful and realistic salary negotiations embrace five principles based on the knowledge that the salary you begin a job with reflects your value to an organization and typically determines future salary increases. Regardless of whether or not you think the salary level is adequate, we suggest that you incorporate these five principles into your job search. This will help you negotiate both professionally and effectively:

1. Research

2. Self-Confidence

3. Recognition of Mutual Needs

4. Calculated Timing

5. Evaluation and Communication

Research

Be careful not to expect an employer to meet your demands just because you think you deserve a higher salary. It is up to you to justify *why* you deserve it. To do this effectively, you will need to spend some time researching your market value. Such information is available online at the various salary sites, such as JobStar at *www.jobstar.org/salary* and other sites mentioned earlier in this chapter. Once you know the current salary range for the type of job you are being offered, you have more leverage with which to negotiate.

However, be careful to know with whom you may negotiate. Through your research, you should determine if the employer will be in a negotiating position. You can't negotiate with someone who isn't empowered to negotiate. Consider whether the employer is even in the position to discuss a salary or whether there is a Personnel department or higher authority that deals with such issues.

Self-Confidence

Self-confidence is a necessary skill applicable to any type of self-directed activity. During the interview phase, it is crucial for you to display self-confidence. It is equally crucial to display and truly feel self-confident when it comes time to discussing salaries. Know yourself. Know what you want. Know what you're worth. How do you know? Research, my friend.

Recognition of Mutual Needs

If you followed the exercise earlier in this chapter, you have already calculated your basic living expenses and your desired income. Combining this information with the information you uncovered in the online salary guides, you should be able to come up with a range with which to negotiate.

The needs of the employer are as important to understand as your own. Recognizing both your needs and calculating them into your negotiation strategy helps you gain empathy, realism, and negotiating power.

Put yourself in the position of the employer to better understand his interests, needs, and perception of you. The employer initially values the position he is trying to fill much more than he values the interviewee. Keeping this in mind, it is up to you to prove that your value equals or exceeds the value the employer places on the position. Thoughtful probing during the interview can help you determine the employer's value of the job, such as asking what his goals are for this position. Self-confidence and good communication during the interview can display your value of the position itself as well as your value to the organization.

If you don't know your value or how to present it to a potential employer, you risk accepting a lower salary than you deserve or a lower salary than the employer may have been willing to pay.

Calculated Timing

Timing is everything. The time at which to employ negotiating tactics is critical. As a rule, salary should never be discussed before an offer has been extended. If an employer asks you during an interview about your salary interest, pleasantly avoid discussion with a sincere response such as "I'm certain you will offer the best possible salary based on my value to your organization." By answering the question, you run the risk of being screened out by mentioning a salary out of the employer's range.

At times, however, it may not be possible to avoid the discussion of salary. Be prepared to discuss your salary expectation in terms of a range, as opposed to a specific figure. Try not to finalize your discussion on salary until you know what they want (you!) and what you want (the job with the right salary!).

A job offer opens the lines for salary discussion and possible negotiation. This is the point in your job search at which the employer places a value on your skills and abilities. Because you have been selected above the other candidates, you have a grasp on the reins, which puts you in a position to negotiate. Now it's time to evaluate the situation and communicate your interest, qualifications, value, and yes, your fee for services.

Evaluation and Communication

In most cases, the salary discussion should be initiated by the employer. Once the employer opens the discussion, it's time for you to professionally address the issue based on your research. One such way to address the issue is by saying something like, "Well, from my research over the past few months, I've figured that a person with my qualifications in a position similar to this is paid anywhere from $28–34,000 a year."

Check into the possible benefits with the organization. Take this into careful consideration when negotiating a salary. If an employer is unable to meet your salary request, perhaps he can increase the compensation package. Sometimes the perks can outweigh the extra $5,000 a year you requested.

Before accepting any job, take time to re-evaluate the situation—even if the employer has met your requests. Most employers will allow you time to think about the offer before giving an answer. After all negotiating is done, reaffirm to the employer your enthusiasm for the job, such as, "I'm very excited about this opportunity. I'd like to take a little time to think about everything we've discussed and would like to get back to you as soon as possible. Would tomorrow be a good time to talk again?"

Most types of negotiations can be overwhelming. The key to a successful negotiation is preparation! Be confident in yourself and your worth to an employer. Research, recognizing needs, and using good judgment in the timing, presentation, and closure are principles sure to satisfy the needs of both you and your future employer.

Putting It All Together

Way to go! You should be well on your way to successfully negotiating a salary for the job offer you've been waiting for. If you followed the guidance in this chapter, you learned that it's next to impossible to make a decision if you haven't done the research on what fee your services command in the current job market, in a specific locale, with a specific type of employer.

You must consider salary, benefits, perks, relocation expenses, and other personal considerations when evaluating a job offer.

The keys to successful salary negotiations are research, self-confidence, timing, an understanding of the employer's needs as well as your own, a reasonable evaluation of the situation, and clear, assertive communication of your expectations.

Next stop: Getting started successfully!

PART V

Strategies for Success

CHAPTER 14

Starting Work: e-Ideas for Success

The day has finally arrived! You're at your new job and you're ready to go. You've got your list of duties and projects, but you're probably feeling a bit uneasy about where to start and how to make sure that you make the best first impression at work with both your boss and your co-workers. This chapter will give you some guidance on how to do this and will show you where to go to get more information online.

Make That First Impression a Lasting One

You've made your first impression with your resume, interview, and your salary negotiations. Now is the time to make your first impression on the job! As we've said before, you never get a second chance to make a good first impression.

There are a few things you can do before you arrive at work on your first day to make sure that your first day, first week, and first month are a success.

First, make sure you have a wardrobe that's appropriate for the environment in which you will work. Even if the dress is less formal, we suggest you dress conservatively for the first few weeks until you've established your reputation with your supervisor, colleagues, and clients.

Be sure to bring a pen, a professional notepad, and a briefcase to carry home reading material. This will send the message that you are serious about getting started and getting on the ball immediately.

Kaplan Careers (*www.studyusa.kaplan.com/view/article/0,1898,1957,00.html*) has some great guidance on how to get organized for your first week at a new job. This site also includes

What You'll Learn in This Chapter:
- ▶ How to make your first impression a lasting one.
- ▶ How to take charge of your career.
- ▶ How to keep a balance between your work and your non-work life.

First and Last

The impressions you give when you begin and end a job are critical to your reputation. People remember you best based on their first impression of you and their last impression of you.

information about setting initial goals and making your first contacts with clients and colleagues over the phone.

Kaplan Careers has an excellent section to help you navigate your first week on the job. Check it out at www.studyusa. kaplan.com/view/ article/0,1898, 1957,00.html.

Try It Yourself ▼ Your first week on the job is critical to developing positive work habits to succeed in your career. You can learn how to successfully develop these habits in your first week by following the guidance at Kaplan Careers.

1. Go to *www.studyusa.kaplan.com/view/article/ 0,1898,1957,00.html.*

2. Read through the one-page article, "Your First Week on the Job," which reminds you that you were hired because you have something of value to bring to the workplace.

3. Click the Set Goals link in the left column and read through this one-page article on how to set specific, quarterly career goals.

4. Click the Get Organized link in the left column and read about the different aspects to being organized in the workplace, such as being decisive, avoiding clutter, and learning to say "No."

5. Click the Work the Phone link in the left column and learn how you can turn the dreaded task of making business calls into an enthusiastic endeavor.

You've done it! You've set some goals, organized your work world, and learned how to communicate effectively by phone.

We suggest that you arrive with a list of goals and priorities in hand. On your first day, and possibly throughout your first week, you will most likely learn about the organization, your work area, your colleagues, your client files, and the organization's policies and paperwork. Take it in stride and know that you don't need to become an immediate expert about everything that is said. You should take notes so that you don't have to ask people to take their valuable work time to re-train you. You can find a great article, called "Wow 'em in a Week," at the Wet Feet site at *www. wetfeet.com/advice/articles/wow.asp*. This article explains how to make a great impression your first week on the job.

Also check out *Career Magazine*'s articles on making the most of your first weeks on the job. This site provides some great ideas to help ease the stress of the transition to your new job. Check it out at *www.careermag.com/newsarts/collegearts/dgordon1.html*.

Taking Charge of Your Career

In today's world of work, *you* are responsible for *your* career success. This means you need to develop and maintain a plan for your career development and your career goals. You can find an outstanding article on career development, called "What Does It Mean to Take Ownership of Your Career: 7 Key Responsibilities," at Gary Recchion's site at *www.aerospacecareers.com/ 060899.html*. This article explains how to develop self-career management skills and also discusses strategies for career success, including continuing your learning, being aware of what's going on in your organization, and building constructive relationships at work.

Most importantly, however, your plan needs to include maintaining the network that you established or expanded during your job search and continuing to grow the network while you're employed. This is the key to career growth and career promotion. If you are thinking about moving up in the organization, you need to identify and meet key people within the organization who can help you achieve this goal, such as hiring managers and senior-level staff. These people should become part of your network. You

Making Sense of Alphabet Soup

One of the hardest things to learn in a new organization is the host of new acronyms. Ask somebody to help you write out all the acronyms they can think of as well as what they mean. Type them up and put them in alphabetical order. Keep the list with you as a handy reference until you know the acronyms well.

Career Self-Reliance

Taking charge of your career is not only smart to do, it's expected by employers today. You are in charge of your career destiny. Don't wait for someone to open doors for you.

need to share career information with them and take an interest in their career success as well.

One of the easiest and most necessary things to do to maintain a network is to join a professional association. My Job Search (*www.myjobsearch.com/network/associations.html*) has links to thousands of professional associations and societies. For Web links to other sites, go back to Chapter 10, "Networking: Online and Offline," to find more online networking resources.

There are many things you can do on the job to continue to grow, develop, and challenge your skills and abilities. The following are a few ideas to get you started:

- Participate in regular activities of your professional association (local as well as regional and national).

- Attend annual conferences or seminars to brush up on the trends in your field.

- Offer to teach a special skill to colleagues.

- Identify a mentor at work who can help you grow in your profession.

- Join a team effort that is tackling a challenge through analysis and creative solutions.

If you're still in college and want to begin your professional development aside from studies, check out Berkeley University's career site (*http://career.berkeley.edu/SchoolsBusiness/faqBusiness.stm#1*) for good advice on how to make yourself attractive to business employers after you graduate. This guidance emphasizes accomplishments aside from grades. Accomplishments can be achieved through extra-curricular activities, full- or part-time work, volunteer work, and contributions to clubs and campus organizations.

CommSciences (Custom Research for Effective Communications at *www.build-site-traffic.com/cca/ccaflexibility1.html*) has an excellent slide presentation regarding the trends in the global economy. It explains what flexibility in the workplace you need to have to stay competitive. It indicates that to survive the global changes, you must be flexible in the workplace, in interpersonal relationships, and in your career. The role of the worker is dramatically shifting from the way we know it today to a new paradigm with a stronger focus on knowledge, different communication styles, and flexible roles in the workplace.

You will find more good advice in Beyond Computing's article, "Learning to Lead" (*www.beyondcomputing.net/index.asp? archive/1998/09-98/career.html*). This article focuses on how to develop your leadership skills, with an emphasis on developing a reputation for getting things done, providing solutions, generating ideas, understanding business needs, managing your time, and building key relationships. These skills are critical in the continually changing economy and global workforce

Work/Life Balance: It's Up to You to Set the Scale

When it seems that work is cutting into too much of your life outside of work, it's important to remember that sometimes it's the employer's fault and sometimes it's not. Regardless, you need to ensure that you have balance in your life, or the job you just invested a lot of time in getting will have you burnt to a crisp before you can update your resume. Don't let this happen to you.

A Life Out of Whack!

If you're telling yourself that you've "got no life," it's time to take a step back and evaluate why your work load is out of balance. You can get that balance back, but it's going to take some effort.

One of the best ways to ensure that you don't fall into a 16-hour-a-day-plus-weekend-work trap is to set your time parameters from the beginning. If you commit to every team project and work until 10:00 p.m. for the first few weeks on the job, you're going to let a lot of people down when you decide to return to a "normal" schedule.

We're not suggesting that you stick to only 40 hours a week. Sometimes your workload demands that you put in a little extra time. What we are suggesting, however, is that you determine what priorities you have. If you went through the assessment stage outlined in Chapter 3, "e-Career Mapping and Job Search Planning," you already know what you value in a job. Now it's time to make sure that you are being true to yourself and not being lost in the bottomless time pit.

You can set a daily routine of reminding yourself to maintain a healthy work/life balance by visiting Managing Work & Family's site (*http://mwfam.com/tip.html*). This site offers a daily tip on how to strive for balance in your home and work lives.

The Managing Work & Family's Web site has a page you should bookmark and visit each day. The page, at http://mwfam. com/tip.html, has a different tip each day on how to manage the balance between work and life.

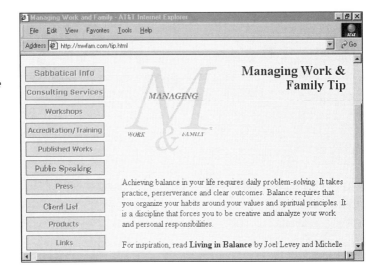

If you are in a high-pressure position, keeping a work/family balance isn't going to be easy—but things we value most in life usually come at some price. Your price for your balance may be learning how to work smarter without working longer, or learning how to say "No" to some projects until you complete others.

We know this isn't easy, but if you want to reap the rewards of meaningful employment and have a life as well, you need to develop a strategy that works for you.

If you have a family, check out the Family & Work Institute site (*www.familiesandworkinst.org*) for great articles and tips on how to manage both work and family commitments.

To find additional resources for work and family issues—even if you're single—check out Work & Family's links to Internet resources (*www.workfamily.com/resource.htm*). Here, you'll find links to sites that offer information, resources, advice, and assistance on the following topics: caregivers, children, families, childcare, colleges and universities, convenience services, eldercare, federal legislation and strategies to address these issues, flexible work options, gender issues, help for employees, publications and magazines, service providers, shift workers, workplace safety, and more. This is probably the best compilation of links to work/life resources that we've found on the Internet.

Putting It All Together

You're on your way to career success! Making that all-important first impression your first week on the job is critical. This chapter provided some outstanding Web sites that will help you develop, grow, and thrive in your career. It also provided tips on what you can do your first week on the job and explained that *you* are in charge of your career—your employer is not.

Because you are in charge of your career, you are also in charge of managing your work with the rest of your life. It's not always easy to do, but if you tap the online resources available to you, you will find support and success in your efforts.

Next stop: Managing change and transitions.

CHAPTER 15

Change and Transitions

These days, changes and transitions are constants in our daily lives. We're getting started in our careers, changing jobs, moving to a new place, starting a family, taking care of others, planning for retirement, or anticipating the next major transition coming our way. How do you manage all of this in today's hectic world? It's not always easy, but we know you can do it—and the Internet can help. This chapter covers a few areas and provides Web sites to help you out in other areas as well.

Changing Careers

We don't mean to tire you out, but just because you recently landed a job doesn't mean you can rest on your laurels. Chances are that you will change jobs or careers again—and sooner rather than later. Most people will change careers anywhere from four to seven times in their life. This doesn't include the job changes within each career! Think about it. List the jobs you've had and then classify them by career field. Chances are, you fit the profile or are well on your way to doing so. You will be able to apply time and again everything you have learned throughout this book and through your online research.

Changing careers, however, can be both exciting and stressful. You're starting something new to you, but you may have already invested so much time and energy into a career that took you up a few notches in pay and level of responsibility. Does changing your career mean you have to start over? Maybe yes, maybe no.

We suggest you take a look at Monster.com's section for career changers (*http://content.monster.com/careerchangers*). This is a great compilation of articles and practical tips for managing a career change, such as addressing the reasons for the career change. Many individuals are thrown into change because of

What You'll Learn in This Chapter:

▶ When to think about changing careers.

▶ What to do if you're relocating within the United States or abroad.

Times Are a-Changin'

You will probably change careers four to seven times in your life, and you will probably change jobs several times within each career!

downsizing, corporate mergers, divorce, having children, or any of a host of other events that initiate change quickly and often unexpectedly. However, you might be thrown into change simply because you're unhappy with your current career.

Regardless of your reason, you can take some simple steps to ensure a successful transition. We suggest the following:

Step One: Take a short time off to reassess your current work situation. Reflect on why you want to change your career. Do you have career interests that can't be addressed in your current position? Are you ready for a change because of your changing interests? Is it possible that you like your career but are not happy with your employer? Is it possible that the job you are doing is in conflict with your personal values? Is it possible that you are stressed because you are overworked? There are many, diverse reasons to change careers. It's important that you identify your reasons if you are to address them fully.

Step Two: After assessing what is contributing to your interest in changing careers, first think about what can be done to address these factors. Perhaps all you need is a new employer or a reduced work load or a more challenging position in the same career field. If this doesn't solve the problem, go to Step Three.

Step Three: Go back to Chapter 3, "e-Career Mapping and Job Search Planning," and Chapter 4, "Finding Yourself in the e-World." These two chapters will help you begin to set goals and assess who you are in relationship to the world of work. You probably have many skills and abilities that can transfer into another career, but you need to have clarity about what your interests are and what makes you tick.

Step Four: Use Chapter 5, "What in the World of Work Is Out There?" and Chapter 6, "Finding the Right Industry, Employer, and Organization," to further research your career interests and potential employers. Make sure that you spend time talking with others in different career fields to find out what they like and don't like about their career or their organization.

Step Five: Review your options and rewrite your career action plan.

Relocation in the United States or Internationally

We already covered some of the online resources available to help you make decisions regarding relocation in Chapter 6 and Chapter 13, "Job Offers: E-valuating and Net-gotiating." There is a lot more out there and a lot to consider if you're considering relocating, but you're not sure where.

Fortunately, the Web has plenty of resources to keep you comparing options for years. To chop off some time, we suggest that you first make a list of your priorities before you begin comparing locations. Take into consideration your preference for city versus country, renting versus owning, cost of living, proximity to recreational activities, proximity to public transportation, crime rates, entertainment and cultural preferences, medical care options, family and friends, and any other considerations that are important to you. Here's what we found online that may help you in making some decisions.

Moving in the United States

Our favorite site for comparing salaries between two cities is HomeFair.com's site (*www.homefair.com/calc/salcalc.html*). This site will provide information on how much you need to earn to keep the same standard of living in a different location. You usually have to provide some information for the site's realty business, but it's well worth getting the information. You can also find information on crime rates in more than 6,000 cities, compare mortgage loans and the cost of renting, and gain access to hundreds of city profiles. You can even search for a home to buy through the site's database of more than a million homes.

HomeFair.com (www.homefair.com/calc/salcalc.html) is one of the best sites we've found on the Web for comparing information about where you live now to where you might move.

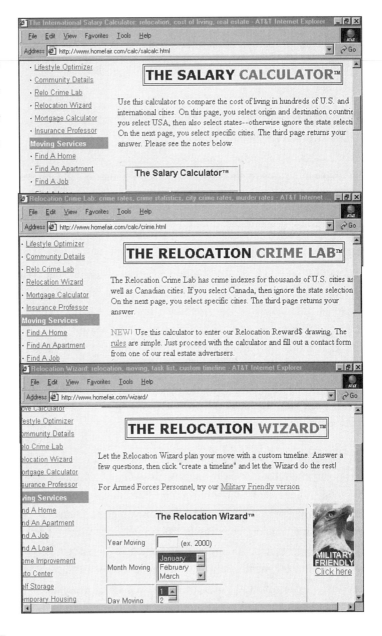

Try It Yourself ▼ You can go online to figure out how much you need to earn to stay at the same standard of living in a different city. Just follow these steps to do a comparison.

1. Go to the HomeFair.com' site at *www.homefair.com/calc/ salcalc.html*.

2. Click the Salary Calculator link in the left column.

3. To compare the cost of living between two cities in the United States, first select the state where you live now (or the first state you want to compare). For our example, select Arizona.

4. Select the second state. For this exercise, choose Virginia.

5. Click Show Cities and select Flagstaff as the city in Arizona and Fairfax as the city in Virginia. Also, choose Own Home for this exercise.

6. Type the salary you are making (or would make) in the first state (or where you live now). For this exercise, type *35000* and click the Calculate button.

As you can see, the Salary Calculator indicates that you would need to make more than $40,000 in Fairfax, Virginia, to have the same standard of living you have with $35,000 in Flagstaff. Pretty handy information to have!

Virtual Relocation (*www.virtualrelocation.com*) is another excellent relocation reference site. Here you can find information on city demographics, mortgage rates by state, moving and storage facilities, schools and education, senior living, vacation properties, weather, and public services.

Money.com has an annual review of places to live. You can access its list of the best places for the year 2000 at *www.money.com/money/depts/real_estate/bestplaces*. San Francisco was rated the number one big city to live in 2000 because of its low unemployment, clean air, and variety of professional sports teams, arts and culture, and recreational activities. Rochester, Minnesota, was rated the number one small city to live in 2000 because of its outstanding medical facilities, its low crime and unemployment rates, and its leisurely lifestyle.

Moving Overseas

It can be a daunting task moving from one state to another. When you think about moving to another country, it can get even more complicated. Fear not. There are lots of online resources to help you make decisions, plan for your move, and ease your transition.

Know Before You Go!

It takes more than buying a ticket and having a passport to make a smooth move to another country. Be sure you take advantage of the wealth of online resources to help you learn what you need to know before you go.

There are some basics to grasp before you buy your ticket. First, you need to find out the visa requirements for the country you will be entering. To obtain a visa, you will need a passport. You can apply for a passport at most U.S. Postal Service offices. Many countries also require different immunizations. You must find out what is required as well as how much time in advance you need to be immunized.

Aside from the logistics, there are some critical pieces of information for you to gather and consider before you move overseas. To reduce the culture shock you'll experience and to increase your chances for a smooth transition to the lifestyle of the new country, you need to learn about the culture and the language of the country where you will be living. You need to learn about the climate so that you can bring appropriate clothing and insect repellant, if necessary. You also should learn about the living conditions so that you can prepare yourself for changes you might not otherwise expect. For example, the country might have frequent power outages. If you depend heavily on your laptop computer, you may want to bring extra batteries to charge daily. You must also find out about medical facilities and the availability of medicines in local pharmacies.

If you know what region or what country you want to move to, you should first take a look at the information provided by the embassy or consulate for that country. You can find links to their sites at the U.S. State Department Web site (*www.state.gov/www/ background_notes*). This site has links to profiles on virtually every country in the world. You can also link to all the U.S. embassies from the home page at *http://travel.state.gov/links.html*. These sites have travel advisories and useful information about the country in which you're interested. You will also find information on visa requirements and necessary immunizations you'll need before you depart.

The Electronic Embassy (*www.embassy.org*), on the other hand, provides links to the embassies of other countries. Some of these Web sites provide detailed information about the country, while others may only provide contact information and a brief list of services. If you know what country you're looking for, this may be a good place to start to find cultural and tourist information.

And, of course, one of our favorite Web sites—Monster.com at *http://international.monster.com/workabroad*—does an outstanding job of providing links related to working abroad, including relocation resources, resources for accompanying spouses, job links, embassies, and consulates, universities, and a whole lot more. This is a definite "must visit" site for you if you're internationally bound!

Monster.com at http:// international. monster.com/ workabroad offers an excellent forum for asking international job experts questions related to international careers.

Putting It All Together

Transitions can make a major impact on your life and career decisions. You need to research and prepare for any life transition. If you checked out some of the online resources and guidance in this chapter, you learned that changing careers can be tough, but it's possible and is becoming more and more common. Even if you're not ready to change careers now, the advice in this chapter is well worth reading, because chances are you'll change careers åagain…and again…and again.

Moving abroad is a lot easier if you're armed with information and can plan for the transition. You need to do more than check for visa requirements and necessary immunization shots. You need to learn about the culture, the living conditions, and the local resources available to you. If you plan ahead, the transition will be much smoother. Next stop: Continuing learning!

CHAPTER 16

Continuing Education and Training

Regardless of your career field, job security, or even seniority, the concept of an individual taking responsibility for his or her life-long learning is becoming an expectation in the work world. It is no longer the employer's responsibility to offer training and education opportunities. You are responsible for maintaining your employability. Both education and professional development support the key concept of employability. If you want to be employable, you need a degree, and you must have marketable skills. To maintain marketable skills, you need to continually learn new skills and upgrade current ones.

Whether you do this through formal education, conferences, workshops, training courses, or online, you need to know what knowledge and skills your career demands. Then you need to know where and how to access professional development opportunities that help you meet these demands. This chapter will help you identify online sources for both online and offline information and opportunities.

What You'll Learn in This Chapter:

- ▶ How continuing your education can make a difference in your career.
- ▶ What distance education opportunities are available.
- ▶ How you can learn by studying overseas.
- ▶ Why you must invest in continued learning.
- ▶ How you can improve and expand your professional skills.

Going to School: Online or Offline, You Just Have to Do It!

If you're considering studying beyond the high school level, we salute you for making a smart decision. It's pretty tough to develop a financially stable life and a marketable career in the United States without some kind of educational credential beyond the high school diploma.

**Plug in to
Education Online!**
Educational institu-
tions across the
board are hooked
up to the Internet
and ready to serve
students, alumni,
and potential stu-
dents.

**How Does Your
School Stack Up?**
School rankings
change yearly, and
the competition is
getting fierce. *U.S.
News* Online is a
great source for stay-
ing on top of who's
hot and who's not.

Whether you're considering vocational training, an associate's
degree, a bachelor's degree, or an advanced degree, you'll find a
lot of useful resources online to help you. You might also find
some courses you can take over the Internet. In fact, now it's even
possible to find full-blown degree programs that you can enroll in
and complete on the Internet! The bottom line is that with the
financial aid and the virtual educational resources now available,
there is little room for excuses for not furthering your education.

Peterson's Education Web site (*www.petersons.com*) is one of the
best sites for identifying colleges and universities for regular in-
person study programs. This site is packed with career education
information, financial aid guidance, English learning programs,
study abroad programs, and other education programs and related
assistance. You can also find an extremely useful state-by-state
listing of higher education institutions nationwide on the
University of Alabama in Huntsville University Pages (*http://
isl-garnet.uah.edu/Universities_g*).

If you're looking for information on undergraduate and graduate
programs in general, including school rankings, we think that *U.S.
News* Online's site (*www.usnews.com/usnews/edu*) provides an
outstanding no-cost information service. This site even offers a
forum you can access to ask questions about college, graduate
school, and financial aid.

*Peterson's
Education Center
is an outstanding
Web site for find-
ing information
about continuing
education. Check
it out at* www.
petersons.com.

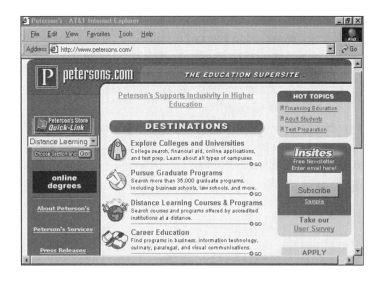

Distance Education: It's Not So Far Away!

Distance learning is a newer option for those looking to continue their education. Courses are offered over the Internet. Some courses offer "live" chat sessions, while others require students to "check in" on a particular site for a class lecture or homework assignments. Some distance education courses even have video feeds for students to access either live or by downloading a video of a professor giving a lecture. This learning forum has been an immense opportunity for many people who do not live close to an educational institution or don't have the time or flexibility to attend daytime classes.

If you're looking for distance-learning opportunities, but want to check out the whys, hows, whats, and wheres, you can find a lot of answers at Peterson's Education Web site (*www.petersons.com*). Click the Distance Learning button to uncover a ton of information about the virtual classrooms that are catching on like wildfire.

The Distance Accreditation and Training Council (*www.detc.org*) is an excellent resource to identify accredited distance-learning programs and institutions. It lists programs from financial management and physical therapy to writing and refrigeration. Try looking up a degree that may interest you.

▼ **Try It Yourself**

1. Go to the Distance Accreditation and Training Council site at *www.detc.org* and click Degree Programs.

2. Scroll through the program options that appear and click an educational institution that offers a degreed subject that interests you (for example, scroll all the way down and click University of St. Augustine for Health Science).

3. Read the description of the program (for example, St. Augustine offers a physical therapy program) and click the link to the Web site to get more information about the program. Alternatively, click the Info link to send an email to the program administrator to request additional information.

▲

Study Abroad: Where in the World Are You Going?

As the United States adapts to its relationship with a global marketplace, study-abroad programs have increased in popularity and in credibility. Studying abroad allows a student to gain educational, cultural, and sometimes even language experience in another country in a safe and organized environment. Needless to say, most students return to the United States much wiser for their efforts.

Many students at universities have the option to study abroad for one or two semesters. However, even if you're not currently a student but are interested in studying abroad, you should certainly explore the educational opportunities available to you. You can find links to more than 6,000 educational institutions in more than 160 countries at General Education Online (*http://wsdo.sao.uwf.edu/~geo*). This site has the most comprehensive collection of educational programs around the globe.

Is It Your Turn to Intern?

More and more employers are demanding experience in addition to a degree—even for entry-level hires. If you are currently studying and don't have relevant work experience, you better be looking for an internship or a cooperative learning program with a company you like.

We strongly encourage you to prepare for an internship interview in the same way you would prepare for a regular job interview. If you don't know what we're talking about, go back through Chapter 12, "Interview Techniques Online." Be sure to ask thoughtful and pointed questions, such as what your specific duties will be and what a typical day will be like. You don't want to be stuck behind a copy machine all day— although you'll probably end up spending some time there, regardless of your work contract.

In an internship, you want to gain real-world experience. If you're not going to get it, don't accept the internship offer and keep looking. If you're in search of internship programs, you'll find some great information and possibilities at both Internship Programs (*www.internshipprograms.com*) and Internships (*www.internships.com/intro.html*). Both sites list internships in mostly Fortune 1000 companies around the country. You can sometimes even find internships abroad. In any case, these sites offer a whole host of good tips for making your internship a success.

The Buck Stops with You: Investing in Your Continued Learning

We used to say that the cost of education skyrocketed. Now we simply and matter-of-factly say that it's an investment—and that's just what it is. Gone are the days of education being only for the fortunate. These days, there's no excuse to *not* find some way to finance an education or continued learning[em]it's time to put the mouse to the pad and start cruising the information superhighway. There you will find terrific sites that detail sources of financial assistance. Yes, there are countless viable ways to cover the increasing expenses of continued learning—you just need to know where to look.

If you're looking for financial aid for higher education, you can find information on scholarships and other financial sources at Federal Student Aid (*www.ed.gov/offices/OPE/express.html*). You can also subscribe to a free scholarship service at FastWeb (*www.fastweb.com*). This site will notify you of scholarships that match your profile. However, the database of scholarships is not comprehensive, so don't rely on this as a sole source for scholarship information.

Other resources for financial aid include College Plan (*www. collegeplan.org/cpnow/pnwguide/pnwguide.htm*), Yahoo! (*http://dir.yahoo.com/Education/financial_Aid*), and College Net (*www.collegenet.com*). College Plan allows you to quickly scan the database of scholarships by simply clicking any of approximately 20 items that may reflect your interests. The site returns a well-organized list that includes the name of the scholarship, the amount it offers, the deadline, and a link to more information about it. Yahoo!, on the other hand, provides a list of links for other sites that offer information about college scholarships.

Finally, you need to check the financial aid pages of your educational institution. Many universities list their scholarships and provide links to online information for financial aid related to their programs.

A Click Can Be Worth $1000!
No longer do you need to spend hours in the library scouring the scholarship books. There is so much information online that, in the course of a weekend, you might be able to finance a chunk of your education!

Formal Education Offers Much, Much More Than Just a Class!

You have much to gain from continuing your education. In addition to acquiring a marketable credential, there are three benefits to returning to school:

- *You extend your professional network*—We've hammered home the importance of networking throughout this book, and we'll continue to drill it here. By now, you know the importance of networking to the success of your career. You can build your network through continuing education opportunities. When you're in school, you will meet other students, professors, trainers, and presenters who work in your career field. You want to meet them and they want to know you. Exchange business cards, stay in touch, share professional information.

- *You stay current on trends in your field*—As a student, you will come across some of the latest and greatest information about trends in the field. Take advantage of the immense resources available to you through the educational institution. Many universities and colleges subscribe to online services that allow you access to information that would otherwise be costly to obtain. Find out what is available to you, and spend some time reading and developing a file of good articles and information. Note resources that are of particular value to your career field.

  Also, as you come across information that may be of interest to someone in your network, remember to send him a copy of it with a note to let him know you are thinking of him. This little gesture goes a long way in growing and nurturing your network.

- *You meet future employers*—Believe it or not, your future employer may be sitting next to you in a class, teaching the class, participating as a guest speaker, or visiting a school-sponsored career fair. Yes, this directly connects to the networking advice we just mentioned. Always keep your eyes and ears open, build bridges rather than burn them, engage in classroom presentations with thoughtful questions, don't disagree with everything a speaker says, and be sure to make a connection before he leaves the room.

Beyond the Bachelor's: The Value of Continuing Education

Career trends being what they are, the savvy worker continues his education beyond a bachelor's degree if his career field demands it for upward mobility. This is the case for many career fields— often, the higher the degree, the higher the salary.

If you're not sure whether or not you should consider continuing your formal education, you need to talk with those in your network, mentors, or professors. You can also do some online research to get a ballpark idea of the value of additional education in a particular field by looking up your career field in the

University of Delaware's Major Resource Kits
(*www.udel.edu/CSC/mrk.html*). The Career services office covers
more than 70 career fields and includes profiles of a day on the
job, links to other sources of information about the field, how to
enhance your marketability in the field, and considerations for
further education and experience.

You can find out the value of continuing your education in your
career field by checking out the great information available in the
University of Delaware's 70 Major Resource Kits. Try it yourself!

▼ **Try It Yourself**

1. Go to the University of Delaware's Career Services pages at
   http://www.udel.edu/CSC/mrk.html.

2. Click your career field. Scroll down to the section on sample
   job titles. You will see a list of titles for those jobs that
   require a bachelor's degree and then the titles of careers that
   often require additional education.

3. Check out some of the links in Other Sources of Information
   for additional information about career growth and how a
   higher degree may help.

4. Bookmark this page so that you can return to it again as
   needed.

In addition to the links to universities at Peterson's Web site
(*www.petersons.com*), you can also find links to graduate schools
in the United States and in other countries at *www.gradschools.
com.*

Many graduate programs (and undergraduate programs, for that
matter) require pre-admissions testing. The Graduate Record
Exam (GRE) is the most frequently requested test, but others may
be required, depending on your circumstances. For example, if
you are applying to a business program, you may be required to
take the Graduate Management Admission Test (GMAT). If
you're applying to law school, you'll be required to take the Law
Schools Admission Test (LSAT). If English is your second language, the school may require you to take an English proficiency
exam called the Test of English as a Foreign Language (TOEFL).
If you're looking for information on higher education tests, you'll
find good guidance, practice questions, and information about

how and where to take the exam by logging on to Educational Testing Service's Web site (*http://etsis1.ets.org*). Note that the LSAT is not on the ETS site but can be found on the Law School Admission Council Web site at *www.lsat.org*.

GradAdvantage (*www.gradadvantage.org*) is probably the wave of the future regarding college applications. It's an online application service for graduate school and MBA programs. It's worth checking out because it might save you a lot of time filling out and submitting graduate applications. If you decide to submit your forms online, be sure to print out a hard copy for your records and request that the site send confirmation of receipt of your application.

Professional Development Through Training, Workshops, and Seminars

Of course, if you're not up for a few more years of education or working on another degree, you can always consider opportunities to increase your skills, such as non-degree programs, workshops, and seminars. Even if you have advanced degrees, you should continue to update your skills and expand your knowledge in key areas within your career field.

One of the best sites for finding learning opportunity programs is America's Learning eXchange (*www.alx.org*), which is sponsored by the U.S. Department of Labor. You can search for seminars, conferences, workshops, classroom courses, distance learning opportunities, Web- and computer-based training, and other educational programs. In addition, you can identify the state in which you want the training. We have found this site to be one of the most valuable resources for identifying professional training opportunities. This site is continually updated and just keeps getting better and better.

Remember, too, that you can always go to universities and colleges for adult education or continuing education courses. You can take one course at a time and usually don't have to go through the lengthy application process. Many courses targeted toward working adults are offered in the evenings or on weekends.

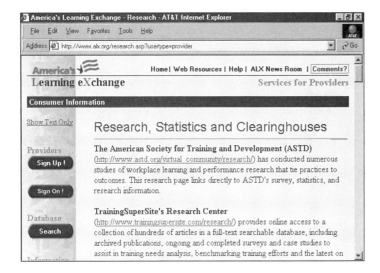

America's Learning eXchange (www.alx.org) is an excellent site to search for professional development seminars, classes, workshops, and conferences.

If you aren't familiar with university or college courses that are designed as part of a continuing education or adult education program, check out Temple University's Web site for online learning.

1. Go to Temple University at *http://oll.temple.edu/oll*.

2. Click the Courses Offered by Department link. Click the Graduate link and look at the variety of courses offered.

3. Click the Undergraduate link and look at the variety of courses. We're sure you will find something that meets your interests and can enhance your knowledge for your career.

4. Click a subject that interests you. Notice how you can read a description of the course as well as link to additional information, such as the syllabus and course materials.

Now that you're familiar with what to look for, check out the Web site of a university or college near you.

Temple University is one example of how universities and colleges nationwide are offering online continuing education programs that are geared toward the adult learner.

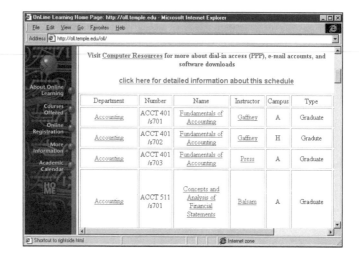

Putting It All Together

Deciding whether or not to continue your education is a major life decision. If you do decide to continue your education, you're making the smart choice. If you checked out some of the online assistance, you have found that you can access online information on thousands of different graduate and undergraduate programs and information on financial resources.

Distance learning opportunities are becoming increasingly more common and more recognized by accrediting institutions.

You can continue your lifelong learning through professional development training opportunities through classroom programs, over the Internet, at conferences, and through other media.

The World Wide Web is the place to find whatever you're looking for. Welcome to the e-world!

PART VI

Appendixes

APPENDIX A
Web Directory

The Internet is teeming with sites and pages that can help you in your job search. The information and opportunities represented by the Internet are mind boggling. We cannot begin to list all the sites related to the job-search process—nor is it our intent to do so. Instead, this appendix makes it easy for you to find Web addresses you have read about in this book and also provides a few additional sites to get you started in your online job search.

If you type one of these Web addresses and a message pops up saying *File Not Found, 404 Access Denied*, or *404 Not Found*, the Web page no longer exists or has changed its address. On the Web, this happens occasionally. You may be able to find the page by using a search engine such as Yahoo! (*www.yahoo.com*) or MetaCrawler (*www.metacrawler.com*). Type the name of the site in the search engine's search box; the search should uncover the site's current address. Be sure to write the correct address in this appendix for future reference.

Chapter 1: Job Hunting in the e-World

Web Address Book
www.webaddressbook.com

This site includes an address book, a calendar with email notification of appointments, a bookmark manager, and a notepad.

Cartoons
www.workforce.com/section/01/cartoons

www.dilbertzone.com

Here you can find work-related cartoons to keep you laughing.

Yahoo! Internet Life

www3.zdnet.com/yil/filters/channels/netezuser

Here you'll find great tips for narrowing your Internet searches.

National Association of Colleges and Employers

www.jobweb.org/catapult/homepage.htm

Here you can find links to colleges and universities. This site is sponsored by the professional association of career counselors and corporate recruiters.

America's One-Stop Career Center System

www.ttrc.doleta.gov/onestop

This site includes links to the more than 650 local One-Stop Centers nationwide.

Newbie-U (New User University)

www.newbie-u.com

This site has great tips for using the Web in the job search.

Wall Street Journal Careers Site

www.careers.wsj.com

WSJ is not just for reading stock quotes anymore! This is a great stop for Internet job-hunting advice.

Monster.com

www.monster.com

This is one of the biggest career sites on the Web. It's an outstanding site for solid career information.

Counseling Net

www.counselingnet.com

This site provides online counseling services and information on how counselors should interact with clients through email or in a chat room.

Counseling
www.counseling.org/resources/codeofethics.htm

This site offers great information about the ethical issues regarding online counseling.

Chapter 2: Using This Book E-ffectively and E-fficiently

Career Kiosk
www.careerkiosk.org

Check out this site for updated links and Web sites if you can't find a link or site listed in this book. Career Kiosk is a Web site run by Susan Musich, co-author of this book.

Chapter 3: e-Career Mapping and Job Search Planning

William Bridges and Associates
www.wmbridges.com

Check out articles on transitions, such as "How You Can Handle Change Better."

Bowling Green State University's Career Planning/Competency Model
www.bgsu.edu/offices/careers/process/process.html

This model is an outstanding guide to the steps involved in career planning and exploration. Start your career planning here by clicking Self-Assessment.

University of Delaware's Major Resource Kits
www.udel.edu/CSC/mrk.html

The Career Services Center compiled kits for more than 70 educational majors. The kits include job titles, profiles of a day on the job, and ways to enhance your marketability in the field.

University of North Carolina at Wilmington

www.uncwil.edu/stuaff/career/majors.htm

Here you'll find a page called "What Can I Do with a Major in…?" for each of more than 35 majors.

College of Mount St. Joseph's Kaleidoscope of Careers

www.msj.edu/academics/career/kocfields.htm

Liberal arts majors will find a great list of majors and titles here.

Michigan's Occupational Information System

www.mois.org/clusters.html

MOIS has an excellent list of career fields and relevant job titles.

University of Milwaukee

http://www.uwm.edu/Dept/CDC/internet-research.htm

Go to the second section on this page to find links to numerous Web sites that give options for career fields and majors.

JobStar

www.jobsmart.org/tools/career/spec-car.htm

Click your career field and review its outlook for the twenty-first century. You will also find information about how to plan for a career in your chosen field.

Mapping Your Future's Career Plan

www.mapping-your-future.org/planning/careerpl.htm

This site will help you develop a career plan. Click the Career Goals link to review the importance of career goals and then click the link to review a sample career plan.

College Grad

www.collegegrad.com/book/6-1.shtml

Read "How to Set Up Your Job Search Control Center." Then go to the bottom of the page and click Next and go through the next eight or nine pages to set up your own job search area.

MetaCrawler

www.metacrawler.com

A great site to find office supplies. Click Shopping. Next, click Office Products, and then click Office Supplies. You'll find of dozens of links to office supply sites.

University of Waterloo's Career Planning Site

www.adm.uwaterloo.ca/infocecs/CRC/manual-home.html

Not only does this site include great career planning guidance, its approach to career decision making is one of the best we've found online—and it's easy to use. If you're not a college student, you may need to modify some of the recommendations.

North Carolina State University's Career Key

www2.ncsu.edu/unity/lockers/users/l/lkj/decision.html

This site lists the steps for effective decision making.

California State University

www.csulb.edu/~tstevens/c15-carp.htm

This site has rules, guidelines, strategies, and checklists to help you make a career decision. Scroll down to the fourth step on making decisions.

Chapter 4: Finding Yourself in the e-World

Career Interests Game

http://web.missouri.edu/~cppcwww/holland.shtml

Here you will find great ideas on careers related to your interests.

The Career Interests Checklist

http://icpac.indiana.edu/infoseries/is-50pl.html

This site offers a quick and easy way to develop a list of possible careers based on your interests.

Cal Berkeley's Career Site

http://career.berkeley.edu/Prep/PrepSkills.stm

Here you can find a great list of work-specific skills.

Washington University's Self-Management Skills Worksheet

http://career-3.wustl.edu/cps/self/manage.htm

This site will help you identify the adaptive skills that best characterize you.

Creative Job Search's Online Guide

http://www.amby.com/worksite/cjs/cjsbook2/skill6d.htm

This site helps you identify the adaptive skills that characterize you. We suggest that you use this list as a complement to the Washington University site listed previously.

Skills Zone

www.pch.gc.ca/Cyberstation/html/szone2_e.htm

The list of transferable skills at this site is one of the most comprehensive such lists online.

University of Minnesota Duluth

www.d.umn.edu/student/loon/car/self/career_transfer_survey.html

This site offers a good example on how to cluster your transferable skills.

Birkman Career Style Summary

www.review.com/birkman/birkman.cfm

This assessment tool will help you learn more about your work preferences. It's one of the best we've seen online. It asks you a series of questions and, based on your answers, offers insights into what work environments may be best for you.

Career Search

http://cbweb9p.collegeboard.org/career/html/searchQues.html

This tool will help you identify your preferred work environment, work style, temperament, and interests. After submitting your information, the program returns a list of careers that match the combination of your answers.

Bowling Green State University

www.bgsu.edu/offices/careers/process/exercise.html

At this site, you can review a list of values and identify those that resonate well within your lifestyle.

Career Perfect's Work Preference Inventory

www.careerpower.com/CareerPerfect/cpWorkPrefInv.htm

This is one of the best Web sites for identifying work values.

University of Minnesota, Morris

http://www.mrs.umn.edu/services/career/Career_Planning

This site offers a nice overview of how your values may influence your work decisions. The first section is a questionnaire; the next section is a values assessment. Finally, the site provides assistance to help you prioritize your values.

The Self-Directed Search

www.self-directed-search.com

This skills and interest inventory can be done online for less than $10. This tool helps you look at how your skills and interests may relate to different careers.

The University of Waterloo

www.adm.uwaterloo.ca/infocecs/CRC/manual/skills.html

This site has a good worksheet to help you identify your achievements.

GeoCities

www.geocities.com/Athens/Academy/5450/3main.html

This site covers various job search and career barriers, from personal and financial to language and technological.

Chapter 5: What in the World of Work Is Out There?

Career Interests Checklist and Career Search

http://icpac.indiana.edu/infoseries/is-50pl.html

and

http://cbweb9p.collegeboard.org/career/html/searchQues.html

These two sites help you identify your interests, values, and skills and provide lists of careers that reflect your interests.

University of Delaware's Major Resource Kits
www.udel.edu/CSC/mrk.html

This site covers 70 majors and provides related job titles. Not only can it spark ideas for jobs and careers to explore, but it gives you a start by providing job profiles and links to information about different careers.

University of North Carolina at Wilmington
www.uncwil.edu/stuaff/career/majors.htm.

This site offers information about jobs and careers related to different majors.

College of Mount St. Joseph's Kaleidoscope of Careers
www.msj.edu/academics/career/kocfields.htm

This site offers information about jobs and careers related to different majors.

Michigan's Occupational Information System
www.mois.org/clusters.html

This site offers information about jobs and careers related to different majors.

University of Milwaukee
http://www.uwm.edu/Dept/CDC/internet-research.htm

Go to the second section on this page to find links to numerous Web sites that give options for career fields and majors.

Occupational Outlook Handbook
http://stats.bls.gov/ocohome.htm

This is an excellent resource on occupational information. Here you can get a realistic picture about a particular career. It is provided by the Department of Labor.

America's Career InfoNet

www.acinet.org

This site provides information about the job market for specific career fields and offers a profile of the occupation by state.

Job Web's Catapult

www.jobweb.org/catapult/homepage.htm

This page links you to career centers in the United States, Canada, Australia, and Great Britain.

My Job Search

www.myjobsearch.com/network/associations.html

From this site, you can link to almost 2,000 associations.

Yahoo! Guide to Professional Associations

http://dir.yahoo.com/business_and_economy/organizations/professional

From this site, you can link to thousands of professional organizations and associations.

Yahoo! Businesses

http://dir.yahoo.com/Business_and_Economy/Companies/

Here you can find an excellent database of businesses by industry.

Telephone Directories on the Web

www.teldir.com/eng

This site helps you find email addresses, telephone numbers, street addresses, and more in any of 350 directories covering more than 150 countries.

Career Chase

www.careerchase.net/INTERVIEWS.htm

Professionals in 20 different career fields answer questions and offer information about their careers. This is a great place to gather ideas for questions to ask your own contacts.

The Liszt

www.liszt.com

This site's database contains contact and profile information for more than 90,000 mailing lists.

Topic.com

www.topica.com

This site does an outstanding job of categorizing thousands of different mailing lists.

Netiquette Home Page

www.albion.com/netiquette

This site offers the rules of the road for communicating in the cyber-world.

Chapter 6: Finding the Right Industry, Employer, and Organization

WetFeet.com

www.wetfeet.com

This site offers excellent information on industry trends, what's good and not so good about an industry, key companies in an industry, job tips, and key positions.

My Job Search-Associations

www.myjobsearch.com/network/associations.html

This site offers links to nearly 2,000 associations.

BizTech Network's @Brint.com

www.brint.com/newswire.htm

This is an excellent site to link to business resources online. Scroll down the page until you find a news source that references your industry or company of interest.

Business Week

www.businessweek.com/search.htm

Here you can search articles from the past five years of the magazine. Only current magazine subscribers can access past articles, but the search may turn up information on a company that makes it worth purchasing the article.

My Job Search

Company research at

http://myjobsearch.com/cgi-bin/mus.cgi/employers/research.html

The directories page at

http://myjobsearch.com/cgibin/mus.cgi/employers/directories.html

These pages make up an outstanding collection of links to online directories and research pages that provide company information.

Hoover's Online

www.hooversonline.com

This is an excellent online directory for researching company information by industry.

Michigan State University's Center for International Business Education and Research (MSU CIBER)

http://ciber.bus.msu.edu/busres/company.htm

Here you will find links to company and business information worldwide. This is an outstanding compilation of international business resources.

Riley Guide

www.dbm.com/jobguide/diverse.html

This site provides links to career resources for women, minorities, military, the disabled, and other groups and audiences.

The Minorities' Job Bank

www.minorities-jb.com

This is a great resource for minorities and women to connect to career information relevant to them.

World Wide Web Virtual Library

www.nttc.edu/gov_res.html

This page on U.S. government information resources allows you to access any government Web site by using its search function.

Govbot

http://ciir2.cs.umass.edu/Govbot

This is an effective and easy-to-use searchable database of U.S. government Web sites.

Piper Resources Guide of State and Local Governments

www.piperinfo.com/state/states.html

Here you can find the Web sites of state and local governments.

Idealist

www.idealist.org

This site has information on more than 20,000 nonprofit organizations in over 140 countries.

Money.com

http://pathfinder.com/money/depts/real_estate/bestplaces

This site offers an annual listing of the best places to live in the United States, including both big cities and small towns. You can also use its screening tool to find a place that matches your own interests.

USA City Link

http://usacitylink.com

This site has a comprehensive listing of cities nationwide, with links to other relevant Web sites.

Job Star

http://jobstar.org/tools/salary/index.htm

This site has links to more than 300 different salary guides, calculators, and surveys. It's the most comprehensive collection we've found online.

Federal Government Pay Scales

www.opm.gov/oca/payrates/index.htm

Here you can find the current salary scales for jobs in the federal government.

Chapter 7: Writing Resumes: The Printed Word

Job Hunter's Bible

www.jobhuntersbible.com

The author of the site is Richard Bolles, author of *What Color Is Your Parachute?* He keeps the site's information updated and is a credible source. A top-notch location!

College Grad Site

www.collegegrad.com/resumes/index.shtml

If you're in college or seeking entry-level work, you should check out the chronological resume sample and the resume templates. The templates cover 28 different career fields and can be downloaded into your word processing program.

Monster.com

http://content.monster.com/resume/samples/resumes

This site has excellent resume samples for various career fields. If your career field isn't represented, check out the sample for financial analysts. This is a great model with which to develop your own resume. The site offers good examples of nicely designed resumes.

http://content.monster.com/resume/resources/phrases_verbs

You can find a great list of action phrases that you can use in writing your resume as well as an alphabetical list of power verbs. Use these verbs to strengthen your accomplishment statements.

JobStar

http://jobsmart.org/tools/resume/res-fu1.htm

Here you'll find great examples of a functional resume.

Career Experience

http://careerexperience.com/resources/resumes/functional_prof.ht
ml

This site offers good sample functional resumes.

Email Addresses

www.emailaddresses.com/email_web.htm

This site allows you to compare functions available on the different free email Web sites.

Yahoo!

www.yahoo.com

This site offers a free email service. Simply click the Mail link at the top of the page and follow the directions from there. Yahoo!'s mail service is known for its capability to handle email graphics, video, and sound.

Distinctive Documents

www.distinctiveweb.com/samples.htm

This site is designed to actually sell resume-writing services, but it also offers outstanding examples of resumes.

Career Lab

www.careerlab.com/art_homeruns.htm

This site offers the best assistance in writing accomplishment statements for your resume. It also offers great information on how to qualify and quantify your experience.

Universities of Virginia and Berkeley

http://minerva.acc.virginia.edu/~career/handouts/vita.html

http://career.berkeley.edu/Phds/PhDCVelements.stm

These sites offer good guidance on how to write a curriculum vitae.

Quintessential Careers

www.quintcareers.com/curriculum_vitae.html

This site includes links to other good Web sites that have curriculum vitae information as well as links to sample CVs.

Eurograduate

www.eurograduate.com/plan.html

Here you will find samples of European-style resumes.

Superior Staffing

www.superiorstaffing.com/newpages/resumebody.html

This site has great design tips for your resume.

Chapter 8: Sending Resumes: The Electronic Word

JobTrak

www.jobtrak.com

This is one of several excellent sites that focus on jobs for graduating college students. The institution must pay for access to it, but it is rated highly by students.

My Job Search

www.myjobsearch.com/cgi-bin/mjs.cgi/resumes/posting.html

This site provides links to more than 70 resume posting sites.

Job Choices Online

www.jobweb.org/jconline/resumes/resumes/Resmatch.shtml

This is a good, easy-to-understand article on how the computer scans your resume.

Career Mosaic

www.careermosaic.com

You can find out about the types of employers that access resumes at that site. Take a look at the guidelines for writing your resume.

ProvenResumes.com

www.provenresumes.com/reswkshps/electronic/electrespg1.html

Come here for great tips on how to write an electronic resume.

Headhunter.net

www.headhunter.net/123res.htm

This is a good site to post your resume if you are interested in jobs in the Human Resources field.

Vacancies in International Organizations

http://missions.itu.int/~italy/vacancor.htm

This site has links connecting you to numerous international organizations.

My Job Search and Riley Guide

www.myjobsearch.com/cgi-bin/mjs.cgi/resumes/posting.html

www.dbm.com/jobguide/resumes.html

Both of these sites offer reviews and information about different sites where you can post your resume.

America's Talent Bank

www.ajb.org/html/atb_home.html

This site does not charge employers to post their jobs nor to view the resumes posted, so chances are that many smaller and mid-size employers will check out these resumes first.

Career Mosaic

www.careermosaic.com/cm/gateway

If you're looking for employment outside the United States, this site offers a resume bank for international employers.

Monster.com

http://international.monster.com

This site allows you to post your resume for employers that have job opportunities in Africa, Central and South America, Canada, Asia, and the Middle East.

Resumix and Webhire (formerly known as Restrac)

www.resumix.com

www.webhire.com

You can get a lot of information about the resume scanning process by visiting these two Web sites. Resumix and Webhire are two of the largest and best-known systems used by employers to scan resumes.

eResumes

www.eresumes.com/tut_keyresume.html

Here you can find good lists of keywords by job category and keywords for personal traits to include on your scannable resume.

Chapter 9: Writing Letters for the Information Age

MSN Careers

http://content.careers.msn.com/gh_cl_htg_intro.html

Here you will find a guide on how to develop the content and format as well as tips for writing letters at all stages of the job-hunting process.

Career Lab

www.careerlab.com/letters/default.htm

If you're looking for sample letters, this is one of the best sites we've seen. You'll not only find information on how to write job search letters, but you'll find excellent examples.

University of Virginia

http://minerva.acc.virginia.edu/~career/handouts/cover.html#sample6

Here you can view an excellent example of an approach letter.

Quintessential Careers

www.quintcareers.com/cover_letter_samples.html

This site provides great examples of cover letters. Try clicking the referral letter. Notice how the letter starts out with an immediate reference to the person who referred the job seeker to the reader.

Chapter 10: Networking: Online and Offline

Networking on the Internet

http://dlis.gseis.ucla.edu/people/pagre/network.html

This site offers great information on how to network.

Wall Street Journal Careers Site

www.careers.wsj.com

This site has some great articles on networking.

California's JobStar

http://jobsmart.org/hidden/index.htm

At this site, you'll find great guidance on networking—both in person and online.

Telephone Directories on the Web

www.teldir.com/eng

This site will link you to more than 350 directories for businesses, individuals, fax numbers, and email addresses in the United States and more than 150 other countries.

Associations Unlimited

www.galenet.com/servlet

This site offers a comprehensive listing of associations. You will need to connect to this site from a library, university, career center, or business that has leased access, because this is a fee-for-service site.

American Society of Association Executives

http://info.asaenet.org/gateway/OnlineAssocSlist.html

Find more than 6,500 associations that have Web sites. This site and the Associations Unlimited Web site previously listed, are the best sites around for identifying what associations are in your career field. Most associations offer a page of links to related Web sites.

Yahoo!'s Guide to Professional Associations

http://dir.yahoo.com/business_and_economy/organizations/
professional

Yahoo! has lists of associations, categorized by industry. This is a good place to find local and regional associations.

American Society for Training and Development

www.astd.org

You can see a great example of an online trade magazine at this site. Click the T&D Magazine link under the Products and Services heading in the left column.

My Job Search

www.myjobsearch.com/network/associations.html

Click the Alumni Associations link to see a U.S. map; click the state where you went to college to see a list of links to online alumni Web sites. This site has links to nearly 500 alumni associations.

Northern Arizona University

www.nau.edu/~alumni/index.html

Here you will find an excellent example of a helpful networking tool for alumni. This site lists the alumni chapters around the country and even allows alumni to update their information online.

The Liszt

www.liszt.com

This is the best Web site to visit to identify listservs in your field. You can search the database of 90,000 lists by words or phrases, or you can search the different lists by topic, such as business or science. When you find a list that interests you, simply read the instructions on how to subscribe, and you're on your way!

Monster.com

www.monster.com

You can meet others online by connecting to a chat room that is hosted by this site. Click the Today's Chats link to start.

America Online (AOL)

www.aol.com

Although most people think of AOL as a specific Internet provider, note that AOL allows access to some of its chat rooms to non-subscribers. However, if you are a subscriber, AOL offers a wide range of workplace topics. It is worth your time to take a look at what's available. After you find the Web page that lists the chat rooms, you can choose which one to enter and participate in a typed discussion or request that an individual have a private discussion with you.

CareerPath.com

http://chat.careerpath.com

When you scroll down the page, you'll see a list of topics and dates and times for the chats. This site has an impressive list of hosts for the chats.

Yahoo! Net Events

http://events.yahoo.com

Here you can search for specific chat rooms on different subjects.

Yack.com

www.yack.com

This site allows you to search for current chats on varied topics.

Synapse

www.synapse.net/~radio/finding.htm

Here you can link to newsgroup search engines.

WomenConnect.com

www.womenconnect.com

A virtual community for women.

Yahoo!

http://dir.yahoo.com/Society_and_Culture/Cultures_and_Groups

Here you can find links to thousands of virtual communities, including minority groups, women, 30-somethings, and others.

Chapter 11: Finding the Perfect Job on the Net

Job Hunters Bible

www.jobhuntersbible.com

This is an excellent guide to the different job sites on the Web. Richard Bolles, author of *What Color Is Your Parachute?*, does an outstanding job of reviewing sites and pointing job seekers in the right direction.

Riley Guide

www.rileyguide.com

This site has extensive listings of links to job listings.

My Job Search

www.myjobsearch.com

This site is excellent to find regional job listings. It allows you to pick a state and then lists the job search sites that focus on job listings in that state. If you're looking for a career-specific site, such as job listings in the engineering/science field, simply click that category and the site presents a listing of job sites for that field. This site also does an excellent job of rating the different general job sites by ease of use, quality of the job search function, and user services. It also provides a detailed review of the different job sites, including the number of job and resume postings and details on how the site operates.

Monster.com

www.monster.com

This site has thousands of new job listings each week. It keeps its job bank freshly updated and provides excellent assistance in identifying specific jobs. This site is wonderfully organized and also allows you to search for jobs based on job category, location, salary, and more. It lists more than 500,000 current job listings from around the world.

The Job-Search-Engine
www.job-search-engine.com

This site is not a job bank, nor does it offer reviews of the different job sites. Instead, it actually searches many of the more popular job sites and returns a listing of jobs from these sites that match your query.

Targeted and Recruiter Job Sites

ExecSearches.com
www.execsearches.com

This free-access site posts executive-level jobs from around the country. Most of the jobs we've seen on this site are in the non-profit arena.

Training and Development—Human Resource Job Mart
at www.tcm.com/hr-careers/career

Lists jobs organized by area of HR specialization, such as employment and recruitment, management, training and development, and more.

The Chronicle of Higher Education
http://chronicle.com/jobs

A top choice for those seeking employment in academia and related organizations. The access to jobs is free, and the jobs are updated weekly.

Regional Sites

CareerPath.com
www.careerpath.com

This site compiles the daily classified want ads from more than 90 newspapers around the country. With more than 400,000 jobs listings, it's an outstanding source to check out the general job market in other regions. It allows you to search by job category, location, or newspaper.

America's Job Bank

www.ajb.dni.us

A compilation of jobs from the 1,800 state employment service offices. There are more than 1,000,000 jobs in both the public sector and the private sector. Because employers don't pay to list the jobs, you can find many job openings at small and medium-size businesses, which is where the job market is expanding significantly.

Duke University's Job Resources by U.S. Region

http://cdc.stuaff.duke.edu/stualum/employment/JobResources/jregion.html

This site is one of the best collections on the Net of job resources by region.

The Riley Guide

www.dbm.com/jobguide/internat.html

This fabulous site provides links to job listings in nearly every country around the world. This is a great site if you're looking for a job outside the United States.

Virtual Career Fairs and University Career Center Sites

College Central

www.collegecentral.com

This site announces career fairs for colleges and entry-level job seekers. You can see which colleges are sponsoring these virtual fairs.

JobTrak.com

www.jobtrak.com

JobTrak.com works with hundreds of universities and thousands of employers to connect students to entry-level positions. Students rate its value as high, and academic institutions are increasingly turning to this service because of its ability to expand their reach to employers. Check out your university or alma mater to see what it has.

Association, Alumni, Nonprofit, and Other Special Interest Group Sites

WiredAlumni.com

http://wiredalumni.com

You can find a listing of online alumni communities at this site.

IdeaList and Opportunity Nocs

www.idealist.org

www.opportunitynocs.org

These are two of the best sites for finding employment opportunities with nonprofit organizations.

American Society of Association Executives

www.asaenet.org

Here you can search and link to thousands of association sites. Association Web sites often have links to job listings relevant to the professional interests of its members.

American Society of Agricultural Engineers

www.asae.org

This site has job listings for agricultural engineering jobs as well as for related careers.

Peace Corps

www.peacecorps.gov

Here you can find all the permanent job openings at this organization as well as many volunteer opportunities.

Environmental Protection Agency

www.epa.gov

If you go to the internal job listing pages on this site, you'll find a current list of job vacancies, including the duties and qualifications for a given position and instructions on how to apply.

Deloitte & Touche

www.us.deloitte.com

This site lists job openings for positions at its central office. However, if you want to work with Deloitte & Touche in Costa Rica, you will find these jobs only at the company's Costa Rica Web site at *www.dtcr.com.*

Email, Listservs, Newsgroups, and Bulletin Boards

Topica.com

www.topica.com

To find links to nearly 200 job listservs, click More Categories and then Employment under the Business section; finally, click Jobs. Although it does not provide a comprehensive listing, this site makes it easy to identify listservs that may post jobs relevant to your career.

Career Magazine

www.careermag.com

Although it does not boast a comprehensive listing, this site collects job listings each day from numerous listservs and newsgroups and makes it possible for you to search them from one location.

Career Mosaic

www.careermosaic.com

This site collects job listings daily from dozens of newsgroups.

Dejanews

www.dejanews.com

This site archives messages from the last two years from nearly 100,000 newsgroups. You can search using keywords. Try typing *job AND* (**name of employer or location**) and see what you come up with!

The Liszt

www.liszt.com

Here you can search for listservs that focus specifically on jobs.

Online Newspapers, Trade Magazines, and Other Electronic Publications

Career Path

www.careerpath.com

This is an outstanding site that compiles the help wanted ads from more than 90 U.S. newspapers. It continues to add more papers regularly.

American Journal Review

http://ajr.newslink.org

This site has links to more than 9,000 newspapers, magazines, broadcasters, and news services in the United States.

All Newspapers

www.allnewspapers.com

Here you will find thousands of links to newspapers and other media around the world. The site is well organized by region and country.

Government Job Search Assistance Pages

America's Job Bank

www.ajb.dni.us

State employment services now compile all their job listings and offer them through this site. You will often find between one and two million jobs posted here, although not all are with the local governments. Many jobs are for private industry.

One-Stop Services Nationwide

www.ttrc.doleta.gov/onestop

The Department of Labor has led the effort to deploy what is called "America's One-Stop Career Center System." This initiative involves more than 600 sites around the country, ranging from actual career centers in most major cities to virtual services in many rural areas.

State Occupational Information Coordinating Committee (SOICC)

www.noicc.gov

You can find links to local job assistance and job listings at this site.

Top Mega-Sites for All Career Fields

Monster.com	*www.monster.com*
Careerpath.com	*www.careerpath.com*
America's Job Bank	*www.amj.dni.us*
Career Builder	*www.careerbuilder.com*
Career Mosaic	*www.careermosaic.com*
HeadHunter	*www.headhunter.net*
Hot Jobs	*www.hotjobs.com*
Job Options	*www.joboptions.com*
Job Bank USA	*www.jobbankusa.com*
6 Figure Jobs	*www.6figurejobs.com*
My Job Search	*www.myjobsearch.com*

Top Sites Listing Jobs for Students and Recent Graduates

JobTrak	*www.jobtrak.com*
Job Direct	*www.jobdirect.com*

Top Sites Providing Links to Career/Industry–Specific Jobs

My Job Search	*www.myjobsearch.com/ cgi-bin/mjs.cgi/specialty.html*
Duke University	*http://cdc.stuaff.duke. edu/stualum/employment/ JobResources/jregion.html*
The Riley Guide	*www.dbm.com/jobguide/ jobs.html#spec*
Yahoo!	*http://dir.yahoo.com/ Business_and_Economy/ Employment_and_Work/Jobs/ Career_Fields*
Snap.com	*www.snap.com/directory/ category/0,16,-65686,00.html*

Top Sites Listing Region-Specific Jobs

Duke University	*http://cdc.stuaff.duke.edu/ stualum/employment/ JobResources/jregion.html*
My Job Search	*www.myjobsearch.com/career/ regional.html*
The Riley Guide	*www.dbm.com/jobguide/ local.html* and *www.dbm.com/ jobguide/internat.html*

Top Sites Listing Jobs for Minorities, Women, and Special Interest Populations

The Black Collegian	*www.blackcollegian.com*
Women in Technology International	*www.witi4hire.com/ candidates/search_frm.phtml*
Hispanic Online	*www.hisp.com*
Saludos	*www.saludos.com*
Latin Professional	*www.latpro.com*
Bilingual Jobs	*www.bilingual-jobs.com*
Minorities' Job Bank	*www.minorities-jb.com/search_page.htm*
DiversiLink	*www.diversilink.com*
Gaywork.com	*www.gaywork.com*

Chapter 12: Interview Techniques Online

Capital University and Western Illinois University's Career Services

www.capital.edu/services/career/csintypes.htm

http://wiuadm1.wiu.edu/mioip/interview/i_type.asp

Both of these sites offer good information about the different types of interviews you need to prepare for.

Jobweb

www.jobweb.org/catapult/student.htm.

If you're interviewing with third-party recruiters at a career fair or in a Human Resources office, check out the guidance this site offers for this interview type.

The Wall Street Journal

http://careers.wsj.com

This site is an excellent reference for finding information on how to prepare for the job interview. Go to the column on the left side of the page and click Job Hunting Advice. Next, click the Interviewing Guidance button in the middle of the page. You should see an outstanding list of great articles.

Career Magazine

www.careermag.com/newsarts/interviewing/1050.html

Here you can read a great article on how to plan for behavioral interviews.

Online Career and Management Consulting

www.dnai.com/~career/ccpan.htm

Learn more about how to handle group interviews and telephone interviews at this site.

Knock 'Em Dead site

www.knockemdead.com/interview/#Stress

Here you can find some great examples of stress interview questions.

Job Web

www.jobweb.org/jconline/quick/tips/tips6-13.shtml

You'll find great tips on how to deal with silence during an interview, how to maintain eye contact, and how to speak clearly and confidently. This site also offers great general information on how to prepare for an interview.

Yahoo!

http://dir.yahoo.com/Business_and_Economy/Companies

You can find links to thousands of companies by using this or any of the other online search engines and directories. When you find the industry you're interested in, click it to see direct links to companies as well as links to online directories of companies.

American Journal Review
http://ajr.newslink.org

This site links you to more than 3,000 U.S. newspapers, as well as Web sites for more than 6,000 radio and television stations. You should be able to find some information about both large and small companies.

Better Business Bureau
www.bbb.com

Here you can look into any complaints that have been filed against a company. You can also get company and charity reports for companies in some areas around the country.

Vault.com
www.vault.com/forums/messageintro.cfm

The Internet now offers its own form of "getting the scoop" on what's happening at thousands of different companies. You can read about hundreds of companies at Vault.com's Electronic Watercooler. Most companies tracked by this site are in the high-tech, human resources, consulting, investment banking, and law industries. However, you will find some interesting topics relevant to most career fields.

Monster.com
http://content.monster.com/jobinfo/interview

This site offers separate interactive practice sessions for college students and mid-career job hunters. The program presents a list of questions for which you choose an answer. Then you are told why your answer was right, why it was wrong, or why another answer would have been better.

Job-Interview.net
www.job-interview.net

Here you can find a great list of practice interview questions.

Career City
www.careercity.com/careercity/content/interview/during/13quest.asp

This site has a list of stress-inducing questions and how you should answer them in an interview.

Bio Online

www.bio.com/hr/search

Here you will find a list of articles on how to prepare for the interview.

Management Recruiters of Scottsdale

www.mriscottsdale.com/candidate/interview.asp

This site provides more information on preparing for the first few minutes of the interview.

Work Search

http://members.xoom.com/worksearch/intres.htm

This site offers the best compilation of top-notch articles about interviewing. The site rates and reviews the articles to help you quickly find the ones that will meet your needs.

Chapter 13: Job Offers: E-valuating and Net-gotiating

JobStar

http://jobstar.org/tools/salary/index.htm

This site compiles more than 300 different salary guides, calculators, and surveys. It's the largest and most comprehensive collection we've found, and we think it's definitely worth a visit.

Abbott, Langer & Associates, Inc.

www.abbott-langer.com

This site provides outstanding salary and benefits survey reports for jobs in information technology, marketing, accounting, engineering, human resources, manufacturing, legal work, nonprofit work, consulting, and a few other fields.

Wall Street Journal Career Site

www.careers.wsj.com

This site is an outstanding resource for articles and data on more than 30 industries.

Economic Research Institute

http://www.erieri.com/cgi-bin/intsurvy.cgi

An excellent compilation of nearly 100 international salary surveys can be found at this site.

Federal Government Pay Scales

www.opm.gov/oca/payrates/index.htm

If you are looking for work with the federal government, this site will help you identify pay scales and wage systems.

Forbes, Inc. Online

www.forbes.com/forbes/Section/Executiv.htm

This site provides great information on executive-level salaries.

My Job Search

www.myjobsearch.com/relocation.html

This site places relocation information at your fingertips.

Riley Guide

www.dbm.com/jobguide/relocate.html

Here you can find great links to other relocation guides, local newspapers, cost of living indices, demographics, real estate information, telephone directories, maps, postal directories, education information, health care information, and weather.

Best Jobs USA

www.bestjobsusa.com/careerguide/relocation/relocation.asp

An excellent relocation guide is at this site.

My Job Search

www.myjobsearch.com/negotiating.html

This site has excellent links to information on how to negotiate a better offer.

Career Perfect's Interview Smart

http://www.careerperfect.com/ISOnline/OPEN.HTM

This site has an outstanding online tutorial to help you learn and practice salary negotiation.

Chapter 14: Starting Work: e-Ideas for Success

Kaplan Careers

www.studyusa.kaplan.com/view/article/0,1898,1957,00.html

This site has some great guidance on how to get organized for your first week at your new job. It also includes information on setting initial goals and making your initial contacts with clients and colleagues over the phone.

Wet Feet

www.wetfeet.com/advice/articles/wow.asp

An excellent article, "Wow 'em in a Week," which explains how to succeed during your first week on the job, can be found at this site.

Career Magazine

www.careermag.com/newsarts/collegearts/dgordon1.html

This site offers articles on making the most of your first weeks on the job. The articles provide some great ways to help ease the stress of the transition.

Gary Recchion's Site

http://www.aerospacecareers.com/060899.html

This site offers articles on taking ownership of your career.

My Job Search

www.myjobsearch.com/network/associations.html

This site has links to thousands of professional associations and societies. One of the easiest and most necessary things to do to maintain a network is to join a professional association.

Berkeley University

http://career.berkeley.edu/SchoolsBusiness/faqBusiness.stm#1

This site provides some good advice on how to make yourself attractive to business employers after you graduate.

CommSciences (Custom Research for Effective Communications)

www.build-site-traffic.com/cca/ccaflexibility1.html

This site boasts an excellent slide presentation regarding trends in the global economy. It explains what you need to stay competitive in the workplace.

Beyond Computing

www.beyondcomputing.net/index.asp?archive/1998/09-98/career.html

Here is an article, "Learning to Lead," that focuses on how to develop your leadership skills.

Managing Work and Family

http://mwfam.com/tip.html

At this site, you can find daily tips on how to strive for balance in your work and home lives.

Family and Work Institute

www.familiesandworkinst.org

This site has great articles and tips on how to manage both work and family commitments.

Work and Family

www.workfamily.com/resource.htm

Here you'll find links to sites that offer information, resources, advice, and assistance on many work/life balance issues for both families and singles. This is probably the best compilation of links to work/life resources we've found on the Internet.

Chapter 15: Change and Transitions

Monster.com

http://content.monster.com/careerchangers

http://international.monster.com/workabroad

These sites' sections on career changes are among the best for managing such a transition. You can also find an excellent forum for asking international job experts questions related to international careers.

HomeFair.com
www.homefair.com/calc/salcalc.html

This site provides information on how much you need to earn to maintain the same standard of living in a different location.

Virtual Relocation
www.virtualrelocation.com/

Here you can find information on city demographics, mortgage rates by state, moving and storage facilities, school and education information, senior living, vacation properties, weather information, and public service information.

Money.com
http://pathfinder.com/money/depts/real_estate/bestplaces

This site offers an annual review of places to live. You can access its list of the best places for the year 2000.

The U.S. State Department
www.state.gov/www/background_notes

This site provides links to profiles of virtually every country in the world.

U.S. Embassies
http://travel.state.gov/links.html

This site has travel advisories and useful information about the country you are considering working in.

The Electronic Embassy
www.embassy.org

This site provides links to the embassies of other countries.

Chapter 16: Continuing Education and Training

Peterson's Education
www.petersons.com

This is one of the best sites for identifying colleges and universities for regular in-person study programs. This site is packed with career education information, financial aid guidance, English learning programs, study abroad programs, and other education programs and related assistance.

University of Alabama in Huntsville University Pages
http://isl-garnet.uah.edu/Universities_g

You can find an extremely useful state-by-state listing of higher education institutions nationwide on the University Pages.

U.S. News Online
www.usnews.com/usnews/edu

This site provides an outstanding free information service. This site even offers a forum for questions about college, graduate school, and financial aid.

The Distance Education and Training Council
www.detc.org

This is an excellent resource to identify accredited distance learning programs and institutions. It lists programs from financial management and physical therapy to writing and refrigeration. Go to the site and click Alphabetical Listing of Degree Topics. Click the subject that interests you and check out what programs are available.

General Education Online
http://wsdo.sao.uwf.edu/~geo

This is the most comprehensive collection online of educational programs around the globe.

Internship Programs
www.internshipprograms.com

www.internships.com/intro.html

Both of these sites list internships, mostly in Fortune 1000 companies around the country. Sometimes you even can find internships abroad. In any case, you'll come across a whole host of good tips for making your internship a success.

Federal Student Aid

www.ed.gov/offices/OPE/express.html

If you're looking for financial aid for higher education, you can find information on scholarships and other financial sources at this site.

FastWeb

www.fastweb.com

You can sign up at this site for free. It will notify you of scholarships that match your profile. However, the database of scholarships is not comprehensive, so don't rely on this as your sole scholarship resource.

College Plan

www.collegeplan.org/cpnow/pnwguide/pnwguide.htm

College Plan allows you to scan the database of scholarships quickly by simply clicking any of approximately 20 items that may reflect your interests. The site returns a well-organized list that includes the name of the scholarship, the amount of the scholarship, the deadline by which you must apply, and a link to more information about the scholarship.

Yahoo!

http://dir.yahoo.com/education/financial_aid

This site provides a list of links to sites that offer information about college scholarships.

University of Delaware's Career Services

www.udel.edu/CSC/mrk.html

This page links you to more than 70 major resource kits. First click the icon that says Major Resource Kits, then click your career field. Scroll down to the bottom of the page to find out about further education for your career field.

GradSchools.com

www.gradschools.com

Here you can you can find links to graduate schools in the United States and other countries.

Educational Testing Service

http://etsis1.ets.org

Here you will find information on higher education tests. You'll also find good guidance, practice questions, and information about how and where to take the exams. Note that the LSAT is not on the ETS site; you can find it on the Law School Admission Council Web site at *www.lsat.org*.

GradAdvantage

www.gradadvantage.org

This site introduces you to what is probably the wave of the future regarding college applications. It's an online application service for graduate school and MBA programs. It's worth checking out because it might save you a lot of time completing and filing graduate applications. If you decide to submit your forms online, be sure to print out a hard copy and request confirmation of receipt.

America's Learning eXchange

www.alx.org

This is an excellent site for professional development seminars, classes, workshops, and conferences. It is perhaps the most comprehensive collection of professional learning opportunities online.

Temple University

http://oll.temple.edu/oll

This site is one example of how universities and colleges nationwide are offering continuing education programs online geared toward the adult student.

GLOSSARY

approach letter   A one-page letter requesting a networking or informational meeting.

ASCII (American Standard Code for Information Interchange)   A plain text format for documents that can be shared and read by most computer systems.

assessments   Tools and resources to help you identify your values, skills, abilities, interests, and needs.

bookmarks   Also known as Favorites. A bookmark is a mechanism for storing the location of a Web site so that you can return to it quickly in the future.

career   The combination of life roles—jobs, education, and avocation—all focused in a related direction.

career advisor   A person who offers guidance and advice to individuals regarding career and job search goals, action, and decisions.

career changer   An individual who moves frequently from one career field to a different career field.

career coach   A person offering services to help individuals set and work toward career and job search goals. Some career coaches are professionally trained as counselors or as coaches, but this is not currently a requirement for this field.

career counselor   A professionally trained individual who helps the job seeker assess his values, interests, skills, and abilities. The career counselor can also help an individual in career exploration, decision-making, and taking action throughout the job search process.

career mapping   Designing and planning a career path following self-assessment and research. At this stage of the job search process, you specify the work you want to do and how you will reach your goal.

chat room   A forum for instant communication between two or more computer users by typing messages that appear on the others' computer screens.

continuing learning   Action taken by an individual to upgrade or maintain his skills continuously through training, workshops, online opportunities, informal education, and formal education.

cover letter   A one- or two-page letter that accompanies a resume or job search application.

credentials   The formal documentation of training, education, and experience that makes one qualified to work in a certain capacity.

cyberspace   The complex, vast system of computers, networks, people, data, and information connected through the Internet.

distance learning   Using the Internet to engage in formal or informal education opportunities.

electronic resume   A job search tool that markets your skills and accomplishments, but which is written and designed to meet the electronic specifications of email, job databases, and scanners.

email   Electronic mail that allows typed messages to be sent from one computer to another computer.

FAQ (Frequently Asked Questions)   A list of questions that are often asked by individuals with regard to a particular Web site, communication forum, or specific document.

flame   Inappropriate comments, often personal in nature, posted through email, newsgroups, chatrooms, and listservs.

government sector   The body of organizations that provide community and social services at the local, city, state, and national level. The government sector is funded mostly by taxes and is governed by elected officials. The U.S. federal government is the largest employer in the world.

HTTP (Hypertext Transfer Protocol)   HTTP is the method by which your computer can be directed to a particular area on the Internet. All World Wide Web addresses begin with *http*, although it is no longer necessary to type these characters in the address.

industry   A group of organizations, employers, and interests related to a common product or service, such as hospitality or health.

interest   Something you enjoy and like doing even if you are not very good at it.

interview   A verbal exchange of questions to assess a job candidate's qualifications for the job and "fit" with the organization. The interview may be conducted in person or over the telephone; rarely is it conducted online.

job   A particular kind of work for an employer.

job database   A Web site that has a system for job seekers to access job openings online. Some databases are searchable by different fields, such as location, salary, or career area.

job search barriers   Characteristics, thoughts, behaviors, or other things that may keep you from finding meaningful employment.

job search office/headquarters   A base you use to organize your files, notes, and other essentials in your search. This is a place that you set up to work on your career planning and job searching.

job search process   A methodical, nonlinear approach for the purpose of achieving employment. The job search process includes self-assessment, research, decision-making, taking action, and managing transitions.

keyword   A specific word that is used to search through text to make a match.

listserv   A group of individuals with a common interest who communicate with each other simultaneously using email.

lurk   The act of being a non-participating individual on a listserv, newsgroup, or chat room.

netiquette   Standard, accepted, appropriate behavior when interacting on the Internet. Most listservs and newsgroups ask new members to read guidelines for appropriate netiquette behavior.

networking   A mutual communication exchange for the purpose of developing contacts, supporting career goals, and sustaining career success. It is usually done in person, but can also be done online through chat rooms, listservs, and email. More than 80% of jobs are obtained through some form of networking. Although some of your networking can now be done online, this doesn't replace the human factor; you still have to meet face to face with others.

newsgroup   A discussion group on the Internet.

nonprofit sector   Organizations and employers that focus on a service without generating profit. Note that the term *nonprofit* does not refer to your earnings potential: You may find that job offerings in the nonprofit sector pay as much as or, occasionally, more than similar jobs in the private sector.

online assessments   Online tools and resources to help you identify your values, skills, abilities, interests, and needs.

private sector   Organizations, companies, and employers that offer a product or service that generates profit.

resume   A one- or two-page document that serves as a job search tool to market your skills and accomplishments, based on your career objective and the needs of the employer.

resume database   An electronic format for storing and retrieving resume information.

resume bank   A forum, electronic or other, for collecting and storing resumes.

references   Selected individuals, usually 3 to 5, who know a job candidate well enough to discuss his skills, abilities, work style, or personality.

salary negotiation   An interaction between an employer and a job candidate to determine and agree on a compensation package that will accompany a specific job offer.

scannable resume   A resume that has been modified to ensure that key words can be identified by a computer that will scan it for the employer.

skill   Something you are good at that can be demonstrated through experience, even if you don't like doing it. A skill can be learned and improved.

surfing   The act of moving from site to site on the Web by clicking the hyperlinks.

thank-you letter   A one-page letter sent to any individual who has spent time with you in an interview, an informational meeting, or at a career fair.

INDEX

K - L

T

U

Tell Us What You Think!

As the reader of this book, *you* are our most important critic and commentator. We value your opinion and want to know what we're doing right, what we could do better, what areas you'd like to see us publish in, and any other words of wisdom you're willing to pass our way.

You can email or write me directly to let me know what you did or didn't like about this book—as well as what we can do to make our books stronger.

Please note that I cannot help you with technical problems related to the topic of this book, and that due to the high volume of mail I receive, I might not be able to reply to every message.

When you write, please be sure to include this book's title and author as well as your name and phone or fax number. I will carefully review your comments and share them with the authors and editors who worked on the book.

Email: `internet_sams@mcp.com`

Mail: Mark Taber
Associate Publisher
Sams Publishing
201 West 103rd Street
Indianapolis, IN 46290 USA

SAMS
Teach Yourself
Today

Sams Teach Yourself
e-Travel Today

Planning Vacations, Finding Bargains, and Booking Reservations Online

Mark Orwoll
ISBN: 0-672-31822-9
$17.99 US/$26.95 CAN

Other Sams Teach Yourself Today Titles

e-Trading
Tiernan Ray
ISBN: 0-672-31821-0
$17.99 US/$26.95 CAN

e-Personal Finance
Ken and Daria Dolan
ISBN: 0-672-31879-2
$17.99 US/$26.95 CAN

e-Music
Brandon Barber
ISBN: 0-672-31855-5
$17.99 US/$26.95 CAN

e-Banking
Mary Dixon and Brian Nixon
ISBN: 0-672-31882-2
$17.99 US/$26.95 CAN

e-Baseball
Bob Temple and Rob Neyer
ISBN: 0-672-31913-6
$17.99 US/$26.95 CAN

e-Auctions
Preston Gralla
ISBN: 0-672-31819-9
$17.99 US/$26.95 CAN

All prices are subject to change.

SAMS

www.samspublishing.com